体裁转换：以中国大学的汉语母语学生为例研究

Genre Transfer: A Case Study of Chinese Writers at a University in China

何梅 著

中国纺织出版社有限公司

图书在版编目（CIP）数据

体裁转换：以中国大学的汉语母语学生为例研究＝Genre Transfer: A Case Study of Chinese Writers at a University in China ：英文 / 何梅著 . -- 北京：中国纺织出版社有限公司，2025.7. -- ISBN 978-7-5229-2773-2

Ⅰ . G643.8；H152.3

中国国家版本馆 CIP 数据核字第 20253BB319 号

责任编辑：郭　婷　吴宇晴　　责任校对：王蕙莹
责任印制：储志伟

中国纺织出版社有限公司出版发行
地址：北京市朝阳区百子湾东里 A407 号楼　邮政编码：100124
销售电话：010—67004422　传真：010—87155801
http://www.c-textilep.com
中国纺织出版社天猫旗舰店
官方微博 http://weibo.com/2119887771
北京印匠彩色印刷有限公司印刷　各地新华书店经销
2025 年 7 月第 1 版第 1 次印刷
开本：710×1000　1/16　印张：20.5
字数：410 千字　定价：99.00 元

凡购本书，如有缺页、倒页、脱页，由本社图书营销中心调换

Preface

Master's students produce and employ various genres through their learning process, among which thesis and thesis defense presentation slides, which are challenging for the students (Peng, 2018; Hertz et al., 2016), are involved. The thesis is an essential component to fulfill the requirements for the award of the degree, while thesis defense presentation slides are significant and supportive for the presentation of the thesis during the defense session. However, to date, little attention has been paid to the rhetorical structure of the whole thesis composed by Chinese writers. Moreover, scant studies have regarded the thesis defense presentation slides as a separate genre, and the rhetorical structure of the genre is still underexplored. In addition, these two genres shape a genre chain of the thesis defense along which the thesis is transferred to the corresponding thesis defense presentation slides.

Nevertheless, no study has examined the genre transfer between these two closely related genres. Therefore, the present study aims to investigate the rhetorical structure of both the thesis and the thesis defense presentation slides as well as the genre transfer between them. Employing Chen and Kuo's (2012) framework, the current research analyzed the moves and steps of 20 theses (MTs) and 20 corresponding thesis defense presentation slides (PSs) produced by Chinese writers from Foreign Linguistics and Applied Linguistics. Furthermore, the changes as an effect of genre transfer and the transfer strategies were investigated by constant comparison of the contents between these two genres. The results demonstrated that the rhetorical structure of the whole MT contained 24 moves and 69 steps which varied in terms of their status. Moreover, 23 moves and 41 steps were identified in the rhetorical structure of the PS. In addition, the findings from the constant comparison of the MTs and the PSs indicated that the majority of the moves and steps were maintained through the genre transfer process, indicating the interdiscursive relationship between these two genres. Nevertheless, as an effect of genre transfer, omission, as well as addition of moves and steps, were observed when the MT was transferred to the corresponding PS. Furthermore, at the textual feature level, most of the texts in the PSs were identical to the original MTs, which manifested the intertextuality between these two genres. The results indicated that 13 single strategies and 22 combined strategies were employed by the students at the textual feature level during the genre transfer process. Based on these findings, the current study provides practical pedagogical implications for the students, the supervisors, and the instructors for the teaching and learning of the MT and PS as well as the genre transfer between them in the present discourse community and other similar ones.

Mei He
2025.02

TABLE OF CONTENTS

CHAPTER 1   Introduction ··1
    1.1   Background of the Study ···1
    1.2   Research Problems ···7
    1.3   Rationale of the Research ···10
    1.4   Research Objectives ··13
    1.5   Research Questions ··14
    1.6   Significance of the Research ··14
    1.7   Scope and Limitations ···16
    1.8   Definitions of Key Terms ··18
    1.9   Summary ···20

CHAPTER 2   Literature Review ···21
    2.1   Genre: Theory and Analysis ···21
    2.2   Master's Thesis ···35
    2.3   Thesis Defense Presentation Slides ··································59
    2.4   Intertextuality, Interdiscursivity, and Genre Transfer ·······66
    2.5   Previous Studies on Genre Transfer ·································70
    2.6   Summary ··74

CHAPTER 3   Methodology ··75
    3.1   Research Design ···75
    3.2   Data Collection ···77
    3.3   Data Analysis ···84
    3.4   Summary ···92

1

CHAPTER 4　Results and Discussion of Moves and Steps of the Thesis······93

    4.1　Overview of the Structure of the Thesis ······93

    4.2　Findings of the Introduction Chapters······94

    4.3　Findings of the Literature Review Chapters ······106

    4.4　Findings of the Theoretical Framework Chapters······119

    4.5　Findings of the Methodology Chapters ······124

    4.6　Findings of the Integrated Results and Discussion Chapters ······135

    4.7　Findings of the Conclusion Chapters ······149

    4.8　Summary······156

CHAPTER 5　Results and Discussion of Moves and Steps of the Thesis Defense Presentation Slides······157

    5.1　Overview of the Structure of the Thesis Defense Presentation Slides······157

    5.2　Findings on the Introduction Sections ······162

    5.3　Findings on the Literature Review Sections ······170

    5.4　Findings on the Theoretical Framework Sections······178

    5.5　Findings on the Methodology Sections ······182

    5.6　Findings on the Integrated Results and Discussion Sections ······189

    5.7　Findings on the Conclusion Sections ······197

    5.8　Summary······201

CHAPTER 6　Results and Discussion of Changes and Transfer Strategies From the Thesis to the Corresponding Thesis Defense Presentation Slides······202

    6.1　The Introduction Pair······202

    6.2　The Literature Review Pair······227

    6.3　The Theoretical Framework Pair······239

    6.4　The Methodology Pair ······248

    6.5　The Integrated Results and Discussion Pair ······261

    6.6　The Conclusion Pair ······273

    6.7　Discussion on the Intertextuality and Interdiscursivity of the Current Genre Transfer ······281

    6.8   Summary ··· 283

CHAPTER 7   Conclusion ··· 284

    7.1   Summary of the Findings ··· 284

    7.2   Pedagogical Implications ·· 294

    7.3   Limitations and Suggestions for Further Studies ·· 297

    7.4   Summary ··· 300

REFERENCES ·· 301

CHAPTER 1 Introduction

This introductory chapter first presents background information about the situated context of this study; namely, the importance of English in China, the Foreign Linguistics and Applied Linguistics master's program in China, and the specific research site. Furthermore, the existing problems and the rationale for this research are stated, followed by the specific research objectives and research questions. Besides, the significance of this research for students, supervisors, and researchers is proposed, and the scope and limitations of the present study are presented. In the end, the definitions of the key terms are provided in advance.

1.1 Background of the Study

1.1.1 Importance of English in China

Among the countless languages in the world, English has played a dominant role since its globalization as a discourse in political, academic, and other perspectives (Chang, 2006; Crystal, 2003; Flowerdew, 2016; Hyland, 2016; Rao, 2019; Swales, 2004; Zhang, 2016). Furthermore, English is the world's prevailing language in language teaching, international conferences, and publications. In the 21st century, over 90% of the journal literature in certain fields is printed in English. Moreover, the most prestigious journals in the globe are in English (Hyland, 2006). In order to understand the disciplines as well as to establish and promote career opportunities, a great quantity of students and academics invest a lot of effort in learning the convention of English academic discourses. Academic English performs as a lingua franca to accelerate the sharing and exchange of thoughts and to disseminate information and knowledge (Rao, 2018). It is also often the case in China where academics need to get published in high-profile English language journals (Hyland, 2016) to improve their academic reputation, and their publication in internationally prestigious journals which is in English relates to their promotion in careers. In addition, graduate students are expected or required to publish research articles in English as well. Thus, great importance has been attached to the study of English in China, especially in the academic fields (Bolton & Graddol, 2012; Rao, 2019; Zhang, 2016).

Since the 1980s in China, English has turned into the dominant language in foreign language teaching in secondary and tertiary education, and until now, it has become prevailing in the curricula of the whole education system (Hu, 2005; Rao, 2018). The official policy, issued in 1991, stated that English should be learned from the third grade in primary school in the national education system (Ministry of Education of the People's Republic of China, 2001). At the tertiary level, regardless of their majors, all students are required to study English to graduate. There are two main streams of English language teaching in China, for non-English majors and English majors (Cheng, 2016). For non-English major students, they need to acquire basic communicative skills and most universities even require them to pass the College English Test before graduation. Moreover, increasing numbers of teaching programs have been taught through the medium of English (Bolton & Graddol, 2012).

As for the education of English majors, three layers have been established in the Chinese higher education system, i.e., bachelor's, master's, and doctoral degrees. The Bachelor's degree attaches importance to the basic aspects of English language learning, that is a solid foundation of English, profound knowledge of English culture, and the communicative use of English in the real world (Teaching Advisory Committee for Tertiary English Majors, 2000). The master's and doctoral degrees in English majors are more inclined to research ability rather than communicative ability. The master's degree for English majors at the tertiary level is the focus of the present study, which will be elaborated on in the following section.

1.1.2　Foreign Linguistics and Applied Linguistics Master's Program in China

In China, two kinds of degrees are provided for English-majored students who are studying for a master's degree; namely, academic degree and professional degree. As for the academic degree, it is under the broad discipline of Foreign Languages and Literature that two specific English-related disciplines are established, i.e., "English Language and Literature" and "Foreign Linguistics and Applied Linguistics", according to *Introduction to the First-level Discipline of Degree Award and Talent Cultivation* (the Sixth Discipline Evaluation Group of the State Council Academic Degrees Committee, 2013). As for the professional degree, Translation orientation and Interpretation orientation are offered. All the students in these English-related disciplines are trained so that they can be qualified as an English teacher or in other English-related jobs in the future. Among these specific disciplines, only students wishing to obtain an academic degree are required to write a thesis in English while those with professional degrees could write a report instead. Furthermore, only those in the discipline of Foreign Linguistics and Applied Linguistics are required to write a thesis in a simple traditional structure. Therefore, the present study selects this discipline as the research context.

"Foreign Linguistics and Applied Linguistics" in this research context is similar to the widely known Applied Linguistics discipline. However, the current study sticks to the local name of this program in the Chinese context. This discipline focuses on the study of English language, drawing on previous linguistic or applied linguistic theories, methods, and findings to the studies of phonetics, phonology, semantics, pragmatics, second language acquisition, discourse analysis, English teaching, cognitive linguistics, and so forth. (The Sixth Discipline Evaluation Group of the State Council Academic Degrees Committee, 2013).

Moreover, the Sixth Discipline Evaluation Group of the State Council Academic Degrees Committee (2014) proposed *Basic Requirements for Doctor's Degree and Master's Degree in First-level Discipline* (Basic Requirements hereafter), serving as a national guideline for postgraduate education. To achieve a master's degree, aside from the possession of basic knowledge, Basic Requirements (2014) states five basic academic abilities that Master of Arts (M.A.) students in Foreign Linguistics and Applied Linguistics are required to possess, i.e., the ability to acquire knowledge, the ability to do scientific research independently, the ability to apply theories into practices, the ability to conduct academic communication, and the ability to use computer technology and multimodal technology. In terms of academic communication ability, M.A. students are demanded to express their academic ideas and to demonstrate their own academic achievements in English, thus they are expected to do presentations of their works both in written form and orally in English. On the basis of the Basic Requirements (2014), all the institutions have the autonomy to conduct a local and feasible regulation or plan to achieve the academic objectives.

In the process of the M.A. journey, there are a diversity of texts or genres that students have to produce and use. Swales (2004) illustrated that these genres expand "from course assignments, term papers, seminar research papers (or prelim papers), posters (in an increasing number of fields), texts of conference presentations, research articles, and on to the dissertation". Furthermore, the presentation involves seminar presentation, conference presentation, classroom presentation, three-minute thesis presentation, and defense presentation, and it may cover handouts, overheads, and PowerPoint slides (Azizifar et al., 2014; Forey & Feng, 2016; Hu & Liu, 2018; Morell, 2015; Wecker, 2012; Zareva, 2016). In addition, Swales (2004) revealed that research grant proposals and conference abstracts are the genres graduate students may produce. Besides, Cryer (2006) proposed that before stepping into thesis writing, students need to deal with research proposals and progress reports. Later, Zareva (2013) concluded that graduate students employ a series of genres which include both written genres (e.g., reflection paper, thesis, etc.) and speech genres (e.g., class discussion, thesis defense, etc.). This is also the case in China where M.A. students need to produce and use these various written genres and speech genres.

During the process of M.A. education, the final ritual for the students is the thesis defense. It is a long-established convention (Roberts & Hyatt, 2019) in which they should attend with their theses and thesis defense presentation slides with corresponding oral commentary. Therefore, in the thesis defense session, the final genres students produced and used are their theses, the written slides, and the oral presentation for thesis defense (Tardy, 2009), three of which are all required to be produced in English. These three genres are in a genre chain along which they interact with each other chronologically. In China, the final requirements for the award of an M.A. degree are divided into two parts: one is the submission and preliminary assessment of the thesis, and the other is the thesis defense by oral examination in which thesis defense presentation slides are involved.

In terms of the thesis, Basic Requirements (2014) demonstrates that it should be produced by M.A. students independently under the supervision of their supervisors, and it is expected to be written in English, no less than 15,000 words. State Council of the People's Republic of China (1981) proposes that M.A. theses ought to have new insights into the research topic, which illustrates the author possesses the capacity to conduct scientific research and the capacity to independently undertake specialized technical work. Furthermore, one or two experts in related fields should be invited to review the theses and detailed comments should be offered as a reference for the defense committee.

In terms of the written slides, i.e., the thesis defense presentation slides, they are a separate genre transferred from the thesis which is another different genre (Tardy, 2009). These slides are produced in English and are utilized to support the oral commentary of the students. All M.A. students are required to present the slides during their presentation in the defense session. The thesis defense presentation slides are a preliminary way to display the thesis. Therefore, there are a good number of slide sets that could be used for research purposes as in the case of the current study. Since this kind of genre is required to be produced by the students, the students need to master its production in order to make it more informative and attractive, contributing to the success of their defense and their obtaining the degree.

1.1.3 The Research Site

The research site of the present research is a university (GZU) in China where M.A. students produce or use the above genres as well. Founded in 1902, GZU is a comprehensive university located in the Southwest of China. It is enlisted into the national construction plan of first-class universities and disciplines of the world, which is also known as the Double-First-Rate initiative, a national strategy to enhance the overall strength and international competitiveness of higher education in China. As of

2022, GZU has 39 colleges, offering 52 master's programs, 19 doctoral programs, and 8 post-doctoral stations, ranging from disciplines in technology and natural sciences to those in humanities and social sciences.

Among the colleges, the College of Foreign Languages (CFL) of GZU offers the most master's programs in Guizhou Province. The program of Foreign Linguistics and Applied Linguistics is one of them. Students in this discipline need to finish their M.A. studies within three academic years, six semesters in total. They are supposed to systematically learn and acquire the basic theories as well as research methods in this field, and then to possess the ability to conduct research in Linguistics, Applied Linguistics, Second Language Acquisition, and English Teaching and Learning as well as to possess the practical ability to undertake English language teaching for English major and non-English major undergraduates in higher education. After the subject learning, students prepare their proposal and are supposed to pass the proposal defense in the third semester. Then, they focus on their thesis writing.

According to the regulation of CFL at GZU, the thesis should be written in English with a minimum of 20,000 words (slightly above the 15,000 words proposed by the Basic Requirements), and to avoid plagiarism, the text copy ratio or similarity index compared with other literature resources should be within 30 percent. After the submission by the students, the theses are delivered by CFL to at least two experts, with the title of Associate Professor or higher, to review. At least one of the reviewers is an external expert. In the period of thesis review, according to the regulation of GZU, in order to roughly evaluate the quality of the theses written by the current batch of the students, 10 percent of the M.A. theses are sent to two external experts to review anonymously for quality inspection. The names of the external experts are kept confidential to the students and the supervisors. If one of the reviewers suggests that the thesis is unqualified, then it will be sent to a third expert. The writer of this thesis can attend the final defense if the third expert suggests a pass, otherwise, he or she needs to revise the thesis based on the comments and resend it three months later to be reviewed anonymously again until it is considered qualified. In the end, the final thesis defense comes.

The final defense committee consists of five expert members with the title of Associate Professor or higher. The Chair of the committee is an external expert from another institution and the candidate's supervisor is excluded from the committee. The Department arranges the defense date and invites the qualified committee members for the whole batch of students in the same discipline. All the student candidates are supposed to defend their theses on the same day with similar committee members scheduled by the Department. At the beginning of the defense, candidates are allowed no more than fifteen minutes to orally present their thesis with the aid of the slides. After the presentation, committee members ask pertinent questions, and the candidates are supposed to answer them. The whole process of the thesis defense lasts for around 45 minutes for each candidate. The candidates achieve a pass if two-thirds of the committee members agree on the quality of the thesis. If the students fail the final defense, they have a second chance to arrange a defense by themselves and their supervisors. One point needs to be mentioned is that apart from the thesis writing and the final thesis defense, to gain the degree, all candidates are required to do a conference paper presentation and publish at least one research article in a journal which is at least included in Science Citation Database, a comprehensive database built in China, or in the international Social Science Citation Index database.

1.2 Research Problems

From the above background information, three academic years for M.A. students are not an easy journey along which they have to produce a chain or a network of genres, both written and oral. To accomplish the requirements and to verify their three-year efforts as well as gain the fruits, the students only have two chances to attend the final thesis defense. Although the students have the second chance to reattend the defense, they have to rearrange it all by themselves, including inviting the committee members, arranging the date, and affording all the costs which is not a small amount. They have to postpone the graduation for one more year if they fail again with the second chance. Therefore, all the students make every single effort to prepare and perform well in the defense which in turn poses much more pressure and challenges to the students. As mentioned earlier, there are three genres the students need to prepare on the defense day, i.e., the thesis itself, the thesis defense presentation slides, and the corresponding oral commentary. They form a genre chain and interact with one another. Thesis defense presentation slides are the intermediate product of the written thesis and the oral presentation; thus, it is written under the requirement that it will be delivered orally. These three genres are evidently interdependent, thus, distinguishing them is beneficial to explore the variations among the three genres (Yates & Orlikowski, 2007) and the differences in their usage to serve different communicative purposes. The present study only focuses on the first two genres, which is the thesis itself and the corresponding thesis defense presentation slides.

For the first genre in the thesis defense, the thesis itself, its writing is challenging for the students, particularly those who are required to write in a foreign language, English (Peng, 2018). As in the cases of Soler-Monreal (2012) and Dastjerdi et al. (2017) where only layout and formatting instructions are provided by the university, students in this discipline in most Chinese colleges, to the present researcher's experience, mainly rely on the skeletal structures suggested by the university or on reading and learning from seniors' works, and largely depend on the supervision and experience of their supervisors. However, these are not enough for the students, so they still feel stressed and challenged when composing their own thesis (e.g., Peng, 2018; Sadeghi & Shirzad, 2015; Wu & Paltridge, 2021). For thesis writing, Swales' Create a Research Space(CARS) model (1990; 2004) for the Introduction of research articles has been applied to writing the thesis Introduction chapter (Bunton, 2002; Maher and Milligan, 2019). Nevertheless, students need more studies which have focused on the whole rhetorical structure of the M.A. theses, especially those written by Chinese writers. To the best of the researcher's knowledge, only three studies have investigated the complete structure of M.A. theses, i.e., Chen and Kuo (2012), Nguyen (2014), and Pramoolsook (2007), however, none of them is from the Chinese context.

The second genre for the students in thesis defense is the thesis defense presentation slides. Thesis and thesis defense presentation slides are two different genres that are governed by different logic (Kress, 2003). To be specific, the thesis is in paper format that operates by the logic of words, while the thesis defense presentation slides are in digital media that adopts the logic of image. Allen and Simmons (2002) stated that images often play a major role in the communication in which prose text is usually illustrated in bulleted lists instead of traditional paragraphs, and it is the screens that arrange the information rather than paragraphs and chapters (Tardy, 2009). Presentation slides, or PowerPoint texts called by some scholars, are increasingly used in a broad array of contexts with various discursive norms and communicative purposes in printed form or digital form (Yates & Orlikowski, 2007). To illustrate, they are used in conferences, seminars, business presentations, and so forth. Moreover, presentation slides are a kind of complex genre that takes consideration into the content, rhetorical structure, visual type, and function that are very unlike the thesis, the more traditional text (Tardy, 2009). There is little or no instruction to students about how to prepare or present slides (Tardy, 2009), thus, the students lack a clear framework for preparing the thesis defense presentation slides (Pieketaleyee & Bazargani, 2018). Given the researcher's own experience as an M.A. student in this context, there is no formal instruction for the students in GZU, or might be the case in other universities as well, to produce presentation slides. The most popular way they learn this genre is to observe the seniors' presentations. Therefore, they obtain scant knowledge about the rhetorical structure of the thesis defense presentation slides, which calls for the support for them in the form of a framework or guideline that they could refer to.

Although thesis and thesis defense presentation slides are two different genres, they are very much related on account that thesis defense presentation slides are a later product of the thesis and they are produced for a similar discourse community. These two genres are in a genre chain of the thesis defense. The students transfer the content and the structures from the thesis into the thesis defense presentation slides. As for creating the presentation slides, Mackiewicz (2008) stated that for students the most difficult parts are making decisions on what should be transferred from the thesis to be the main points of the slides and rewording them persuasively in the new rhetorical context. Therefore, the exploration of how students transfer other genres into presentation slides is of significance so as to help them effectively create presentation slides and then reduce the pressure on them. In the present case, in what ways the students select the content from the thesis into the slides is unclear. The most challenging part for the students is how to condense a 20,000-word thesis into a set of presentation slides that are required to be delivered orally within 15 minutes. However, up until now, the transfer between thesis and thesis defense slides leaves a vacancy in the research field of genre relationships. Therefore, there is still a gap that has yet to be filled.

In reality, the students and supervisors place more attention on the thesis writing which is a kind of genre that puts a great deal of stress on the students (Russell-Pinson & Harris, 2019). As for the thesis defense presentation slides, the students possess scant knowledge of this complex genre with regard to its audience expectations, rhetorical structures, and generic characteristics. Furthermore, the norms and conventions of this genre depend to a large extent on the discourse community. Nevertheless, the students attain little or no formal instructions, or even explicit guidelines, within the discipline context (Tardy, 2009). The major source for them to learn about this genre is to observe the thesis presentation slides of seniors and then produce it based on their own understanding.

1.3 Rationale of the Research

In response to the research problem proposed above, the present study is committed to demystifying, or at least further understanding, several puzzles that lie behind M.A. thesis writing, thesis defense presentation slides, and most importantly, the transfer between these two different but related genres in a genre chain, which are insufficiently explored or even absent.

Firstly, compared with remarkable investigations conducted on research articles, less attention has been paid to the M.A. thesis (Li & Zhang, 2021; Maher & Milligan, 2019; Flowerdew, 2015; Paltridge, 2002; Samraj, 2008; Swales, 2004), especially its whole organization and those written by Chinese authors. The reason why scant research has been conducted on the whole structure of the M.A. theses, to a large extent, is that the theses have daunting length and many variations among disciplines

(Paltridge, 2002; Swales, 2004). In the inadequately explored field, the structure of certain parts of M.A. theses has been analyzed, such as Acknowledgements (Hyland, 2004; Zhang, 2012), Introductions (Samraj, 2008; Maher & Milligan, 2019), Literature Review chapters (Kwan, 2006; Nguyen & Pramoolsook, 2014), Methods (Nguyen & Pramoolsook, 2015a), Results and Discussions (Nguyen & Pramoolsook, 2015b), Discussions (Nodoushan & Khakbaz 2011) and Conclusions (Hewings, 1993). In addition, some scholars provided a detailed analysis of specific sections, for example, Statement of the Problem in the Introduction chapter (Jalilifar et al., 2011) and Commenting on results in the Discussion chapter (Basturkmen, 2009). These studies present a general view of the schematic structures of some specific chapters of M.A. theses. In regard to the structure of the complete M.A. theses, to the researcher's knowledge, only three studies investigated it. To be specific, Pramoolsook (2007) explored the rhetorical structure of the M.A. thesis produced by Thai students in Biotechnology and Environmental Engineering when investigating the genre transfer between theses and research articles. In addition, Chen and Kuo (2012) conducted the research on the rhetorical structure of complete theses in Applied Linguistics. Following their model, Nguyen (2014) analyzed the move-step structures in English TESOL master's theses written by Vietnamese. Therefore, the rhetorical structures of the whole M.A. theses are still underexplored, especially those written by Chinese and in the discipline of "Foreign Linguistics and Applied Linguistics".

Secondly, for thesis defense presentation slides, only one study, to the best of the researcher's knowledge, has investigated it as a separate genre, i.e., Pieketaleyee and Bazargani (2018) analyzed the rhetorical structure of the Introduction and Literature Review on the thesis defense presentation slides. Previous studies mainly regarded the presentation itself as a genre (e.g., Dubois, 1980; Hu & Liu, 2018; Morell, 2015; Rowley-Jolivet & Carter-Thomas, 2005; Yates & Orlikowski, 2007). As for the presentation slides, except for several studies that considered conference presentation slides as a genre (e.g., Atai & Talebzadeh, 2014; Diani, 2015), most scholars viewed them only as a significant visual device during presentations to provide visual aid and keep the audience informed and interested (Dubois, 1980; Rowley-Jolivet, 2002).

Genre theory suggests that the identification of a genre depends on its communicative purposes, discourse community, and rhetorical structures (Bhatia, 1993; Swales, 1990). Therefore, thesis defense presentation slides are a separate genre since they have their particular communicative purposes, discourse communities, and generic structure, which is in line with Tardy (2009) that presentation slides are a unique genre on account of their pervasive use in the academic context and professional practice. Given the fact that presentations with slides are increasingly utilized as a predominant way to display articles and theses (Pieketaleyee & Bazargani, 2018), it is necessary to investigate the rhetorical structure of this increasingly important and demanding genre. However, studies on thesis defense presentation slides as a separate genre are scant.

Thirdly, since very few studies have analyzed thesis defense presentation slides as a separate genre, the rhetorical structure of this kind of genre is unclear. Much attention to presentation slides has been paid to those in the teaching context to examine their effect on the learning of students (e.g., Baker et al., 2018; Levasseur & Kanan Sawyer 2006; Nouri & Shahid 2005; Pi & Hong, 2016; Zdaniuk et al., 2019). Besides, several scholars investigated the students' slide design (Chen, 2021; Shin et al., 2020), slides format (Castelló et al., 2020), categories of visuals in the slides (Rowley-Jolivet, 2002; Azizifar et al., 2014), and the integration of slide-text into lectures' spoken expositions (Hallewell & Crook, 2020). In addition, general strategies in designing slides were suggested by a few studies (e.g., Berk, 2011; Mackiewicz, 2008) and the perception of students towards presentation slides was explored as well (Apperson et al., 2008; Bucher & Niemann, 2012). Nevertheless, most students are still unfamiliar with the rhetorical structure of the thesis defense presentation slides, thus, they find it challenging when producing this kind of genre. For supervisors and researchers, they may have tacit knowledge of the rhetorical structure of this genre, however, they may need the support from concrete and explicit findings that this present study could offer as well.

Finally, for thesis writing, the students have the skeletal structure provided by the university and the supervision from their supervisors at least, however, when transferring from the theses into the thesis defense presentation slides, little or no instruction is provided (Tardy, 2009). Genres are interrelated with each other and are intertextual in nature (Bhatia, 2004; Bullo, 2017; Ho, 2011; Wu, 2011). Moreover, one genre could evidently show the features from another genre or other genres, thus, these genres are related both intertextually and interdiscursively (Bhatia, 2010; 2012). Thesis defense presentation slides are produced based on the original theses, thus these two genres are interrelated at the intertextual level and the interdiscursive level. Bremner (2008) pointed out that the comprehension of the intertextual links which play a role in shaping genres is beneficial to learners for their rhetorical awareness of the genres involved. Unfortunately, to date, studies in the intertextuality and interdiscursivity, or the transfer, between these two genres could be absent, so little has been known about the changes from one to another and what strategies students would employ when conducting such transfer.

1.4 Research Objectives

To address the above concerns, which pivot around the transfer from M.A. theses to their corresponding thesis defense presentation slides conducted by GZU master's students in Foreign Linguistics and Applied Linguistics, four research objectives are set out to govern the whole research in order to make a particular contribution to the exploration of genre transfer, the ultimate goal of the present study:

1. To identify the moves, steps, and their structures of the whole M.A. theses in Foreign Linguistics and Applied Linguistics written by GZU master's students;

2. To identify the moves, steps, and their structures of the corresponding thesis defense presentation slides produced by GZU master's students;

3. To find out the changes the students made as the effect of genre transfer from M.A. theses to thesis defense presentation slides and;

4. To explore the strategies the students employed when transferring M.A. theses to thesis defense presentation slides.

1.5　Research Questions

For the accomplishment of the four research objectives established in the previous section, the following research questions are formulated respectively:

1. What are the moves, steps, and their structures of M.A. theses written by GZU master's students in Foreign Linguistics and Applied Linguistics?

2. What are the moves, steps, and their structures of the corresponding thesis defense presentation slides produced by GZU master's students?

3. What are the changes the students made as the effect of genre transfer from M.A. theses to thesis defense presentation slides?

4. What are the strategies the students employed when transferring M.A. theses to thesis defense presentation slides?

1.6　Significance of the Research

By finding out the answers to the above research questions, the present research could make some contributions to the field, which would benefit student writers, supervisors, writing teachers, and writing researchers.

Firstly, thesis is one of the crucial genres in the M.A. learning process, which, to a large extent, determines whether a graduate student could receive the degree or not (Chen & Kuo, 2012). Writing a thesis effectively is challenging for both the non-native English students, and even the native ones (Basturkmen, 2009; Bitchener & Basturkmen, 2006; Bitchener et al., 2010; Nodoushan & Khakbaz, 2011; Paltridge, 2002; Sadeghi & Shirzad, 2015; Seloni, 2014; Wu & Paltridge, 2021). The exploration of the rhetorical structure of complete theses in the specific discipline provides the novice students with a clear picture of what makes up an acceptable thesis, so the stress felt by the students (Peng, 2018; Wu & Paltridge, 2021) would be reduced to some extent as suggested that making the writing knowledge explicit to the inexperienced writers through genre analysis might be an effective way to cope with the challenges on them (Putri & Kurniawan, 2021; Ren & Li, 2011). Hence, the students could compose their own theses more effectively to be acceptable to their discourse community.

Besides, it is of potential use for supervisors to utilize the findings as some guidelines to prepare the supervisees for effective writing of the genre. In addition, the present study would offer some pictures of thesis writing from the perspective of the Chinese context.

Secondly, as mentioned in the previous section, very few studies have considered thesis defense presentation slides as a separate genre, therefore, little is known about their communicative purposes and rhetorical structure. The present study dealing with them as a specific genre adds to our knowledge of how this kind of genre is produced in the teaching and learning context. It will also raise students' awareness of this particular genre and build up their rhetorical knowledge (Bhatia, 1993; Tardy, 2009), and then students will have a clearer view of the audience's expectations of them. Furthermore, the analysis of the rhetorical structure would largely benefit the students since they receive no or few instructions from their discipline learning. Besides, unique as it is, presentation slides are pervasive in various contexts and it is meaningful to include this kind of genre in a writing course (Tardy, 2009). Hertz et al. (2016) suggested that students should be taught how to design slides, especially how to present effectively with PowerPoint slides. Therefore, this present study will provide practical materials used as empirical evidence for English writing teachers to address and promote this particular genre in English as a Foreign Language context, as the case in China.

Thirdly, apart from the rhetorical structure of the two different genres, i.e., thesis and thesis defense presentation slides, the present study will attach great importance to the transfer between these two very much related genres. From the thesis to the thesis defense presentation slides, a large text of around 20, 000 words is condensed into a 15-minute presentation with slides, which places much stress on the students. The findings on the genre transfer in this study would not only provide a distinct description of how the students make and handle a transfer between these two genres, but also generate some useful suggestions for the students and the English writing teachers. The endeavor of exploring the transfer will save the students much time in selecting contents from the thesis and arranging them in a persuasive way that would be more accepted by the intended discourse community. Findings as to the strategies the students employed while transferring would add some insights into understanding this particular process in both a text-based and an author-informed manner. All the findings of the present study would inform the development of teaching materials for writing teachers or provide guidelines for students to support their production of these two particular genres.

Finally, in addition to the pedagogical implications, the results of the present study may provide some theoretical perspectives since genre transfer has been underexplored in the existing literature. Many different but related genres have been produced and used in the academic contexts as well as the professional practice. The investigation of the present study might inspire and benefit similar studies on other genre pairs and enrich the knowledge of genre analysis.

1.7 Scope and Limitations

The present research mainly aims to investigate the rhetorical structure of the thesis and the corresponding thesis defense presentation slides, and the genre transfer between these two genres conducted by Chinese writers in the Chinese context. Considering the undertaking time and the access to the data, the study will be conducted within the following scope and limitations.

During the thesis defense, there are three genres the students need to prepare in advance as mentioned in the previous section, that is the thesis itself, the thesis defense presentation slides, and the corresponding commentary, among which two underlying transfers undertake. One is from the thesis to the thesis defense presentation slides, and the other is from the thesis presentation slides to the oral commentary. Although the thesis defense presentation slides are delivered in the digital channel, the present study regards this particular genre as a written product (Tardy, 2009). Furthermore, only the first transfer from the thesis to the thesis presentation slides will be explored. The second transfer is out of scope as a result of the heavy workload in the investigation on the first transfer and the difficulty of collecting the oral data, especially from the students who have already graduated. More importantly, the present study will be mainly conducted on the basis of textual analysis, therefore, the genre transfer between these two genres is more product-oriented but will be supplemented by some interviews with the supervisors and the writers.

Moreover, given that numerous universities offer master's degrees in Foreign Linguistics and Applied Linguistics in China, a large learning context, it is not feasible for the present researcher to include all of the universities and even not practicable to conduct a random sampling to collect the data that could represent the whole population since each university has its own requirements on the thesis writing although it is under the national requirements for M.A. thesis. Therefore, the present research will select only one single research site, i.e., the English Department in the College of Foreign Languages of GZU, which lends itself a case study for the present research.

By means of this kind of single-site research, the present case study will demonstrate a thorough and detailed understanding of the specific educational context being investigated. However, the findings could not be fully generalized into other contexts owing to the fact that this single site cannot be considered as a representative sample of the whole population. Nevertheless, the master's programs in this particular discipline, Foreign Linguistics and Applied Linguistics, are offered by an enormous number of universities under the same national requirements, although the universities themselves have their own regulations for the award of the degree. Thus, the results of the present study can provide certain insights, to some extent, to other colleges offering similar programs.

Furthermore, three layers of analysis will be included in the whole investigation. To be specific, the first layer is the investigation of the rhetorical structure of Genre A (the thesis), the second is the exploration of the rhetorical structure of Genre B (the corresponding thesis defense presentation slides), and the last one is the comparing of rhetorical structures and the textual features between Genre A and Genre B. In addition, these text-based analyses will be triangulated and enriched by the interviews with the supervisors and the writers. Given the workload of this three-layered analysis, only 20 pairs of the thesis and the corresponding thesis defense presentation slides will be collected as the sample, following previous related studies. Besides, to capture the current tendency and the recurrent structure accepted by the discourse communities, the data will be collected merely among the graduates from the academic years 2017 to 2021.

1.8 Definitions of Key Terms

To better find out the answers to the research questions raised in the previous section and conduct the present study, the following key terms are defined to provide their operational meanings specific to this research.

Foreign Linguistics and Applied Linguistics is a program offered by the majority of the universities in China. It is similar to the international program in Applied Linguistics. At GZU, the topics include those related to cognitive linguistics, applied linguistics, second language acquisition, discourse analysis, English teaching and learning, and so forth.

Genre refers to a successful class of communicative events which are conducted by members of a specific discourse community (Bhatia, 1993; Swales, 1990). This specific discourse community shares a set of communicative purposes which serve as the privileged criterion to generate the categories of genre. In addition, the schematic patterns and language choices are shaped by the communicative purposes as well. Therefore, communicative purposes, the discourse community, and the schematic patterns work together to determine a specific genre. The definition of genre from Swales (1990) and Bhatia (1993) is powerful and widely adopted, so the present study employs their definitions as well. Hence, in the present study, thesis and thesis defense slides are two different genres in that each has its own particular communicative purposes, rhetorical structures, and discourse communities.

Genre transfer, in this study, refers to the changes or modifications appearing, and the strategies employed by the writers when producing one corresponding genre based on the original genre. To be more specific, it means the changes or modifications of the rhetorical structure and the textual features in the thesis defense presentation slides compared with the original thesis, and the strategies the writers employed when they produced the thesis defense presentation slides based on the thesis.

Genre transfer strategies are defined by the current study as the techniques the students used to conduct the genre transfer from the M.A. thesis to the corresponding thesis defense presentation slides. Once the techniques are identified, they could be utilized as the strategies for others to adopt or as practical materials for teaching purposes. Therefore, the present study adopts the term "strategy" rather than "technique" for the consistency of the writing.

M.A. thesis, in the present study, is the final product that M.A. students in Foreign Linguistics and Applied Linguistics submit to the defense committee members during their thesis defense. According to the State Council of the People's Republic of China, M.A. theses ought to add some new insights into the research topic and should be around 15,000 words long.

Move is a text segment serving a specific communicative function that contributes to achieving the overall communicative purposes of a genre (Biber et al., 2007). In this study, move refers to phrase(s), sentence(s), or paragraph(s) which performs a specific communicative function to accomplish the overall communicative purposes of the thesis or the thesis defense presentation slides.

Rhetorical structure refers to the moves, steps, and the recurrent move-step sequences within one genre so as to achieve the overall communicative purposes of that genre. It has been termed, or used alternatively, by other scholars with slight differences as "generic structure" (Bunton, 2002; Frow, 2013; Kathpalia & Khoo, 2020), "discourse structure" (Bhatia, 2012), "schematical structure" (Basturkmen, 2009; Flowerdew & Forest, 2009; Swales, 1990; Zhang, 2018), "organizational pattern" (Fairclough, 2006; Hyon, 1996). The present study selects the term "rhetorical structure" (e.g., Flowerdew, 2005; Putri & Kurniawan, 2021; Yeung, 2007; Yoon & Casal, 2020) for the purpose of focusing more on the writing and the functions of the moves and steps.

Step is a sub-text within a move through one or more of which the communicative function of the move is accomplished.

Textual features, in the current study, are the distinct characteristics of texts in one genre at the formal and textual level, which display writers' ways of placing texts to present information, such as bulleted lists and diagrams that show the texts in another form. Moreover, they are related to how the texts from one genre are being presented in another genre.

Thesis defense presentation slides are an independent genre. In the present study, they are a set of slides mainly containing contents that are extracted from the original thesis with certain modifications by the students to support and facilitate their oral commentary during the thesis defense. For convenience in the analysis, the present study regards the thesis defense presentation slides as a written product rather than a digital one.

1.9 Summary

This chapter first introduced the context the present research situated in from a general view on the importance of English in China to the specific master's program being focused on and then narrowed it down to the single research site this study selected. On the foundation of the background, the research problems and the related rationale were delivered. Furthermore, the specific research objectives were generated from the research problems to guide the whole study and the research questions were raised next. In addition, the potential significance of conducting this particular study was stated as well as the scope and limitations. In the end, some key terms were defined under the current context. The next chapter will make an effort to review the related theories and to synthesize the previous studies on similar topics having been done by other scholars for the purpose of building up not only the theoretical foundation but also the research network with other pertinent studies. Moreover, the frameworks for analyzing the rhetorical structures of the two genres proposed in the present study will be provided in detail.

CHAPTER 2 Literature Review

This chapter lays the theoretical foundation for genre and genre analysis in which definitions of the genre, the concept of discourse community, the genre study traditions, and move analysis are provided and discussed. Next, the pertinent studies on the two focused genres of the present study, i.e., thesis and thesis defense presentation slides, are reviewed in terms of their definitions, communicative purposes, intended audience, and rhetorical structures, respectively. During the review of the pertinent investigations on the rhetorical structure of these two different but corresponding genres, research gaps will be indicated. Finally, the related concepts of intertextuality, interdiscursivity, and genre transfer are investigated, followed by a discussion of several studies on genre transfer.

2.1 Genre: Theory and Analysis

2.1.1 Definitions of Genre

Since the end of the last century, the definition of genre has been explored by numerous scholars from different perspectives which, in turn, has enriched its development. Martin proposed that genre is "a staged, goal-oriented social process" (Martin et al., 1987) in which members of a culture interact with each other to accomplish their goals through more than one step. Moreover, stressing goals as well, Swales (1990) extended the definition of genre to include the discourse community and emphasized the patterns of the texts. As a scholarly resource of genre analysis, Swales (1990) provided readers with a very comprehensive definition of the genre, as follows:

A genre comprises a class of communicative events, the members of which share some set of communicative purposes. These purposes are recognized by the expert members of the parent discourse community, and thereby constitute the rationale for the genre. This rationale shapes the schematic structure of the discourse and influences and constrains the choice of content and style. Communicative purpose is both a privileged criterion and one that operates to keep the scope of a genre as here conceived focused on comparable rhetorical action. In addition to purpose, exemplars of a genre exhibit various patterns of similarity in terms of structure, style, content, and intended audience.

From the above definition, more attention is paid to the communicative purpose which is regarded as the key factor when deciding whether a text belongs to a genre category or not. However, Swales (2004) suggested that given the possibility of a genre evolving over time, communicative purposes cannot be used as the only factor to define a genre. Besides the communicative purposes, the definition indicated that there are certain patterns among the instances of a genre.

Based on Swales' (1990) definition, Bhatia (1993) elaborated the definition of the genre, as follows:

Genre is a recognizable communicative event characterized by a set of communicative purpose(s) identified and mutually understood by the members of the professional or academic community in which it regularly occurs. Most often it is highly structured and conventionalized with constraints on allowable contributions in terms of their intent, positioning, form, and functional value. These constraints, however, are often exploited by the expert members of the discourse community to achieve private intentions within the framework of socially recognized purpose(s).

This definition provides a clear picture of the genre from several aspects. On the one hand, the communicative purpose is the primary factor that influences a genre's nature and construction, thus, differences in communicative purpose are likely to shape different genres. On the other hand, to achieve the communicative purpose(s) of one genre, the writers are not totally free to use any resources. Instead, they are constrained within the conventions of that genre which has a relatively standardized structure to conform to. In addition, it is the reaction of one group of people to the recurrent situation that shapes the genre and gradually forms a conventionalized internal structure to fulfill certain specific communicative purposes. In other words, genre is the cumulative result of producing and using texts in a group of people or a discourse community as proposed by Swales (1990) which will be elaborated on the following section. Therefore, members of that discourse community are much more knowledgeable about the communicative purposes and the internal structure than the apprentices of and the outsiders from that discourse community. In turn, people who want to enter this discourse community need long exposure or training to be accepted by this community. More importantly, Bhatia (1993) stressed that genre is dynamic rather than static from the tactical perspective of genre construction.

Apart from these two elaborated definitions of genre, various definitions have also emerged. Miller (1994) defined genre as "a form of social action". Holmes (1997) stated that genre is "a class of texts characterized by a specific communicative function that tends to produce distinctive structural patterns" . Furthermore, Paltridge (2014) just briefly regarded genres as "communicative events". Besides, Hyon (2018) concluded that a genre is "a category of texts characterized by similarities as well as — to some extent — differences across its members" .

From different aspects, these definitions provide a distinctive angle to examine language use in the teaching and learning contexts. The recurrent characteristics of a genre from these definitions are communicative purposes, target audience, and schematic or rhetorical patterns. Therefore, in the present study, genre refers to "a kind of successful communicative event that owns its particular communicative purposes, schematic patterns, and members of a certain discourse community which, in turn, become the criteria to determine the scope of that genre". The concept of discourse community will be presented in the following section.

2.1.2 Concept of Discourse Community

To better understand the definition of genre, there is one aspect that needs to be further elaborated, that is, discourse community. From the social perspective, a discourse community is a group of people who use discourse to form a social behavior, to maintain and extend its knowledge, to initiate new members into it, and as a result, that discourse constitutes the knowledge of the group (Herzberg, 1986, as cited in Swales, 1990). Subsequently, Swales (1990) further explored and appropriated the notion of discourse community based on this social view, and then defined that "discourse communities are socio-rhetorical networks that form in order to work towards sets of common goals". By distinguishing the concept of speech community and discourse community, Swales (1990) emphasized that the common goals are the predominant factor in influencing the development and maintenance of the discoursal characteristics of one discourse community, thus, the privileged determining factors of the community's linguistic behavior are functional rather than social. For the established members of a discourse community, they are characterized by the familiarity with the particular genres which are employed to fulfill those common goals.

For an easier and clearer identification of a discourse community, Swales (1990) suggested a list of sufficiently explicit criteria, as follows:

1. A discourse community has a broadly agreed set of common public goals.

2. A discourse community has mechanisms of intercommunication among its members.

3. A discourse community uses its participatory mechanisms primarily to provide information and feedback.

4. A discourse community utilizes and hence possesses one or more genres in the communicative furtherance of its aims.

5. In addition to owning genres, a discourse community has acquired some specific lexis.

6. A discourse community has a threshold level of members with a suitable degree of relevant content and discoursal expertise.

In essence, this set of criteria is mainly generated from the concept of genre in a discourse community since genres are the properties of the discourse community. To put it in simple terms, the present study views discourse community as a group of people who are obviously or potentially involved in the production and use of a particular genre. The concept of discourse community is mostly investigated in the

English for Specific Purpose(ESP) tradition of genre analysis. This tradition and the other two genre analysis traditions will be discussed in the next section.

2.1.3 Three Traditions of Genre Analysis

The definition of genre has been explored from different perspectives as stated in the prior section, and scholars from each perspective have further developed and established distinct approaches to analyze genre, making the literature of genre colorful and complicated. Therefore, to better view genre landscape, initiated by Hyon (1996), genre research studies are mainly divided into three traditions or schools, based on their focus, approaches of the analysis, and genre-based pedagogy (Bawarshi & Reiff, 2010; Fakhruddin & Hassan, 2015; Hyland, 2002; Johns, 2002). These three traditions are the Systemic Functional Linguistics, the English for Specific Purposes, and the New Rhetoric. They are not absolutely different from one another as overlapping exists among them (Johns et al., 2006). Other possible candidates for the genre tradition were suggested, such as the Brazilian approach to genre (Vian, 2012; as cited in Swales, 2012) and the Academic Literacies movement which is also known as the "New London School" (Swales, 2012). However, they are not widely acknowledged among scholars of genre studies. Therefore, the present study will focus on the review of the three traditions of genre studies. Genre theories in each tradition are highly situated, and it is helpful for researchers to gain insights into different genre conceptions regarding their implications for research and pedagogies (Hyland, 2002).

2.1.3.1 The Systemic Functional Linguistics

This tradition, also known as "the Sydney School", underpins its theoretical framework within the larger language theory of Systemic Functional Linguistics (SFL) founded by Michael Halliday which states that language forms are shaped by the surrounding social context and its three key features; namely, field, tenor, and mode, which work together to determine a register of language. Built on Halliday's work, Martin (1984) associated genre, functioning at the layer of the context of culture, with a register which functioned at the layer of the context of the situation. Further, he defined the genre as a "staged, goal-oriented and purposeful social activity that people engage in as members of their culture". In this tradition, scholars emphasize the social purposes of a genre and its structural patterns to construct meanings in culture. Thus, it aims to explore the organization and structure of language within a particular context, and how the social purposes are linked to text structures and are realized by them.

Originally, scholars in this tradition mainly focused on English education in primary, secondary level, and adult education intending to help students effectively participate in academic and workplace contexts (Hyon, 1996; Yunick, 1997). In recent years, plenty of studies adopted this tradition to explore genres in diverse contexts and languages (e.g., Abdel-Malek, 2020; Gardner, 2012; Humphry & Economou, 2015; Mitchell et al., 2021; Yasuda, 2017).

In order to identify the purposeful, interactive, and sequential features of genres and how the language choices are influenced by social purposes, genre analysis in this tradition seeks not only to find out the distinctive stages or moves of genres, but also to investigate the lexical, grammatical patterns and cohesive choices which fulfill the function in each stage of genres (Hyland, 2002). Moreover, the SFL explores the ways a genre's context is constructed by the field, tenor, and mode of a register, and the ways these three register layers are realized in a genre by ideational, interpersonal, and textual choices which are known as the meta-functions of a register (Martin, 1997; Yasuda, 2017). By means of analyzing these three layers and meta-functions of a register, the SFL tradition believes that it can provide a systematic comprehension of the construction of genres and their realizations in a particular social context. Therefore, the most common trajectory in this tradition falls into one or more steps within the following: a) to identify the social purposes through the investigation of the generic structural elements and possible stages of a specific genre; b) to analyze the field, tenor, and mode of the texts which work together to determine the context; c) to analyze the meta-functions of the texts, and d) to explore a genre's semantic, lexicogrammatical and phonological/graphological features (Fakhruddin & Hassan, 2015).

In this tradition, form, function, and social context of a genre are linked together, thus providing a great deal of implications for genre instruction and genre-based pedagogy in various contexts, and proposing several instructional frameworks, especially the Teaching/Learning Cycle (Hermansson et al., 2019; Thongchalerm & Jarunthawatchai, 2020). In this cycle, different stages are proposed, i.e., three stages, four stages, and five stages. For the three-stage cycle, the main stages are *Deconstruction*, *Joint Construction*, and *Independent Construction*, which is informed by context setting and field building through the whole cycle (Humphery & Macnaught, 2011; Rothery & Stenglin, 1995). In terms of the four-stage cycle, *Setting the Context*, *Modelling and Deconstruction*, *Joint Construction*, and *Independent Construction* are put forward (Callaghan & Rothery, 1988; Hermansson et al., 2019; Rothery, 1996). Moreover, in the five-stage cycle, an extra stage Linking related texts is added as the last stage based on the four-stage cycle (Feez, 1998; Hyland, 2007). These three cycles differ in the number of the stages, but the three key stages are the same. These cycles emphasize the notion of scaffolding (Paltridge, 2001) and make a significant impact on the teaching of various genres.

2.1.3.2 The English for Specific Purposes

English for Specific Purposes (ESP) is a widespread term covering diverse areas of English studies, such as academic English and professional English. With an emphasis on the functions and rhetorical structures of texts as well, genre in this tradition refers to a kind of communicative event determined by communicative purposes within a particular discourse community whose members employ particular rhetorical structures and lexical features to fulfill these communicative goals (Swales, 1990). A discourse community is introduced in this tradition as a group of individuals sharing some common communicative purposes. By means of exploring the communicative purposes and formal language features of a genre which is situated in particular discourse communities, the major aim of this tradition is to explicate the appropriate language resources and skills for language learners so that they can be accepted by certain discourse communities. The ultimate goal is to better understand the underlying features of the construction of genres and the ways they achieve their communicative purposes (Bhatia, 1993; Paltridge, 2002; Swales, 1990).

With these mentioned goals, the ESP tradition serves a different target audience. Scholars in this tradition focus more on international students who are at a more advanced level of education, often the graduate level (Bawarshi & Reiff, 2010). Moreover, except for the academic genres, Bhatia (2004) extended the analysis to explore genres in professional settings. With the main focus on non-native English speakers, this kind of tradition seeks to help them get familiar with the functions and conventions of various genres that they need to produce or use in their disciplines and professions.

A typical analysis approach in this tradition is move analysis, beginning with the identification of a genre in the context of discourse community and then with the definition of communicative purposes which the genre will accomplish. This approach pays much attention to the communicative purposes of genres within particular discourse communities. Moreover, the analysis proceeds to investigate the organization, or the schematic/rhetorical structure of the genre which is expressed by a sequence of moves, and then turns to explore the linguistic features of each move (Bawarshi & Reiff, 2010). The most popular instantiation of move analysis is the Create a Research Space (CARS) model proposed by Swales (1990). Furthermore, Bhatia (1993) demonstrated a more detailed genre analysis with seven steps in total which could be adopted in a combination of several steps or in a non-sequential way. Genre analysis in ESP provides fascinating insights into the understanding of the functions, forms, as well as the context of diverse genres in numerous areas (e.g., Matzler, 2021; Xu & Lockwood, 2021; You & Li, 2021) and helps new members better produce genres which are new or unfamiliar to them (Tardy, 2016).

Genre analysis findings from this tradition provide profound generic resources for teachers and learners in terms of genre instruction and genre-based pedagogy. With the needs analysis of students, ESP teachers could be better prepared for the courses best suiting students and then help raise their genre awareness (Hyon, 2016). Rhetorical structures and linguistic features of a variety of genres are identified to support teachers and learners to recognize each genre and to actively participate in the construction, interpretation, and use of genres.

2.1.3.3 The New Rhetoric

Originally, the New Rhetoric genre investigation mainly consisted of North

American researchers and practitioners who embraced a rhetorical tradition (Hyland, 2002). Unlike the other two traditions, much significance is attached to the context in which genres are produced and used, thus genre in this tradition is viewed as a kind of social action responding to the recurrent situations (Coe & Freedman, 1998; Miller, 1984). In addition, Coe (2002) asserted that from the New Rhetoric perspective, a genre is the functional relationship between a text type and a situation rather than either of them alone. Therefore, it is the social context surrounding texts that improves the understanding of how genres are being constructed, interpreted, and acted, hence, the starting point of this tradition is to investigate the contexts of genres rather than their formal features.

The New Rhetoric genre analysis was initiated in first language teaching to investigate genres in universities and first language composition aiming to support university students and professional beginners to have a better understanding of the social functions and contexts of genres (Hyon, 1996; 2018).

Emphasizing the social and cultural contexts in which genres occur, this tradition adopts an ethnographical approach to analyze texts which provides rich descriptions of the surrounding academic and professional contexts of genres and the social functions genres serve within these contexts (Hyon, 1996; Hyland, 2002). By this kind of ethnographical method, it tends to gain insights into the attitudes, values, and beliefs of the communities in which genres are produced and used. Moreover, Johns (2013) proposed some analysis topics and questions to conduct a detailed contextual genre analysis, such as questions related to ecology, production, representation, activity, and distribution.

Scholars in this tradition contend that genres are dynamic rather than static since they are gradually evolving over time in the context and they possess a complicated nature in reality. Therefore, it is impossible to teach written genres in the classroom (Hyland, 2004). Although the focus of this tradition is not on the teaching orientation, it brings another aspect for learners to understand genres more thoroughly beyond the text.

2.1.3.4 Summary of the Three Traditions

In reality, the nature and construction of genres are complicated. These three traditions bring abundant insights into understanding a variety of genres from different perspectives and they share some similarities and differences. All of them admit the value of language use to embody the social function of the specific context in which genres perform. Moreover, they all attempt to analyze the interrelationship between function and language use in a particular context and then apply the findings to language learning contexts.

Nevertheless, the three traditions differ in their educational contexts, intellectual foundations, and emphasis on a particular side of the relationship between language use and its social functions (Yunick, 1997). The ESP tradition primarily focuses on non-native English speakers in academic and professional contexts, while the SFL tradition and the New Rhetoric tradition are more applied to the first language composition. However, nowadays, these three traditions are all applied to various educational contexts, hence, this distinguishment among them is vague now.

As for their intellectual foundations, the SFL tradition obviously draws from the works in Systemic Functional Linguistics, while the New Rhetoric tradition situates itself into the non-linguistic schools, such as post-structuralist social and literary theories, and developmental psychology (Yunick, 1997). Similar to the SFL tradition, scholars in the ESP genre analysis adopted the works from Hallidayan linguistics as well but they focus more on the linguistic models of genres rather than involving the analysis of register variables of field, tenor, and mode, or the analysis of the meta-functions of language use.

On the continuum of language use, or texts and social purposes, or contexts, the New Rhetoric inclines toward the social purposes end to explore the social context in which genres are produced and used; thus, they view that genres are dynamic in nature and cannot be taught in classrooms as static products. However, the SFL genre analysis inclines more towards the texts end to investigate the discoursal structures and linguistic features of genres. Genre analysis in the ESP stands in the middle of the continuum to identify the moves and linguistic features adopted to achieve communicative purposes within a discourse community.

In addition, different aims of genre analysis result in different methods in looking at genres. The New Rhetoric tradition applies an ethnographical approach to grasp the attitudes, values, and beliefs of the context in which a genre occurs, while the other two employ a textual analysis method to demonstrate the rhetorical structures and linguistic features of a genre and then with the supplement of interviews, observations, and other documents to understand the context of a genre.

In a word, the New Rhetoric tradition pays much attention to the context with which genres actively interact, adopting a non-linguistic analysis to explore the dynamic nature of genres. Nevertheless, the ESP and the SFL traditions focus more on the text aspect using a linguistic approach that views genres as static products at the time, and then generalize the findings into genre teaching and learning in other similar contexts.

In the present study, the ultimate goal is to investigate the transfer between two target genres, i.e., the thesis and the corresponding thesis defense presentation slides, which results in changes and modifications of the rhetorical structures and linguistic features. By exploring the move structure of each genre and comparing both of them, the ESP tradition will be adopted as the theoretical and analytical framework throughout the whole process. Register variables (field, tenor, and mode) and meta-functions of texts will not be taken into consideration as those in the SFL tradition. Besides, compared with the New Rhetoric, the ESP tradition is situated more in the English as a Foreign Language(EFL)/English as a Second Language(ESL) educational contexts which the present study focuses on. In the ESP genre analysis, the identification of the rhetorical structure of texts is through the investigation of a sequence of moves and steps, which is typically termed as "move analysis" (Biber et al., 2007; Paltridge, 2013). The notion of move analysis will be elaborated on in the next section.

2.1.4 Move Analysis

Move analysis in genre studies was first introduced and developed by Swales in 1981 (as cited in Moreno & Swales, 2018) aiming to depict the schematic patterns of research articles, which is applied to investigate the rhetorical structures of other genres in ESP afterward. It is a text-based analytical approach assuming that the discoursal structure of texts consists of a series of moves and steps in sequence. In addition, it aims to reveal the form-function interaction between texts and text structures, and at the same time, to enhance our comprehension of the cognitive structures on how writers construct the content of genres (Ntalala et al., 2018).

A move, or a rhetorical move, refers to "a discoursal or rhetorical unit that performs a coherent communicative function in a written or spoken discourse" (Swales, 2004). In other words, moves are the segments or units of a text which serve distinct communicative functions, and which make up the whole text to fulfill the ultimate communicative purposes of this kind of genre that exists in a certain discourse community.

Within each move, there are multiple constituent elements (You & Li, 2021) to accomplish the specific communicative function of the move. These constituent elements are called "step" or "rhetorical strategies" as in Bhatia (1993). Steps are subdivisions of a move (Franken, 2020) or subunits of a move (Tseng, 2018). They are in some combination or join together to realize a particular move to which they belong (Biber et al., 2007). In a word, steps constitute a move that combines with other moves in a sequence to achieve the communicative purposes of the genre that are shared among the members of a particular discourse community. Usually, more specific terms are assigned to interpret steps than those in moves (Moreno & Swales, 2018).

Biber et al. (2007) put forward the general procedures to conduct a move analysis. In the beginning, after collecting the data, it is significant to have an overall comprehension of all the texts' rhetorical purposes. Then, the second procedure is to examine the communicative function of each text segment from its local context and look for the possible move categories. This procedure is the hardest one since multiple readings and reflections are necessary until distinctive move categories come out. The third procedure is to search for the common themes in terms of their functions and semantics and then group them to reflect the particular steps through which a move could be realized. These themes either share certain similarities or occur in approximately the same location among the texts. After identifying the possible common move categories and steps, the next needed procedure is to measure the validity of the definitions of moves and steps through the pilot-coding with fine-tuning from time to time. The fifth procedure is to provide clear definitions and examples of each move and step to form the coding protocol. The next procedure is using the protocol to code all the texts in the data with inter-rater reliability. During this procedure, any revealed additional moves or steps need to be put in the protocol and then further discussion and analysis are needed if there is a discrepancy between the inter-coders. Moreover, the coding protocol is revised by the new moves or steps, or by the further discussion of the discrepancies. The problematic part needs to be re-coded if there is any. Finally, the linguistic features of each move or step could be further explored. These steps are conducted in a top-down manner, whereas they can be undertaken in a bottom-up manner as well by which linguistic features of the texts are firstly analyzed and then the move types or the framework emerge from the analysis of the linguistic feature patterns. It is significant to point out that no strict rules or procedures are set for the conduction of move analysis (Biber et al., 2007) as long as typical move and step patterns are identified. The whole process of move analysis is underpinned by the grounded theory approach to some extent, in the present researcher's opinion. Grounded theory is a kind of inquiry design in which themes or categories are generated from the data, thus a general, abstract theory grounded in the data is derived (Creswell & Creswell, 2018). Similarly, in the move analysis, the move categories and step categories are generated from the data as well.

Generally, move identification is a qualitative approach and is mainly conducted manually based on the prominent communicative purpose of each move. However, Biber et al. (2007) proposed a framework for corpus-based move analysis to integrate quantitative counts in analyzing texts. There are a few differences between corpus-based move analysis and traditional move analysis. On the one hand, corpus-based move analysis is conducted in a relatively large text sample, and all the moves and steps are coded electronically in order to run the computerized counts and calculations. On the other hand, it is easier to investigate the linguistic features of each move and offer details to understand the ways communicative functions are fulfilled from a linguistic perspective. These quantitative counts in corpus-based move analysis provide the potential for generating general trends about the move types and patterns. Recently, most ESP genre studies have been conducted through this kind of analysis (e.g., Cotos, 2019; Khany & Malmir, 2020; Ntalala & Orwenjo, 2018; You & Li, 2021). In short, corpus-based move analysis combines both qualitative and quantitative analysis, thus it is more like mixed methods research, which will be adopted by the present research. It is qualitative since all moves and steps are first identified and tagged manually by the researchers with subjective judgments toward the communicative functions of text segments, while it is quantitative because it involves computerized counts on the frequencies of moves and steps and other linguistic items that are the focus of investigations.

Apart from the corpus-based move analysis, scholars recently put forward corpus-driven, or bundle-driven move analysis which uses lexical bundles, generated automatically depending on their length, frequency, and text distribution, as move indicators to automatically identify the moves of a large number of texts (Li et al., 2017; 2020). This kind of analysis integrating automatic computational technology with corpus could make great contributions to the identification of moves and help reduce the researcher's bias. However, move identification depends on not only the lexical bundles but also the human's cognitive judgment of the text segments about their communicative functions which could only be clear after consideration of the local context (Tseng, 2018). Thus, this kind of move analysis needs further development to enhance its reliability of the move identification.

The typical instantiation of move analysis is the CARS model proposed by Swales (1990) which serves for the construction of the Introduction of research articles. There are three moves in this model with some steps in each move. The first move in this model is *Establishing a Territory*, in which the author sets the research context by one or more steps of *Claiming centrality*, *Making topic generalization*, and *Reviewing previous items of research*. The second move is *Establishing a Niche* through the steps of *Counter-claiming*, *Indicating a gap*, *Question-raising*, or *Continuing a tradition*. The last move is *Occupying the Niche* realized by *Outlining purposes*, *Announcing present research*, *Announcing principal findings*, and *Indicating RA structure*. This CARS model enjoys wide applications in different disciplines, even the RAs written in other languages.

From the previous move studies (Biber et al., 2007; Khany & Malmir, 2020; Moreno & Swales, 2018; Tanko, 2017), moves possess several characteristics. The first characteristic is that moves have distinctive boundaries that can be identified, and they vary in their length from one sentence to several paragraphs. Moreover, there may be a few steps, or no step at all, to realize one move. In addition, the frequency of each move is different in that some are considered conventional or obligatory, while some are optional. Besides, some moves are more likely to recur in a cycle or do not occur in a fixed sequence occasionally.

2.2 Master's Thesis

2.2.1 Definitions, Communicative Purposes, and Intended Audience

Generally, a thesis is a kind of formal document (Casanave, 2019), or a report of research (Joyner et al., 2018) that M.A. candidates write to accomplish their M.A. journey and apply for an academic degree (Putri & Kurniawan, 2021). It is a significant component of postgraduate education in most of the world. The thesis is a lengthy text that roughly ranges from 10,000 to 20,000 words (Thompson, 2013). Moreover, it looks scholarly since it is situated in the literature and contains a lot of citations from previous studies (Joyner et al., 2018). Besides, it is written in a formal way and the writers endeavor to be as objective as possible.

The thesis serves several communicative purposes within the discourse community it is produced and used. First of all, students write to report or to inform the results of their research (Joyner et al., 2018). Besides, it is produced by students to convince examiners not only of the authoritative voices in their works but also of the appropriate self-positioning based on their research topics and disciplines (Casanave, 2019; Thompson, 2012), and then to persuade examiners that they deserve to be members of the academic community (Paltridge & Starfield, 2007). In addition, a thesis is written for assessment purposes (Paltridge 2002; Thompson, 2013). Furthermore, from the university faculty's perspective, a thesis is perceived as a way to demonstrate that the candidate possesses the ability to conduct research, and as a widely accepted form for accomplishing their mission of "generating and disseminating new knowledge" (Joyner et al., 2018). For the students themselves, writing a thesis is to obtain a master's degree, and it is also a way of learning.

In the discourse community of the thesis, the M.A. students are obviously the writers and there are a couple of groups of readers as the intended audience. Firstly, the most immediate audience is the supervisors and the examiners in the committee (Paltridge & Starfield, 2007; Thompson, 2013). They read the thesis carefully and provide feedback, thus, they might be the persons who know the most about the thesis aside from the students themselves. Therefore, thesis writers are expected to display their knowledge of the field and show that they are capable of conducting research independently. Secondly, the less immediate audience is the faculty members, hence, the thesis needs to meet the requirements of the institution in terms of the content and the form (Joyner et al., 2018). Finally, the potential audience might be the members of the profession (Joyner et al., 2018), such as other junior M.A. students or probably other researchers in the field.

"Thesis" and "dissertation" are both adopted to refer to the report of research in different contexts. In the US context, the research reports written by M.A. students are viewed as "thesis", while in the UK context, they are called "dissertation". As for those written by doctoral students, "dissertation" and "thesis" are used in these two different contexts, respectively (Paltridge, 2002; Thompson, 2013). In Australia and New Zealand, the term "thesis" refers to the research reports produced by both M.A. students and doctoral students (Thompson, 2013). In the Chinese context, the US tradition is adopted in that the thesis is written by M.A. students while the dissertation is written by doctoral students. Therefore, the present study will adopt the term "thesis" to refer to the research report produced by M.A. students.

2.2.2 Structures of Master's Thesis

Although a thesis possesses particular communicative purposes and target audiences, there is more than one structure or pattern to produce such text. Dudley-

Evans (1999) depicted that the traditional organization of a thesis or dissertation is the IMRD structure which includes Introduction, Methods, Results, and Discussion. Later, this structure was expanded to include Literature Review and Conclusions, shortened as the ILrMRDC structure (Paltridge, 2002; Swales, 2004). Furthermore, Thompson (1999) divided the traditional organization into a simple pattern and a complex pattern. These two patterns differ in that the latter one reports on more than one study thus the IMRD structure recurrently appears in the middle part with a general Introduction in the beginning and a general Conclusion in the end. Except for the traditional type, Dong (1998) stated that some doctoral dissertations are produced by compiling several publishable research articles. In addition, Dudley-Evans (1999) found another structure of the thesis, that is a "topic-based" thesis with an Introduction in the beginning, followed by several chapters which demonstrate sub-topics of the investigated topic, and then finished with a Conclusion.

By comparing the structures suggested in the handbooks with the actual practice of thesis writing, Paltridge (2002) concluded that theses and dissertations usually have four structures; namely, Traditional: simple, Traditional: complex, Topic-Based, and Compilation of research articles. Moreover, based on this framework, Anderson et al. (2020) found that the majority of the dissertations in their study fall into the traditional-simple category, but two new hybrid dissertation structures emerge; namely, Hybrid SM (simple/manuscript) and Hybrid TM (topic/manuscript). The former type is in a standard traditional-simple structure and the latter one looks like a standard topic-based structure. However, previously published sections are embedded in certain dissertation chapters or are the entire dissertation chapter without change or with slight modification. This can be explained by that the dissertation writers may transfer certain parts of their work into research articles during their writing without modification (Pramoolsook, 2007).

Thompson (2013) pointed out that the adopted thesis/dissertation structures vary to some extent in different disciplines or contexts. Hence, it is significant to explore the structures within a specific discipline. Therefore, the present study is situated in a specific discipline, i.e., Foreign Linguistics and Applied Linguistics.

2.2.3 Previous Studies on Master's Thesis

The majority of the studies on M.A. theses focused only on one single chapter. Scarce attention has been paid to the rhetorical structure of the whole M.A. theses (e.g., Chen & Kuo, 2012; Nguyen, 2014). Since Ph.D. dissertations have a similar rhetorical structure to master's thesis (Dastjerdi et al., 2017) and on account of both sharing similar communicative purposes, structures, and target audiences (Chen & Kuo, 2012), consequently, related studies on Ph.D. dissertations are also reviewed in the present section.

2.2.3.1 The Introduction Chapter

The first study to explore the rhetorical structure of the Introduction of M.A. theses was conducted by Dudley-Evans (1986) who proposed a six-move model with two or three possible steps in some moves through investigating seven M.A. theses in Plant Biology. This model has some similarities with Swales' (1990) CARS model for the research article Introductions which has three moves and several steps in each move. The first three moves in Dudley-Evans' (1986) indicated a gradual progression from the wide field to a general topic, and then to a particular topic, which is similar to the first move *Establishing the territory* in the CARS model. After the first three moves, writers define the scope of their particular topic by either introducing research parameters or summarizing previous studies. Then, in Move 5, the writer's own study is indicated by a gap or a possible extension of previous studies, which is similar to *Establishing a niche*, the second move in the CARS model, both of which make the writer's study situated in the wider literature. The last move in both models is similar in which objectives of the research are revealed. The link between the writer's study and the wider field is more emphasized in Move 2 in Swales' (1990), thus, Bunton (2002) drew from the three moves in the CARS model and all the steps in both models to explore the rhetorical structure of dissertation Introductions.

Examining 45 dissertation introductory chapters across eight disciplines, Bunton (2002) found that nearly all texts in the corpus contained the three moves in CARS model and almost in a cyclical way in which the Move1-2 cycle was more frequently used than Move 1-2-3 as demonstrated in the framework. As for the steps, all the 14 steps proposed by both Dudley-Evans (1986) and Swales (1990) were found in his corpus. However, 10 new steps were identified. The reason why more steps were found may be because of the wider coverage of the disciplines and the size of Ph.D. dissertations which are longer than research articles and M.A. theses. Based on these findings, Bunton (2002) proposed a model for dissertation Introduction writing which groups the moves and steps into "Often present" and "Occasionally present".

Furthermore, Samraj (2008) conducted a contrastive analysis of 24 M.A. theses, eight of which were each from three disciplines (Biology, Philosophy, and Linguistics). Move analysis and semi-structured interviews with several subject specialists were conducted. Adopting Swales' (1990) CARS model as the framework and modifying it from the findings of the research article Introductions and dissertation Introductions, Samraj (2008) found that there were variations in terms of the moves and steps among the disciplines. Only the writers from Linguistics consistently employed Move 2 (*Establishing a niche*) to justify their studies. Moreover, the theses from Linguistics showed the most intradepartmental differences and demonstrated more textual variations.

In addition, Nguyen and Pramoolsook (2014) explored the M.A. theses written by Vietnamese students in TESOL. Adopting Bunton's (2002) model to analyze the 12 theses in their corpus, all the three moves were found but only 15 out of the 24 steps proposed in the model were identified in their corpus. Nevertheless, they found a new step *Chapter Summary* in their data which indicated the three-part writing instruction (Introduction-Body-Conclusion) the students received in their university.

Recently, Kawase (2018) compared the dissertation Introductions of Applied Linguistics with those of other disciplines through analyzing the moves and steps of 20 Introductions using Bunton's (2002) model. These 20 Introductions were all from the dissertations with the ILrMRDC(Introduction, Literature review, Methodology, Results, Discussion, and Conclusion) structure selected from English-speaking universities. The findings revealed that the writers in Applied Linguistics more frequently demonstrated research questions/hypotheses and research subjects/material while they infrequently utilized the step *Problem/need* to establish a niche and the methodology description was less presented.

Besides, Maher and Milligan (2019) employed the framework adapted from the models of Swales (1990) and Samraj (2008) to investigate the moves and steps of 16 thesis Introductions produced by Mechanical Engineering students. Almost all the moves and steps were identified in their corpus which suggested that the CARS schema seems to be applicable to the production of the thesis Introductions in this discipline.

Furthermore, Zainuddin and Shaari (2021) adopted the CARS model of Swales (1990) to explore the doctoral dissertation Introductions written by Malaysian ESL writers and then focused on the constituent steps of Move 1 *Establishing the territory*. They found all the three moves in the model were obligatory, but much attention was afforded to Move 1 according to the frequency of the occurrence. Among the three steps of Move 1, Step 2 *Topic generalizations and background information* was the most frequently adopted one. Moreover, they identified three sub-steps to realize Step 2. Their findings suggest that the writers need to provide a great deal of background information when introducing their research topic.

Apart from exploring the thesis/dissertation Introduction written in English, those written in other languages were also investigated. To explore the rhetorical structure of the Spanish dissertation Introductions in Computing, Carbonell-Olivares et al. (2009) adopted Bunton's (2002) model to identify the moves and steps. Their findings showed the presence of most of the steps from the adopted model while a couple of steps and sub-steps were found as well. Furthermore, following their framework, Soler-Monreal et al. (2011) compared the Spanish dissertation Introduction with the English dissertation Introduction in Computing and claimed that in the Spanish context, the first move *Establishing the territory* and the third move *Occupying the niche* were obligatory, while the second move *Establishing the niche* was optional. On the contrary, English dissertation Introductions were more produced in the range from the first move to the third move.

In summary, the reviewed studies above made great contributions to the understanding of the production of thesis or dissertation Introductions in several disciplines. From the methodological perspective, these studies mainly utilized move analysis to identify the moves and steps of the Introductions, while one study adopted move analysis as well as interviews with specialists to enhance the understanding of the rhetorical structures of Introductions (e.g., Samraj, 2008). These studies proposed several move-step models which had certain similarities with Swales' (1990) CARS model, which embodies the robustness of this model despite its aim to support the production of the research article(RA) Introductions rather than the thesis Introduction. The modified CARS model by Bunton (2002) had a wider coverage of steps than the other models. Moreover, the findings of these studies indicated that there are certain variations in terms of the moves and steps across different disciplines and cultural contexts.

2.2.3.2 The Literature Review Chapter

Genre analysis of the particular chapter Literature Review (LR) remains scarce. To confirm whether Introduction and LR are the same genre or not as suggested by other studies, Kwan (2006) explored the rhetorical structure of the LR chapter from 20 dissertations in Applied Linguistics produced by English native speakers and compared the findings with Bunton's (2002) model for dissertation Introduction. Based on Swales' CARS model, Kwan (2006) found that LR chapters were usually presented in an Introduction-Body-Conclusion structure, and within the Body part which was conducted by several thematic units, three moves from the CARS model were employed recursively. Among the thematic units, the pattern of Move1-2 was the most frequently identified. When comparing the moves and steps with Bunton's (2002) model, most of the steps were found and several new steps were also identified at the same time, for example, *Asserting confirmative claims about knowledge or research practices surveyed*. The findings suggested that the LR chapter and Introduction in the dissertation have some similarities while they are not entirely the same in the structure. It should be mentioned that Kwan (2006) prefers the term "strategies" rather than "steps" since they were not in a fixed order or pattern.

Recently, the framework of the LR chapter proposed by Kwan (2006) has been adopted to investigate that of thesis or dissertations from other similar disciplines and cultures. Based on this framework, Xie (2017) analyzed 25 thesis LR chapters written by Chinese English-major students and revealed that all the three moves listed in the framework were identified in the corpus. Move 1 and Move 2 were all obligatory, whereas Move 3 was conventional. Unlike Kwan (2006), the main objective of this study is to examine the evaluation of the moves so that the Introduction and the Conclusion parts were excluded, hence only the Body part was investigated. Within Move 1, Strategy 1A (*Surveying the non-research-related phenomena or knowledge claims*) and Strategy 1C (*Surveying the research-related phenomena*) were found in all the theses. Among the strategies of Move 2, it was found that Chinese students preferred Strategy 2B (*Gap indicating*) rather than Strategy 2A (*Counter claiming*) as identified in Kwan's (2006) corpus of doctoral dissertations. The reason may be that finding paucity or scarcity is academically less demanding than criticizing the weaknesses and problems in the literature. In other words, the less epistemically equipped master's students tend to indicate the gap as the motivation of their research. Furthermore, the results showed that the strategies of Move 3 were all optional.

In addition, Rawdhan et al. (2020) compared 60 LRs written by both Iraqi and international master's students in Applied Linguistics, which found that the Introduction-Body-Conclusion structure was rare in the Iraqi LRs compared with the international counterparts. Instead, the Iraqi LRs were more structured by Introduction-Body. Regarding the moves, Move 1 was conventional while Moves 2 and 3 were optional in both corpora. Nevertheless, the frequencies of Moves 2 and 3 were far less in the Iraqi corpus. The findings show that when compared with the international LRs, the Iraqi students tended to provide the theories and knowledge claims of their topic in the LRs without critiquing the relevant studies and situating their research in the field.

The Introduction-Body-Conclusion configuration was found in both of the corpora. The result revealed that the thematic section in the Body part was obligatory, and the Introduction was essential although it was not obligatory. However, the Conclusion part was optional. Among the introductory texts, almost all of them were untitled in both of the corpora, which is different from the findings of Kwan (2006) that most of them were titled "Introduction". The difference was suggested to be because of the preferred writing conventions between these two different academic communities which contained Chinese-speaking native writers and English-speaking native writers, respectively. In addition, compared with Kwan (2006), this study went further to explore the moves and steps in the Introduction and the Conclusion parts with the framework for the thematic units in the Body part. The findings indicated that Move 2 was frequently used by master's writers, while Move 3 was more preferred by doctoral writers. Furthermore, the analysis of the thematic sections revealed that these two groups of writers utilized the moves and steps in similar ways.

It can be concluded that genre analysis in LR chapters received rare attention. However, Kwan's (2006) model seems to provide an appropriate template for the production or investigation of this chapter. All the three above studies counted the frequency of the moves or steps, however, they counted it in a different way. Kwan (2006) and Rawdhan et al. (2020) counted all the thematic units and then regarded a move or step as obligatory if it appeared in all the thematic units. On the other hand, Xie (2017) considered it is obligatory if it is found in all the theses. Differently, You and Li (2021) calculated the percentage of the move or step in its total occurrence without examining its status as obligatory or not. The three methods of calculating frequency have their own strengths. The first one is helpful for the writers to consider whether they should contain a move or step in one thematic unit or not. The second one is better to examine the distribution of moves or steps in the corpus, and the last one is insightful to see the proportion of each move or step in the data.

2.2.3.3 The Method Chapter

Similar to the Literature Review, the Method chapter of the M.A. thesis has been scarcely explored. Nguyen and Pramoolsook (2015a) carried out a move analysis on 24 TESOL theses written by Vietnamese graduate students. Appling Chen and Kuo's (2012) framework to investigate the moves and steps, their findings showed some similarities and differences with those found in Chen and Kuo (2012). All five moves were found in both corpora and the first four moves were sequenced in a linear way. The similarities indicated that this group of Vietnamese writers produced the Method chapter in compliance with the norms found in the international writers of Chen and Kuo's (2012) study. However, the newly identified moves in Nguyen and Pramoolsook

(2015a) revealed that the Vietnamese writers adapted themselves to the local discourse community at the same time.

In the same vein, Mosquera and Tulud (2021) adopted Chen and Kuo's (2012) framework to investigate 30 Methodology chapters produced by Philippine M.A. students in Language Teaching. They modified the framework by adding two moves, i.e., Move 2 *Presenting the design of the study* with three steps, and Move 5 *Establishing the ethical considerations and trustworthiness of the study* with five steps. Moreover, they omitted the independent move *Referring to other studies* in the original framework. The findings indicate that the moves were similar among the Methodology chapters. However, the writers preferred varied steps to realize these moves.

In summary, the two studies above reveal that there are variations in terms of the moves and steps in the Methodology chapters composed by students in similar disciplines with different cultural backgrounds. Scant studies in this chapter suggest that more attention needs to be paid to the investigation of it.

2.2.3.4　The Discussion Chapter

To date, to the best of the researcher's knowledge, no study which focuses only on the single Results chapter of the thesis or dissertation has been found, thus, the review of this chapter is absent. This may be because writers prefer to combine their Results and Discussion into one chapter, therefore, the theses that contain a separate Results chapter are hard to collect. In this section, the studies on the Discussion chapter are presented first, and then the studies on the Integrated Results and Discussion chapter are demonstrated.

To explore the rhetorical structure of the Discussion chapters of theses, Dudley-Evans (1986) investigated seven theses written by native English speakers from the discipline of Plant Biology. The results showed that this chapter was generally presented in three parts, Introduction, Evaluation of results, and Conclusions and future work. Eleven moves were identified in his corpus within which Move 2 *Statement of result* was compulsory. In addition, certain moves were employed in a cyclical way which usually began with Move 2 and was followed by other moves. Dudley-Evans (1986) suggested that, unlike the Introduction, the moves in the Discussion chapter seldom occur linearly, thus, the identified moves are a set of possible moves or move lists rather than in a sequence.

Furthermore, in comparing the moves identified in the Discussion chapter both in the theses and the research articles, Hopkins and Dudley-Evans (1988) proposed a slightly revised version of the move list of Dudley-Evans (1986) which some moves were removed from or added to. Similarly, Move 2 *Statement of result* was found to be obligatory and some moves occurred in cycles. However, they stated that in the thesis Discussion, the cyclical move pattern was mostly related to the reported result. To illustrate, for unsatisfactory results, the students tended to adopt Move 3 *Unexpected outcome* followed by Move 4 *Reference to previous research (Comparison)*, or Move 5 *Explanation of unsatisfactory results*. On the other hand, for the satisfactory results, they were likely to use Move 7 *Deduction* and Move 8 *Hypothesis* supported by Move 9 *Reference to previous research (support)* and Move 10 *Recommendation*. Besides, Hopkins and Dudley-Evans (1988) demonstrated that a certain move was expected to precede another move. For example, Move 3 usually preceded Move 4.

Dudley-Evans (1994) further modified his move list identified in 1986 by thoroughly investigating one thesis Discussion. First, the three-part structure was slightly modified as Introduction-Evaluation-Conclusion, of which Evaluation is the major place where move cycles usually occurred and it was the main part for writers to present significant results with detailed comments and to propose their main claims. Differently, only nine moves were identified compared with his original work among which three moves were newly found and added; namely, Move 3 *Finding*, Move 7 *Claim*, and Move 8 *Limitation*. The move *Finding*, an observation generated from the research, is similar to the move *Statement of result* but without the presentation of actual figures. The move *Claim* was integrated by the move *Hypothesis* and the move *Deduction* from his previous list.

The moves identified from the Discussion sections in research articles are also applied to the investigation of moves in the thesis Discussion chapter. Nodoushan and Khakbaz (2011) adopted the seven-move framework proposed by Yang and Allison (2003) for research article Discussion written by Iranian students to analyze the rhetorical structure in thesis Discussion and then compared the results with those of Rasmeenin's (2006, as cited in Nodoushan & Khakbaz, 2011) study of non-Iranian writers. The findings showed that the most frequent moves were Move 2 *Reporting results*, Move 4 *Commenting on results*, and Move 7 *Deducing from the results*. By statistical analyses, the results revealed that the move frequency in this chapter was significantly different between Iranian EFL students and non-Iranian ones.

Apart from these studies on the single Discussion chapter, Dastjerdi et al (2017) examined the rhetorical structure of the Integrated Results and Discussion chapter from 40 theses in both hard and soft disciplines by combining Kanoksilapatham's (2005, as cited in Dastjerdi et al, 2017) models for RA Results section and for RA Discussion section which contained 4 moves, respectively. The findings showed that this chapter was mainly presented with the results and then the comments on them. Besides, disciplinary variations were found between the soft sciences and the hard sciences. The steps of *Referring to previous research* and *Making overt claims or generalizations* were more frequently used in the soft disciplines, whereas the step *Invalidating results* was identified more in the hard disciplines.

In addition, one study was found to investigate the separated Results chapter and Discussion chapter, and the combined Results and Discussion chapter written by Vietnamese master's students. Having collected 24 theses, Nguyen and Pramoolsook (2015b) observed that 13 of them have separated Results chapter and Discussion chapter, while the remaining 11 had these two chapters combined as one. Thus, they analyzed their rhetorical structures respectively adopting Chen and Kuo's (2012) framework. In the Results chapter, Move 5 *Evaluating the study* and Move 6 *Deductions from the study* were absent in their data. However, they identified three new steps; namely, *Section introduction*, *Next section introduction*, and *Summary of each section*, which formed a sub-cycle in a move. As for the Discussion chapters, it was found that interpretations were provided toward all the findings in their corpus. Moreover, in the combined chapters, their findings were similar to the results of Dastjerdi et al. (2017) in that research findings were predominantly followed by interpretations. In addition, the majority of Vietnamese writers tended to compare their results with pertinent studies. In the end, Nguyen and Pramoolsook (2015b) suggested that explicit instructions on the production of these two chapters are necessary for non-native English writers.

In a nutshell, recent studies on the thesis Discussion chapters are rare. Moreover, several studies on the combined or integrated Results and Discussion chapters suggest that it is sufficient to combine the frameworks of a single Results chapter and a single Discussion chapter to investigate the combined chapter. Besides, it reveals that cultural variations are expected in the rhetorical structures of this chapter or the combined one (e.g., Dastjerdi et al., 2017; Nguyen & Pramoolsook, 2015b).

2.2.3.5 The Conclusion Chapter

When analyzing the Conclusion chapters in six MBA theses, Hewings (1993) found that this particular chapter generally served three main functions, namely, Reporting, Commenting, and Suggesting. Besides, the Commenting generally presented evaluations, deductions, or speculations about the results.

A detailed investigation of the rhetorical structure of the Conclusion chapters is conducted by Bunton (2005) from the general chapter titles to the specific steps through a corpus of 45 dissertations collected from both science and technology disciplines (ST) and humanities and social sciences (HSS). The results showed that most of the dissertations use one or even two chapters to perform the concluding role with various titles. Only around half of them were simply titled "Conclusion" or "Conclusions". Moreover, the majority of them focused more on the thesis itself whereas others focused more on the field and mentioned the thesis' findings or contributions to the whole field. Thus, Bunton (2005) classified them into thesis-oriented and field-oriented, and then proposed two models for the thesis-oriented Conclusions (one for ST and one for HSS), and one for the field-oriented ones. As for the thesis-oriented Conclusions, both of the two models had the first two moves as *Introductory restatement* and *Consolidation*. Nonetheless, ST Conclusion chapters often ended with *Future research*, but HSS Conclusion chapters were usually finished with *Practical implications and recommendations*. At the step level for Move 1, the HSS Conclusions mainly restated the research purposes, research questions, or hypotheses. Instead, the ST Conclusions restated the work carried out. As for the field-oriented Conclusions, they were more presented in a Problem-Solution-Evaluation structure and had a wider range of steps. Besides, Bunton (2005) also pointed out that apart from the variations in moves and steps in different disciplines, there are variations between disciplines regarding the chapter titles, length, references, and number of sections.

Furthermore, Soler-Monreal (2016) explored the moves and steps in Computer Science dissertation Conclusions by adopting Bunton's (2005) model for ST. The findings indicated that Conclusions in this discipline were mainly produced in one chapter with three moves frequently identified among the five moves from the model. In addition, recurrent move-step patterns were identified in the corpus.

To sum up, little attention has been paid to the move analysis in the thesis Conclusion chapter. From the above review, it seems that Bunton's (2005) framework is applicable to investigate this chapter in other research contexts, as in the case of Soler-Monreal (2016). Furthermore, disciplinary variations are also found in this chapter.

2.2.3.6 The Whole Thesis

As for the whole rhetorical structure of the thesis, to the best of the researcher's knowledge, only three studies have explored it, i.e., Pramoolsook (2007), Chen and Kuo (2012), and Nguyen (2014).

Focusing on the genre transfer from dissertation to research articles, Pramoolsook (2007) investigated six theses and their corresponding research articles written by Thai students in Biotechnology and Environmental Engineering. The investigation of the rhetorical structure of the theses was conducted chapter by chapter based on the models from the previous studies (e.g., Abstract: Hyland, 2000; Introduction: Bunton, 2002). The findings showed that the traditional simple (ILrMRD) type of dissertation organization was adopted by the writers and there were some disciplinary variations in terms of the moves and steps across the chapters between Biotechnology and Environmental Engineering.

Furthermore, Chen and Kuo (2012) developed a complete framework of moves and steps from previous studies (e.g., Abstract: Lores, 2004; Introduction: Bunton, 2002; Literature Review: Kwan, 2006; Method: Lim, 2006; Results, Discussion, and

Conclusion: Yang & Allison, 2003) to analyze the whole thesis in Applied Linguistics. In the end, they proposed their own framework. It should be mentioned that in order to investigate the rhetorical functions of the citations, Chen and Kuo (2012) added an independent move *Referring to other studies* in each chapter aside from the Literature Review chapter. Their framework will be adopted by the current study because of its applicability, the wide nationalities of the writers being investigated, and the wide coverage of the steps identified. Hence, their study is reviewed in detail in the subsequent paragraphs.

After examining the macro structures of the 20 theses in their corpus, Chen and Kuo (2012) found that 15 theses are structured in the traditional simple pattern (ILrMRDC) and there was a slight variation in the rhetorical chapter headings among them. Further, they analyzed the moves and steps of these 15 theses chapter by chapter utilizing their developed framework. There were 4 moves for Abstracts in their framework; namely, *Introduction* (AI), *Method* (AM), *Results* (AR), and *Conclusion* (AC). The findings suggested that the first three moves were obligatory and they usually occurred in a linear pattern, while the last move was optional. Moreover, the AI move in most Abstracts mainly indicated the research purpose or the centrality of the research topic for which, in the present researcher's opinion, it is more inclined into Hyland's (2000) framework which contains 5 moves; namely, *Introduction*, *Purpose*, *Method*, *Product*, and *Conclusion*.

As for the Introduction chapter of the theses, most of them had an independent Introduction chapter and Literature Review chapter while four theses embedded Literature Review in the Introduction, which is similar to Bunton (2002)'s corpus. Chen and Kuo (2012) combined all the steps in a list under each move (Table 2.1) which were proposed by Bunton (2002) as "often present" and "occasionally present", and modified the terms assigned to some steps, such as modifying the move *Method* in Bunton (2002) into *Indicating research method*. Moreover, a new step *Indicating scope of research* was identified in their corpus, but the step *Research parameters* was absent under Move 1 in their framework compared with Bunton (2002). After a thorough examination of the moves and steps in the data, Chen and Kuo (2012) found that the move pattern of M1-M2-M3 was frequently adopted in most of the theses, but the step sequences tended to be more diverse.

Table 2.1   The Move-Step Framework for Thesis Introduction Chapter in Applied Linguistics (adapted from Chen & Kuo, 2012)

Moves	Steps
Move 1: Establishing a territory (T)	a) Providing topic generalization/background b) Indicating centrality/importance of topic c) Defining terms d) Reviewing previous research
Move 2: Establishing a niche (N)	a) Indicating gap in previous research b) Question-raising c) Counter-claiming d) Continuing/extending a tradition
Move 3: Occupying the niche (O)	a) Indicating purposes/aims/objectives b) Indicating scope of research c) Indicating chapter/section structure d) Indicating theoretical position e) Announcing research/work carried out f) Describing parameters of research g) Stating research questions/hypotheses h) Defining terms i) Indicating research method j) Indicating findings/results and Indicating models proposed k) Indicating applications l) Indicating value or significance m) Providing justification n) Indicating thesis structure
Referring to other studies	**a) Providing background information** **b) Providing definition of terms** **c) Providing support or justification**

(*Note: New moves or steps identified and proposed by Chen and Kuo are in bold.*)

For the Literature Review Chapter, Chen and Kuo (2012) adopted the framework proposed by Kwan (2006) and they found that similarly almost all the theses were organized in the three-part structure which includes Introduction, Body, and Conclusion (Table 2.2). In the Introduction, they indicated the organization of this chapter and justified the thematic units to be reviewed. In the Conclusion part, they intended to provide a summary of the review of the thematical units and situated the present study in the review literature. In the Body part, in terms of the steps, *Surveying the non-research-related* and *Surveying the research-related* had the highest frequencies and these two steps usually occurred in pairs and cycles. Moreover, they were often preceded by a newly identified step *Concluding a part of Literature Review and/ or indicating transition to reviewing a different area.* Thus, these three steps were frequently utilized in order or cycles to completely review a thematic unit in the Body part.

Table 2.2 The Move-Step Framework for Thesis Literature Review Chapter in Applied Linguistics (adapted from Chen & Kuo, 2012)

Moves	Steps
Introduction	Indicating organization of the review chapter(s) and justifying the themes (areas) to be reviewed
Body part (each thematic unit)	
Move 1: Establishing one part of the territory of one's own research by	a) Surveying the non-research-related phenomena or knowledge claims b) Claiming centrality c) Surveying the research-related phenomena
Move 2: Creating a research niche	a) Counter-claiming (weaknesses and problems) b) Gap-indicating (paucity or scarcity) c) Asserting confirmative claims about knowledge or research practices surveyed d) Asserting the relevancy of the surveyed claims to one's own research e) Abstracting or synthesizing knowledge claims to establish a theoretical position or a theoretical framework **f) Concluding a part of literature review and/or indicating transition to review of a different area**
Move 3: Occupying the research niche by	a) Indicating research aims, focuses, research questions, or hypotheses b) Indicating theoretical positions theoretical frameworks c) Indicating research design/ processes d) Interpreting terminology used in the thesis
Conclusion	**Providing a summary of the review of the themes and relating the review to the present study**

(*Note: New moves or steps identified and proposed by Chen and Kuo are in bold.*)

Compared with the first two chapters, few studies explored the Method chapter in research articles or theses/dissertations, which might be caused by the disciplinary variations in research methodology (Chen & Kuo, 2012). Therefore, Chen and Kuo

(2012) adopted Lim's (2006) elaborate move-step structure for the Method section of Management research articles with some modification or addition of moves and steps to make it more appropriate to examine the theses in Applied Linguistics (Table 2.3). According to Lim (2006), a new move *Introducing the method* was added, which contains two steps: *Indicating chapter/section structure* and *Providing an overview of the study*. Besides, under the move *Delineating methods of data analysis*, a new step *Explaining variables and variable measurement* was inserted.

Table 2.3 The Move-Step Framework for Thesis Method Chapter in Applied Linguistics (adapted from Chen & Kuo, 2012)

Moves	Steps
Move 1: Introducing the Method chapter	a) Indicating chapter/section structure b) Providing an overview of the study c) Indicating theory/approach
Move 2: Describing data collection method and procedure(s)	a) Describing the sample (participants, location, time, etc.) b) Describing methods and steps in data collection c) Justifying data collection procedure(s)
Move 3: Delineating methods of data analysis	a) Presenting an overview of the (data analysis) design b) Explaining specific method(s) of data analysis c) **Explaining variables and variable measurement** d) Justifying the methods of measuring variables or data analysis
Move 4: Elucidating data analysis procedure(s)	a) Relating (or recounting) data analysis procedure(s) b) Justifying the data analysis procedure(s) c) Previewing results
Referring to other studies	a) **Providing background information** b) **Providing definition of terms** c) **Providing support or justification**

(*Note: New moves or steps identified and proposed by Chen and Kuo are in bold.*)

After applying the modified framework to analyze the Method chapters in the corpus, the findings indicated that the steps *Describing methods and steps in data collection* and *Describing the sample* occurred in all the theses which were obligatory. In addition, some pairs of the steps were frequently utilized by the writers. For example, the pair of *Describing methods and steps in data collection* and *Justifying data collection procedures* was frequently found. In terms of the moves, the last move *Elucidating data analysis procedures* had less frequency than the first three moves which may be as a result of inclusion or combination into the Results chapter. Moreover, Chen and Kuo (2012) suggested that on the one hand, thesis Method chapters in Applied Linguistics focus more on data collection method(s)/procedures and the samples; on the other hand, they unlikely have a fixed way to present research methodology in this discipline.

As for the Results chapter, Chen and Kuo (2012) employed Yang and Allison's (2003) framework for research articles with some modifications (Table 2.4). Move 1 *Preparatory information* in Yang and Allison (2003) was replaced by *Introducing the Results chapter* with two steps of *Providing background information or how results are presented* and *Indicating methods used or statistical procedure applied*. Moreover, two steps were added under the move *Reporting results*: *Locating graphics* and *Reporting major findings*. Besides, one step *Making conclusions of results* was added under the move *Summarizing results*, which is not necessary since only one step under the move indicates that the communicative functions of the segments are already embraced by the move.

Table 2.4 The Move-Step Framework for Thesis Results Chapter in Applied Linguistics (adapted from Chen & Kuo, 2012)

Moves	Steps
Move 1: Introducing the Results chapter	a) Providing background information or how results are presented b) Indicating methods used or statistical procedure applied
Move 2: Reporting results	a) **Locating graphics** b) **Reporting major findings**
Move 3: Commenting on results	a) Interpreting results b) Comparing results with literature c) Evaluating results (including strengths, limitations, generalizations, etc. of results) d) Accounting for results (giving reasons)
Move 4: Summarizing results	**Making conclusions of results**

Cont.

Moves	Steps
Move 5: Evaluating the study	a) Indicating limitations of the study b) Indicating significance/advantage of the study
Move 6: Deductions from the (research) study	a) Recommending further research **b) Drawing pedagogic implications** **c) Making suggestions**
Referring to other studies	a) Providing background information **b) Providing definition of terms** **c) Providing support or justification**

(*Note: New moves or steps identified and proposed by Chen and Kuo are in bold.*)

The findings in this chapter revealed that two steps (*Reporting major findings* and *Providing background or indicating how results are presented*) were obligatory in that they occurred in all the theses. Besides, three other steps have high frequencies and occurrences as well (*Interpreting results, Indicating method or statistical procedures applied, and Locating graphics*). Moreover, these top five frequent steps and the step *Comparing results with literature* formed several step pairs/sequences or cycles with high frequencies. Chen and Kuo (2012) concluded that thesis Results chapters were similar to those of research articles which focus more on reporting and commenting on research results. In terms of the step pairs, the frequent occurrence of *Locating graphics* and *Reporting major findings* suggested that in Applied Linguistics the graphics played a significant role in reporting results, and writers in this discipline preferred to locate the graphics before demonstrating the major findings from the graphics.

After reports on the specific findings, the Discussion chapter proceeded to interpret and evaluate these specific findings from a general view, which was in a rhetorically reversed way as Introduction that goes from general to specific (Chen & Kuo, 2012). With a slight modification of Yang and Allison's (2003) framework for the research article Discussion, Chen and Kuo (2012) also have seven moves in their framework (Table 2. 5). Differently, Move 1 in their framework was *Introducing the Discussion chapter* rather than *Background information* as in Yang and Allison (2003).

Table 2.5 The Move-Step Framework for Thesis Discussion Chapter in Applied Linguistics (adapted from Chen & Kuo, 2012)

Moves	Steps
Move 1: Introducing the Discussion chapter	Providing background information (such as purpose, design, research questions/ hypotheses, etc.) or how discussions are presented
Move 2: Reporting results	Reporting major findings
Move 3: Summarizing results	Making conclusions of results
Move 4: Commenting on results	a) Interpreting results b) Comparing results with literature c) Accounting for results (giving reasons) d) Evaluating results (including strengths, limitations, etc. of results)
Move 5: Summarizing the study	Summarizing the study briefly
Move 6: Evaluating the study	a) Indicating limitations b) Indicating significance/advantage c) Evaluating methodology
Move 7: Deductions from the (research) study	a) Making suggestions b) Recommending further research c) Drawing pedagogic implications
Reference to other studies	**Providing support or justification**

(*Note: New moves or steps identified and proposed by Chen and Kuo are in bold.*)

10 out of 20 in their corpus had a separate Discussion chapter and the investigation of these Discussion chapters indicated that the step *Reporting major findings* occurred in all the theses which tended to be an obligatory step. Besides, Chen and Kuo (2012) regarded the other four steps of high frequencies as quasi-obligatory steps since their occurrences were above 80%. Moreover, the step *Interpreting results*, *Accounting for results*, and *Comparing results with literature* were often in a combination of *Reporting major findings*, which revealed that the communicative purposes of Discussion in theses intended more to summarize and comment on the results, and then to compare them with pertinent studies. Regarding the moves, the first four moves were identified more frequently than the others. In addition, step pairs or three-step sequence patterns

with high frequencies were also found in this chapter.

As the last chapter in a thesis, few genre-analysis studies have been conducted on Conclusions (Chen & Kuo, 2012). Drawn from Yang and Allison's (2003) framework for the research article Conclusions, Chen and Kuo (2012) developed a framework for the thesis Conclusions chapter to which a new move *Introducing the Conclusions chapter* was added as Move 1 and contained four moves in total at last (Table 2.6). Moreover, a new step *Making suggestions* was added under the move *Deductions from the (research) study*.

Table 2.6 The Move-Step Framework for Thesis Conclusion Chapter in Applied Linguistics (adapted from Chen & Kuo, 2012)

Moves	Steps
Move 1: Introducing the Conclusions chapter	Restating purpose, design, research questions/hypotheses, results, or indicating how conclusions are presented
Move 2: Summarizing the study	**Summarizing the study briefly**
Move 3: Evaluating the study	a) Indicating significance/advantage b) Indicating limitations c) Evaluating methodology
Move 4: Deductions from the (research) study	a) Recommending further research b) Drawing pedagogic implications **c) Making suggestions**
Referring to other studies	**Providing support or justification**

(*Note: New moves or steps identified and proposed by Chen and Kuo are in bold.*)

The same as the Discussion chapter, the Conclusion chapter was only found in 10 theses of the corpus as an individual chapter. The findings demonstrated that the step *Summarizing the study briefly* was obligatory while the other three highly frequent steps (*Drawing pedagogic implications*, *Recommending further research*, and *Indicating limitations*) were quasi-obligatory. Step sequence patterns or cycles were seldom found in this chapter.

Chen and Kuo (2012) provided a complete and comprehensible framework for investigating the moves and steps of the whole master's thesis. Later, Nguyen (2014) adopted their framework to explore the TESOL theses written by Vietnamese students.

Apart from the moves and steps in each chapter, Nguyen (2014) also examined the citation types and functions found in her corpus. However, since citation is not in the scope of the current study, only the findings of the rhetorical structure are reviewed.

Collecting 24 TESOL theses from three Vietnamese universities as the data, Nguyen (2014) analyzed their rhetorical structure chapter by chapter and then compared the findings with those of Chen and Kuo (2012) to find out the similarities and differences. Firstly, in the Introduction chapters, 7 steps out of the 28 found in Chen and Kuo (2012) were absent in this corpus. However, Nguyen (2014) identified two new steps, *Summarizing the chapter* and *Introducing the next chapter content*. Secondly, in the Literature Review chapters, the Introduction-Body-Conclusion structure was also identified with thematic units in the Body part. Unlike Chen and Kuo (2012) who found Move 1 obligatory, the result showed no obligatory moves were employed by the Vietnamese writers. In addition, apart from being found at the very beginning of the chapter, introductory texts were also identified at the beginning of Move 1 to lead in the related content of each thematic unit. Thirdly, in the Methodology chapters, the independent move *Referring to other studies* was found to be obligatory, which is different from Chen and Kuo's (2012) finding that *Describing methods and steps in data collection* was obligatory. Moreover, a new move *Chapter summary* was identified, and a three-step sequence of *Instruments-Purposes-Justifications* was found to be frequently employed by the writers. Fourthly, in the Results chapters, a different obligatory cycle (*Locating graphics-Reporting major findings*) was identified. Besides, two new steps, *Section introduction*, and *Section summary*, were found in the corpus. Fifthly, in the Discussion chapters, the highest frequent step cycle was *Making conclusions of results-Interpreting results*, and a few instances of three-step patterns were identified. Sixthly, 11 out of the 24 theses in the corpus had an Integrated Results and Discussion chapter. Combining the frameworks of the separate Results and the Discussion, Nguyen (2014) found that this integrated Chapter had a linear structure of moves, and the step sequence of *Graphics-Findings* was frequently used by the writers. Lastly, in the Conclusion chapters, Move 4 *Deduction from the study* was found to be obligatory.

From Nguyen's (2014) study, it reveals that despite several new moves or steps being found, the framework proposed by Chen and Kuo (2012) is applicable to analyze the theses written by Vietnamese students; however, differences among the employment of moves and steps are demonstrated, which indicates there are variations across different cultural contexts in terms of the rhetorical structure of the thesis.

2.2.3.7 Summary of Studies on Master's Thesis

From the above sections of genre studies on master's thesis, it is shown that most of the studies only focus on one or two chapters of the thesis while scarce studies tend to investigate the thesis as a whole. Among all the chapters of the thesis, the Introduction chapter gains much more attention than other chapters, and it is mainly analyzed on the basis of Swales'(1990) CARS model. For the less explored chapters, the Methodology chapter and the separate Results chapter in the thesis receive little attention. As for the whole rhetorical structure of the thesis, the findings of Chen and Kuo (2012) indicated that moves in theses are more elaborate than those of research articles in that almost all the chapters have an introductory move at the beginning of the chapter.

To sum up, all the studies add significant insights into the understanding of the particular genre, the M.A. thesis. Moreover, the studies indicate that there are variations in moves and steps across disciplines and cultural contexts. Therefore, genre studies on thesis in a specific discipline or cultural context would broaden our horizon on this particular genre. Furthermore, Chen and Kuo (2012) provided a comprehensive and complete framework for exploring the whole structure of the thesis, thus, their framework will be adopted by the present study since it is verified by Nguyen (2014). In addition, the focused discipline of the present research, Foreign Linguistics and Applied Linguistics, is similar to Applied Linguistics as situated by their study. An elaboration on the selection of this discipline and Chen and Kuo's (2012) framework is provided in *Section 3.3.1* of Chapter 3.

2.3 Thesis Defense Presentation Slides

2.3.1 Definitions, Communicative Purposes, and Intended Audience

Thesis or dissertation defense, which is alternatively known as "oral examination" or "viva", has been viewed as a kind of academic spoken genre. At plenty of universities around the world, it is conducted with the dissertation or thesis evaluation to award students the degree they apply for (Lin, 2020). The main communicative purpose of the defense is not only to authenticate authorship and examine the originality of a thesis or dissertation (Phillips & Pugh, 2010), but also to conduct an academic conversation between the candidates and the committee for the sake of certifying the membership of candidates in their chosen specialization (Swales, 2004). During the thesis defense, the candidates showcase their theoretical foundation and academic competence (Liu & Liu, 2021). Moreover, Swales (2004) suggested that there are four main phases during the defense, that is, "preliminaries" "the defense proper" "in-camera session", and "closing segment". The main part is the second phase in which candidates deliver an oral presentation on the basis of their research to the committee and the audience, and then they are expected to answer rounds of questions from the committee. In the third phase, committee members evaluate the written work and the oral performance of the candidates in private and then announce the defense results in the last phase. In China, the thesis defense procedures are similar to the four phases identified by Swales (2004). However, the present study only focuses on "the defense proper", the second phase of the thesis defense. To be more specific, only the presentation slides, which are projected on the screen during the oral presentation in "the defense proper" session, will be investigated.

Thesis defense presentation slides are an independent genre related to the written thesis. They are a kind of visual aid (Yates & Orlikowski, 2007) to support the oral commentary of the students in "the defense proper" stage of the thesis defense. Therefore, the primary communicative purpose of thesis defense presentation slides is to support or facilitate the oral presentation (Schoeneborn, 2013; Wecker, 2012; Yates

& Orlikowski, 2007). Moreover, they are used to structure and string the components of the oral commentary during the presentation (Dubois, 1980; Weissberg, 1993). Sometimes, they are utilized as speaking notes as well (Hertz et al., 2016).

As a corresponding genre to the thesis, thesis defense presentation slides have a similar but narrower intended audience than those of the thesis. The most immediate target audience is the committee members who have already read the students' theses before the thesis defense. Another audience is the supervisors to whom the students show that they are ready for the defense and look for some feedback. The fellow students or the faculty members might be the potential audience who intend to attend the students' thesis defense; however, they may not be in the author's mind when creating the slides.

2.3.2 Types of Slides

Weissberg (1993) divided the presentation slides into discourse marker slides and content slides. As for the former, they are used as framers and transitions, or labels to frame the presentation or to prompt topic shifters. On the other hand, content slides are diversely utilized to present illustrators, citations, lists, schematic diagrams, data, and so forth. Besides, Atai and Talebzadeh (2012) demonstrated there is usually a title slide at the beginning and a Thank You slide at the end.

Furthermore, Rowley-Jolivet (2002) stated that there are two channels of communication during a presentation, that is, the verbal channel and the visual channel. The visual channel (what is shown) refers to the slides or transparencies being projected onto the screen accompanied with the speaker's oral commentary, the verbal channel (what the speaker says). By the analysis of the visuals during the conference paper presentation from the disciplines of Medicine, Geology, and Physics, Rowley-Jolivet (2002) proposed four typologies of visuals in slides; namely, Scriptural, Numerical, Figurative, and Graphical. Scriptural visuals in slides mainly contain text, while the Numerical visuals are often mathematical formulae and numerical tables. In addition, Figurative visuals are more about photos, X-rays, or MRI images, whereas maps, graphics, and diagrams belong to the Graphical category.

These four types of visuals in slides are represented by a Scriptovisual Pyramid (Figure 2.1) with each type in a pole or angle (Rowley-Jolivet, 2002). This pyramid shape sufficiently represents the four types, and it is flexible to explain the hybrid visuals in the slides. To illustrate, the flowcharts utilizing diagrammatic form to present text could be put along the Scriptural-Graphical axis.

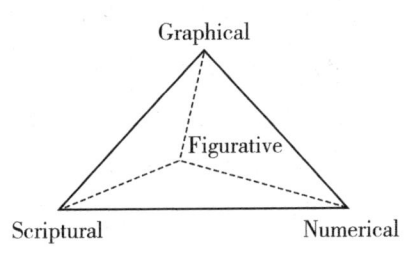

Figure 2.1   The Scriptovisual Pyramid (Rowley–Jolivet, 2002)

2.3.3 Previous Studies on Thesis Defense Presentation Slides

Previous genre studies have paid much more attention to the oral commentary during the presentations in different spoken genres, such as three-minute thesis presentations (Hu & Liu, 2018), seminars (Aguilar, 2004), conference presentations (Hertz et al., 2016; Rowley-Jolivet & Carter-Thomas, 2005), and lectures (Thompson, 1994). Scant studies focus on the thesis defense presentations, especially the thesis defense presentation slides per se. To the best of the researcher's knowledge, only one study (Pieketaleyee & Bazargani, 2018) has investigated the rhetorical structure of the thesis defense presentation slides. Besides, Azizifar et al. (2014) explored the types and functions of the thesis defense presentation slides.

Pieketaleyee and Bazargani (2018) collected 50 PowerPoint presentations prepared by language-teaching students based on their thesis for their defense sessions and then investigated the moves and steps employed by the students in presenting the Introductions and Literature Reviews of their original thesis. In their study, they analyzed "the written form of PowerPoint genre". In other words, they analyzed the presentation slides as a written genre rather than a digital one, which will be adopted by the present study as well.

Moreover, on the assumption that the information needed for preparing the thesis defense presentation slides is extracted from the corresponding thesis, Pieketaleyee and Bazargani (2018) adopted the framework proposed by Chen and Kuo (2012) for analyzing the thesis' moves and steps to identify the rhetorical structure of the slides. The findings showed that the basic macrostructure of the presentation slides was in line with that of the thesis; namely, Introduction, Literature Review, Method, Results, and Discussion. The move analysis in the Introduction sections of the presentation slides revealed that three conventional moves (*Establishing a territory*, *Establishing a niche*, and *Occupying the niche*), which is in concordance with Swales' (1990) CARS model, were frequently used by the writers. Compared with Chen and Kuo's (2012) framework, all four moves from the framework were found in the corpus. However, fewer steps under the moves were identified, and some steps were completely missing in the presentation slides, such as *Continuing a tradition* under the second move and *Describing parameters of research* under the third move.

As for the Literature Review sections of the presentation slides, the findings indicated that all the five moves from the framework of Chen and Kuo (2012) were identified as well. However, very few presentation slides contain the first move *Introduction* and the last move *Conclusion*, which was suggested by Pieketaleyee and Bazargani (2018) that these two moves are obligatory for writers to produce the thesis while they are considered unnecessary when creating the slides, and the writers do not want to load the audience with too much information. In addition, as the longest chapter in the thesis, a limited number of slides were utilized to present the Literature Review, of which a maximum of three slides was found in the corpus to depict this chapter. Pieketaleyee and Bazargani (2018) indicated that this may be a result of the limited presentation time during the thesis defense.

The study of Pieketaleyee and Bazargani (2018) revealed that compared with the thesis, fewer moves and steps were identified in the presentation slides, and this may be influenced by the time limitation of the thesis defense so that the students only present the main parts of the thesis in the slides.

Apart from the moves and steps of the thesis defense presentation slides, Azizifar et al. (2014) analyzed the types and functions of this genre, the "visual language" as they called, by collecting 70 PowerPoint defense session presentations produced by the students in Applied Linguistics. The results indicated that the fundamental parts of a thesis, Introduction, Literature Review, Methodology, Results, and Discussion and Conclusion, were also presented in the slides. Adopting the four typologies of visuals (Scriptural, Numerical, Graphical, and Figurative) proposed by Rowley-Jolivet (2002), their findings demonstrated that students in this discipline mainly adopted scriptural slides to visualize themselves to their discourse community members. These scriptural slides were not only used as boundary devices to shift the topics, but also utilized to introduce the title, and demonstrate the research questions, hypotheses, or conclusions. The next frequent slides were numerical which were mainly employed to display the statistical tables and results. The other two types of slides were less identified in their corpus.

Aside from these two studies on the thesis defense presentation slides, another move study, i.e., Atai and Talebzadeh (2012), on presentation slides in the conference is also reviewed in this section because the conferences for writers to present research articles are similar to the thesis defense session for graduate students to present their thesis. Previous studies indicated that the move-step structures of research articles could be applied to analyzing the rhetorical structure of the thesis as well (e.g., Bunton, 2002; Dudley-Evans, 1986; Kwan, 2006; Maher & Milligan, 2019; Nodoushan & Khakbaz, 2011; Samraj, 2008). On account of the pertinent studies on the rhetorical structure of the thesis defense presentation slides are scarce, thus, to better situate the present study into the wider literature, the studies on the rhetorical structure of the similar genre, conference presentation, are reviewed.

With a corpus of 438 slides which constituted 20 Applied Linguistics conference presentations, Atai and Talebzadeh (2012) analyzed the moves and steps adopted in the presentation slides. The findings indicated that the traditional organization IMRD or IMRDC of the written scholarly reports (i.e., research articles) were presented in the slides, which is in accordance with Zareva's (2013) study on the TESOL graduate students' presentations that writers preferred to stay close to the original written academic genres when conducting their presentations. In addition, the results revealed that the framework for analyzing the written genres was available to account for the slides' rhetorical structures. Therefore, drawn from previous studies on RA Introduction (Swales, 1990), RA Method (Lim, 2006), and RA Results, Discussion, and Conclusion (Yang & Allison, 2003), Atai and Talebzadeh (2012) adopted the framework proposed by these studies to explore the moves and steps of each section in the conference presentation slides. The results revealed that each section and its constituent moves or steps were realized by one slide or a series of slides. Nevertheless, the Introduction section and the Results section were demonstrated with the highest number of slides, while Discussion or Conclusion had the least number of slides.

In the Introduction section of the presentation slides, Atai and Talebzadeh (2012) found that the three moves in the CARS model (Swales, 1990) were all identified in the corpus, but more slides were utilized to realize the first move *Establishing the territory* and this move occurred in all the presentations. As for the Method section, all the three moves in Lim's (2006) model were recognized as well. The second move *Delineating procedures for measuring variables* occurred in all the slide sets followed by the first move *Describing data collection procedures*. In this section, writers not only reported basic information about the participants and data collection procedures but also showed their familiarity with the conventional research methods of the discipline. Furthermore, the findings from the Results section demonstrated that writers in this soft science usually utilized numbers, graphics, charts, and tables to increase their empirical credibility for their findings. Compared with the framework of Young and Allison (2003), Move 2 *Reporting results* occurred in all the presentations, but the last three moves from the framework were absent in the corpus. In addition, many writers had Discussion embedded in this Section rather than present it separately. Accordingly, few slides were used, and few moves or steps were found in the Discussion section as a result the writers in Applied Linguistics were not so willing to devote more to the Discussion due to the limited time of the presentation.

Besides, Atai and Talebzadeh (2012) adopted the typologies of slides proposed by Rowley-Jolivet (2002) to explore the types of slides in their corpus and confirmed that the four types of slides were utilized by Applied Linguistics writers in their presentations. However, since this discipline is a kind of soft sciences, more scriptural slides have found in the corpus, and numerical slides are the second most frequently used slide type. Graphical slides and figurative slides were less found. Moreover, some hybrid slides were identified in the corpus of which Scripto-graphical and Scripto-numerical slides occurred the most.

Another study also focusing on the conference presentation slides was conducted by Diani (2015). Collecting 56 slide sets produced by native and non-native English speakers at three Applied Linguistics conferences, Diani (2015) found that the scriptural slide was the most predominant slide type in the presentations. The other three slide types were also found in the corpus. It is interesting to notice that this study did not mention the hybrid slides which were found in other similar studies. Furthermore, adopting Swales's (1990) IMRD model to investigate to what extent the slides may reproduce the model, the findings showed that the four sections of the original research articles were all identified in the slides. In the Introduction slides, Move 1 *Establish a territory* and Move 3 *Occupying the niche* were obligatory, whereas Move 2 where a niche is established is optional. As for the Methods slides, they mainly displayed the information about the research design in one or two slides. Moreover, Diani (2015) indicated that this kind of information may be embedded in the slide which stated the research aims of the study. With regard to the Results section, it occurred in all the slide sets with a variety of the slide number ranging from 6 to 35. In terms of the Conclusion section, 54 out of 56 slide sets included it. Only Move 2 *Statement of results* was identified to be obligatory.

To sum up, genre analysis studies on presentation slides are scant, especially on the thesis defense presentation slides whose preparation places much stress and challenges on most master's students. In terms of the rhetorical structure of the thesis defense presentation slides, to the best of the researcher's knowledge, only one study has touched upon it and only focused on two sections (Introduction and Literature Review) of it. Moreover, the previous studies reviewed above suggest that the rhetorical structure of the original written genre, the thesis, is available for accounting for that of the corresponding presentation slides as well. Hence, the present research is about to explore the rhetorical structure of the thesis defense presentation slides based on that of its original written genre, the thesis. These two genres form a genre chain along which the former genre (the thesis) is transferred into the later genre (the corresponding thesis defense presentation slides) from the perspectives of intertextuality and interdiscursivity, which will be discussed in the next section.

2.4 Intertextuality, Interdiscursivity, and Genre Transfer

Intertextuality, firstly coined by Kristeva (1969, as cited in Ngai et al., 2020), has been explored by a number of scholars for a long time. Kristeva (1969) asserted that the history of other texts can be found in any text within itself in that "every text is from the outset under the jurisdiction of other discourses which impose a universe on it". Furthermore, Kristeva (1980) referred to intertextuality as the phenomenon that "several utterances, taken from other texts, intersect and naturalize one another". Devitt (1991) stated that "no text is single, as texts refer to one another, draw from one another, create the purpose for one another". In other words, all texts are intertextual in nature to some extent (Bhatia, 2010; Candlin & Maley, 2014). Intertextuality illustrates that a text is explicitly or implicitly related to texts from the past to present, or probably, to the future (Bazerman, 2004). Furthermore, Bhatia (2010) contended that intertextuality refers to that a text is interrelated to other texts at the textual level. Similarly, Wu (2011) maintained that a text usually draws upon other texts in terms of their textual features, typically through quotation and citation. The definitions of intertextuality share the notion that one text is connected with other texts at the textual level.

Apart from the different definitions, there are different categories of intertextuality. Through the exploration of communication in a tax account community, Devitt (1991) identified three categories of intertextuality; namely, referential intertextuality, functional intertextuality, and generic intertextuality. The first one indicates that within one text, there is a direct reference to other texts or documents. The second one illustrated that one text is shaped by and interacted with the surrounding texts in a larger system. The last one refers to that writers exploit previous text types to respond to similar rhetorical situations in a specific community. Besides, Fairclough (1992) divided intertextuality into manifest intertextuality and constitute intertextuality. Manifest intertextuality refers to the phenomenon that other texts are explicitly presented in a new text at the textual level, while the constitute intertextuality of a text refers to "the configuration of discourse conventions that goes into its production" (Fairclough, 1992). Furthermore, Bhatia (2004) provided six detailed categories of intertextuality. They are "texts providing a context" "texts within and around the text" "texts explicitly referred to in the text" "texts implicitly referred to in the text" "texts embedded within the text", and "texts mixed with the text". These categories enrich our understanding of this particular intertextual phenomenon.

To better understand the relationship between or among genres, another notion, interdiscursivity, was put forward. Fairclough (1992) used the term "interdiscursivity" to replace the "constitute intertextuality" and defined it as "a matter of how a discourse type constituted through a combination of elements of orders of discourse". In other words, interdiscursivity is the incorporation of characteristics of various genres, discourses, or styles into one text to achieve specific communicative purposes. Moreover, Bhatia (2010) stated that genre is constituted by both text-internal and text-external aspects. The first one refers to the intertextuality, while the second one relates to the interdiscursivity which is the utilization of text-external features, generic resources of another genre, into the construction of a new genre, essentially contextual in nature. Through the investigation of professional communications, Bhatia (2010) put forward four levels to analyze any instance within the professional context; namely, text, genre, professional practice, and professional culture. Interdiscursivity is the interactions between and across genres, professional practices, and professional cultures. Similarly, Koller (2010) regarded interdiscursivity as "the transfer of particular linguistic features that are typical of one discourse (or genre) to texts that represent another one". The interdiscursive performances usually generate a hybrid, embedded, or mixed genre (Deng et al., 2021).

The major difference between intertextuality and interdiscursivity is that the first one mostly pays attention to the textual level, while the second one predominantly focuses on the appropriation of conventions of genres, discourses, and styles. In other words, intertextuality focuses on the actual surface forms of texts, whereas interdiscursivity investigates the whole language system to which a text is referred (Wu, 2011). These two concepts differ in the way of viewing the text (Deng et al., 2021). On the one hand, intertextuality considers text as the representative of a genre. On the other hand, interdiscursivity regards it as the representative of professional practices and culture. From another perspective, Mäntynen and Shore (2014) referred to the intertextual performances as the explicit transfer and transformation of specific texts, instead, the interdiscursive ones related to the transfer and transformation of the implicit features and conventions of genres. Any text is inherently intertextual and interdiscursive (Deng et al., 2021; Fairclough, 1992; Ho, 2011).

To realize intertextuality and interdiscursivity, several strategies or techniques were identified. As for the intertextual manifestation, Devitt (1991) identified four methods being utilized by the tax accountants in their discourse community. These four methods were explicit quotations, unmarked quotations, paraphrases, or interpretations. Further, Bazerman (2004) suggested six strategies of intertextual representation as follows:

1. Direct quotation.

2. Indirect quotation.

3. Mentioning a person, document, or statement.

4. Comment or evaluation of a statement, text, or voice.

5. Recognizable phrasing, terminology, or "voice" of a group of people or document.

6. Echoing certain ways of communicating discussions or types of documents.

The first four strategies are more explicit than the last two, thus they are more identifiable. The first four were considered as intertextual strategies or techniques and the last two were viewed as interdiscursive techniques (Deng et al., 2021; Koskela, 2013). Furthermore, Tardy (2011) mentioned citations, summaries, or paraphrases from other texts as intertextual manifestations. These strategies provide us with a special angle to see how a text is constructed and related to other texts.

Both intertextuality and interdiscursivity shed light on our understanding of the interrelationships between various genres. Moreover, they work as a useful analytical tool when analyzing genres (Bhatia, 2004; Bremner, 2008). Genres are not isolated by themselves. Instead, they are interrelated and textually linked with other genres so that form a "genre chain" (Swales, 2004), "genre set" (Devitt, 1991), or "genre system/ network" (Bazerman, 1994; Swales, 2004). A genre chain is a progression of genres in chronological order (Günther et al., 2015; Swales, 2004; Zhang, 2018). Along this chain, genres are influenced and linked by each other and then usually are the "products of constant hybridization" (Mäntynen & Shore, 2014). In addition, the genres within a chain involve "systematic transformations from genre to genre" (Fairclough, 2003). As for the genre set, it is part of the total genre network which an individual or individuals engage in so that it serves as part of their occupational or institutional practice (Devitt, 1991; Swales, 2004). Further, Bazerman (1994) expanded the notion of the genre set into the concept of the system of genres and defined it as "interrelated genres that interact with each other in specific settings". Moreover, the genre system contains "the full set of genres that instantiate the participants of all the parties" (Bazerman, 1994). Swales (2004) used "genre networks" to cover this concept and regarded it as "the totality of genres available for a particular sector". These terms indicate the interrelationship and interaction among the genres and in which intertextuality and interdiscursivity have functioned.

In the present study, the thesis anticipates the forthcoming thesis defense presentation slides, and it influences the production of the slides, thus they are in chronological order and form a ring of the genre chain of "thesis defense genres". In this genre chain, certain parts of the thesis are extracted for the production of the slides, which involves the process of "recontextualization" proposed by Linell (1998). Recontextualization was defined as "the extrication of some part or aspects from a text or discourse, or from a genre of texts or discourses, and the fitting of this part or aspect into another context, i.e., another text or discourse (or discourse genre) and its use and environment" (Linell, 1998). Following Pramoolsook (2007), the present study adopted the term "genre transfer" which was put forward by Hyland (2000) to indicate this kind of translation or transformation process between genres because this term explicitly indicates the relationship between genres and covers the perspectives of intertextuality and interdiscursivity.

Moreover, thesis and thesis defense presentation slides could be regarded as both texts and genres. Therefore, the investigation of genre transfer between these two genres involves both the exploration of intertextuality and the examination of interdiscursivity. Intertextuality in the present research refers to the text-internal connection between the thesis and the corresponding thesis defense presentation slides, thus focusing primarily on the textual level to examine how the text of the thesis is being appropriated by the thesis defense presentation slides. Nevertheless, interdiscursivity aims to identify the text-external interaction between these two genres from the genre perspective which mainly focuses on how the rhetorical structure of the thesis is presented in the slides.

2.5 Previous Studies on Genre Transfer

To the best of the researcher's knowledge, there is no study investigating the genre transfer between the master's thesis and its corresponding thesis defense presentation slides. Nonetheless, to better situate the present research into the wider literature, the studies of genre transfer between other pairs of genres are reviewed in this section.

The earliest studies carried out to investigate the genre transfer were reported in Swales (1990). Dubios (1986, as cited in Swales, 1990) explored the genre transfer between the research articles in journals and the corresponding news items in local papers. The changes and modifications through the transfer process were at the language level. For example, the jargon in the research articles was removed in the news items. Moreover, changes were found at the structure level as well, such as the main conclusions being relocated into the opening section of the news.

Fahnestock (1986, as cited in Swales, 1990) investigated the genre transfer from research reports to popular accounts. The identified changes between these two closely related genres were the translation of epideictic language into ordinary language, the loss of cautious peer reviews, and the greater effort to attract the readers' interest. Apart from different audiences, these changes were caused by a different purpose of these two genres in that the research reports are to celebrate instead of validating the facts.

Furthermore, Myers (1990) conducted a detailed analysis of the genre transfer between the biology research articles for a professional audience and the popularizing articles in prestigious science magazines. These two genres indicated two views of science. The major differences and modifications were found at the levels of narrative structure, syntax, and vocabulary. For example, a narration of science was changed into a narration of nature. In addition, the syntax and vocabulary that emphasize the disciplinary conceptual structure were translated into those stressing the externality of nature to scientific practices.

Moreover, Mohamed (2000, as cited in Pramoolsook, 2007) examined the genre transfer between two academic genres, i.e., dissertation and research articles. To identify the differences between these two genres in terms of the argument structure, the problem-solution rhetorical pattern analysis was utilized to analyze ten Egyptian dissertations and 33 corresponding research articles were published successfully. Various changes to the semantic elements of the organizational pattern and the related strategies were identified. At the top semantic elements of *Question and Answer*, four possible strategies the writers employed were *Focus-Restate, Focus-Reshape, Extend-Restate,* and *Extend-Reshape*. In addition, at the middle-level semantic elements, such as *Setting* and *Response*, the major textual modifications were text condensation and reorientation.

By the same token, Pramoolsook (2007) conducted a study on the genre transfer from thesis to research article. The data included six pairs of these two genres, with three each from Biotechnology and Environmental Engineering. Through move analysis and text comparison of these two sets of data, the findings showed that the changes and modifications related to the rhetorical structure as well as the content and language. For example, at the rhetorical structure level, the Environmental Engineering theses had separate Introduction and Literature Review, while being transferred into the research articles, the Literature Review chapters were omitted, with some related information was relocated into the Introduction sections. At the content and language level, the major changes and related strategies were the omission, addition, and relocation of texts. In addition, those findings were validated and clarified by the structured interviews with the supervisors and the writers of those theses and research articles included in the data. These changes may be caused by several factors. For example, the RA writing is influenced by the gatekeepers, such as the editors and reviewers, thus, their opinions are taken into consideration when producing the RAs. In other words, thesis and research articles have different communicative purposes, target audience, and rhetorical structures and conventions, which work together to influence the genre transfer between these two genres.

Besides, the genre transfer in the genre system of medicinal product information has been explored as well. Piorno (2012) investigated the genre transfer from the source genre, the summary of product characteristics (SPC), to the target genre, the package leaflet (PL). The source genre is an expository genre aiming at experts and professionals, while the target genre is an instructional genre for lay readers. Through comparing the templates of these two genres, the target genre was simpler and shorter in terms of structural changes. In addition, putting the original texts in the SPCs and the corresponding texts in the PLs side by side, several changes and strategies were identified. For example, the passive sentence was transferred into an active one. The findings revealed that these changes and shifts mainly intended to facilitate patients' readability of the PL, to have power implications on the patients' actions, as well as to get close to readers of the PL.

Recently, Zhang (2018) explored the transfer between the university press releases and the corresponding news stories in two mass media websites. After collecting 90 science news stories each from the university websites and two media websites, move analysis was firstly conducted to identify the move structure of the university releases and then used this structure as a framework to investigate the moves and steps of the news stories in the two media websites. The findings showed that they employed similar structures. Moreover, through the log-likelihood analysis of the frequencies of each move and step, it was found that only several steps had statistically significant differences. A closer examination revealed that the traditional structure IMRD of research articles was first integrated into the university releases, and then into the mass media news without significant changes except for the removal of the promotional elements, such as the funding acknowledgment.

In summary, studies focusing on genre transfer are scant. The existing research makes a great contribution to the understanding of the genre chains and the transfer between the genres along the chain. The above studies show that there are no stable analytical procedures or methods to explore the phenomenon of genre transfer. However, these studies indicate that comparative analysis is frequently used to investigate the changes and modifications between the genres. Moreover, the changes are mainly at the structure level as well as the content and language level which are regarded as an effect of genre transfer. These changes indicate that there arc similarities between the genre pairs in terms of the structures as well as their content and language, which implies the appropriation of the text and convention of one text or genre into another text or genre and embodies the theories of intertextuality and interdiscursivity as mentioned in *Section 2.4*. However, no study, to the researcher's best knowledge, has combined or integrated these two theories into the investigation of the genre transfer along the genre chain. Therefore, the current study which explores the genre transfer with the combination of these two theories will provide new insights into the future studies of genre transfer.

As for the genre pairs, the research articles and the news stories have been mainly explored. However, few studies paid attention to the genre transfer along the academic chains (e.g., Mohamed, 2000; Pramoolsook, 2007). In addition, no study has investigated the genre transfer between the thesis and the thesis defense presentation slides, which places certain stress on the master's students. Therefore, the present research aims to examine the genre transfer between this genre pair in terms of their rhetorical structure and language features.

Overall, the current study hopes to fill the gaps identified in the previous sections. Firstly, scant studies have investigated the rhetorical structure of the whole M.A. theses, especially those written by Chinese students. This study will add new insights into the understanding of this academic genre that places a lot of challenges on the students and make the students more familiar with its conventions expected and shared by the members of the discourse community. Secondly, the thesis defense presentation slides as a genre have gained little attention, thus, their rhetorical structure is unclear to the writers who find difficulties in producing this kind of genre and who may underestimate its functions. The present study could raise the writers' genre awareness about it. Thirdly, the thesis and the corresponding thesis defense presentation slides in the genre chain of the thesis defense very much interrelate and interact with each other. However, the transfer between these two different but closely related genres is still a gap in the literature. The current research could fill this gap based on the theory of intertextuality and interdiscursivity, so that the strategies the students employed to conduct the genre transfer process will be identified, which will benefit the learners, teachers, and material designers. In a word, this study could make contributions to the genre studies of the M.A. theses, the corresponding thesis defense presentation slides as well as to the studies of intertextuality, interdiscursivity, and genre transfer.

2.6 Summary

Putting the present study in the wider literature, the theoretical foundation of genre and genre analysis are presented in this chapter, on the one hand. The pertinent studies on the understanding of the two genres in question and their rhetorical structures are reviewed to indicate the research gaps, on the other hand. Moreover, these related studies are supposed to provide certain insights into the results and discussions of the present study in later chapters. The next chapter will present in detail the research methodology designed to fulfill these identified gaps.

CHAPTER 3 Methodology

This chapter firstly depicts the overall research design of the present study, and then gives details on how the needed data were collected, including the sampling criteria and the sample size. Furthermore, details on corpus creation and corpus management are demonstrated. In addition, the specific data analysis procedures to answer each of the research questions are elaborated, and the measurement of inter-coder agreement is described as well. Finally, the preliminary findings of the pilot study are presented, followed by the suggestions for the main study.

3.1 Research Design

The present study is a case study in nature. A case study is a kind of methodology and a type of research design or a kind of method or strategy (Yin, 2003b) which focuses on an issue through the exploration of a bounded system /a case or multiple bounded systems /cases over time, employing detailed, in-depth data collection with multiple sources of information (Creswell, 2007; Duff, 2018). The bounded system could be an individual, a school, or a community (Cohen et al. 2007). Besides, from another perspective, a case study is "the study of an instance in action" (Adelman et al., 1980, as cited in Cohen et al. 2007), however, the instance in this definition is similarly "of a bounded system" (Cohen et al. 2007).

From the definitions, the recurring characteristics of a case study are the bounded or singular nature of the case, multiple sources of data or triangulation, and in-depth analysis (Creswell, 2007; Duff, 2018). These three characteristics could be the criteria to determine whether a study belongs to case studies or not. The present research mainly aims to explore the genre transfer from the thesis to the corresponding thesis defense presentation slides conducted by a group of master's students in one bounded system (GZU) through an in-depth analysis of their theses and the corresponding thesis defense presentation slides which is then triangulated by the documents as well as the interviews with the supervisors and the writers. Hence, it is proposed that the present study possesses the three features of a case study and thus is claimed to belong to a case study indeed.

Furthermore, case studies can be divided into three categories based on their primary purposes; namely, exploratory, descriptive, or explanatory (Yin, 2003a). An exploratory case study mainly focuses on the need to create a framework or on the determination of the feasibility of the expected research procedures, while a descriptive case study aims to provide a complete description of a phenomenon within its bounded system. In addition, explanatory case studies intend to identify the cause-effect relationships to explain the potential reasons behind the event. Given the lack of a priori assumptions (Negretti & Kuteeva, 2011) about the genre transfer between the two focused genres in question, the present study falls into the category of an exploratory case study.

Case studies possess certain advantages. A case study is attractive as a result of a high degree of completeness, depth of analysis, and readability (Duff, 2018). It is feasible for analytic rather than statistical generalization (Robson, 2002). However, it allows generalizations either about an instance or from an instance to similar instances (Cohen et al., 2007) in that the findings of a case study can provide insights for researchers to understand and interpret other similar cases or situations (Cohen et al., 2007; Nisbet & Watt, 1984; Robson, 2002). Drawn from the strengths of case studies, the present study adopts an exploratory case study research design.

Beyond the case study, the present research employs mixed methods research design to answer the proposed research questions. Mixed methods research design is a kind of approach involving both qualitative and quantitative data collection as well as merging these two forms of data together to better understand the research phenomenon (Creswell & Creswell, 2018). This kind of research design absorbs the strength of qualitative data and quantitative data while reducing the limitations of either one of them so that additional insight is yielded. In the present study, for the identification of moves and steps in the two focused genres, move analysis, a kind of qualitative research, is employed, while for the frequency of each move and step to determine whether it is obligatory or optional, quantitative analysis based on the corpus is utilized, following Basturkmen (2009), Dastjerdi et al. (2017), and Zainuddin and Shaari (2021). Besides, to figure out the changes as an effect of genre transfer between the two different but closely related genres, a detailed textual analysis, which is also a kind of qualitative study, is used to conduct the mapping of the moves and steps as well as the textual features between the two corpora. Furthermore, as a means of data triangulation, qualitative analysis of the interviews with the supervisors and the writers is employed to clarify and enrich the findings from the analysis of the texts. Thus, the present research incorporates qualitative research methods and quantitative research ones together as a mixed methods research design in a way that qualitative research is supplemented by quantitative research in order to better achieve the research objectives.

3.2 Data Collection

All the data of the present study have been collected from the research context GZU. GZU is selected as the research site and sources of data since the present researcher used to be a master's student of this discourse community and has the accessibility as well as the understanding of the data obtained from this context. Being a previous master's student in the research site makes the present researcher familiar with the context and later could provide some ethnographic information and perspective for the study (Ho, 2011). The first kind of data collected from GZU is the documents about the master's program in Foreign Linguistics and Applied Linguistics which is the focused discipline of the present study, such as the training plan of the program, the requirements of awarding a master's degree, and the format requirements of the thesis. These documents could provide certain contextual information and background about the master's program the present study focuses on and from which the data are drawn.

Furthermore, the data which are the primary data for analysis of the present study include the master's theses and their corresponding thesis defense presentation slides. Besides, interviews with the supervisors and the writers have been conducted as a source of in-depth information that sheds more light on the textual analysis results of these two genres.

3.2.1 Master's Theses (MTs)

Four criteria are established to collect the master's theses in GZU to be used as a data set of this current study. Firstly, the theses should come from the master's students who graduated from the academic years 2017 to 2021. In other words, only the theses within these five years were collected, following Xie (2017). As genres keep evolving and new rhetorical practices keep emerging (Hyland, 2004; Swales, 1990), it is the intention of the present study that to obtain the current tendency and to find out the recurrent rhetorical structures of the theses produced in this context. Therefore, the present study, which started in 2021, selected the data from the period of the past five years from 2021 back to 2017. The researcher has confirmed with the Director of the English Department of GZU that the requirements for the thesis writing and for the degree rewarding within these five years are the same, with only some slight variations on the courses offered. Secondly, only the theses produced by the master's students in the discipline of Foreign Linguistics and Applied Linguistics were selected as the data. This is because, apart from the familiarity of the present researcher with this discipline, almost all theses are written in the first language of the students (i.e., standard Chinese) in China, and only the master's students at schools or departments of foreign languages are obliged to write their theses in a foreign language. Therefore, only those in English-related disciplines (i.e., Foreign Linguistics and Applied Linguistics, English Literature, and Translation and Interpretation) are required to compose their theses in English. Among the three disciplines, merely those in the Foreign Linguistics and Applied Linguistics follow the traditional ILrMRDC structure. Thirdly, only the thesis versions that students utilized to create the thesis defense presentation slides for their final defense were collected, not the final revised version after the defense. The reason is that after the defense, the students may add certain information into or revise some parts of the theses which are not identifiable in the corresponding slides. Finally, to make the present study more concise and consistent, only the traditional simple type of theses (ILrMRDC) was collected, which is a pervasive structure in thesis writing (Anderson &

Okuda, 2021; Chen & Kuo, 2012). To conclude, the theses that meet all the four criteria were selected to build the corpus of master's theses for the current analysis.

At the beginning, after gaining the permission of the gatekeepers, i.e., the administrator and the Director of the English Department who have access to the students' information from GZU, the present researcher collected the contact information of the potential authors of the M.A. theses since only they possess their thesis defense presentation slides. Then, the researcher contacted each of them one by one via WeChat (a popular social application in China) to make sure they clearly understood the purposes of the present research and to ask for their permission and cooperation in sharing their theses and the corresponding thesis defense presentation slides for the current research.

There are 52 master's students who successfully graduated from GZU within the academic years 2017 to 2021. After contacting all of them, 13 of them were unwilling to share their theses and thesis defense presentation slides because of the confidentiality concerns and 9 of them said they could not find their thesis defense presentation slides due to improper preservation. In the end, 30 of the potential authors were willing to provide their theses and thesis defense presentation slides. However, 4 out of the 30 participants withdrew in the middle of the data collection process. Therefore, only 26 pairs of theses and the corresponding thesis defense presentation slides were collected with the signed consent forms from the authors.

In the pool of the collected 26 theses, 6 theses embedded the Methodology chapter in other chapters, such as in the Introduction chapter or in the Theoretical Framework chapter, thus they were excluded. In the end, 20 theses (2 from 2021, 2 from 2020, 5 from 2019, 5 from 2018, and 6 from 2017) met the criteria set by the present researcher and thus were collected to form the corpus for this current study. The structures of the 20 selected theses belong to the traditional simple type ILrMRDC (Paltridge, 2002). However, they are slightly different in that the Results chapter and the Discussion chapter were combined into one single chapter as an integrated Results and Discussion chapter. Hence, the structure of the theses is more of the ILrM[RD]C type. Moreover, 12 out of the 20 in the corpus have a separate chapter entitled Theoretical Framework located between the Literature Review chapter and the Methodology chapter. According to an informal interview with a GZU supervisor, who has 12-year experience of guiding students how to write a thesis, the Theoretical Framework chapter is a part of the Literature Review, and it could be a separate chapter if the thesis writers consider that more space or more attention needs to be put in the adopted theories. This decision was in line with Kwan (2006) that the chapters between Introduction and Methodology were all considered as Literature Review. Therefore, the Theoretical Framework chapter was analyzed and presented separately using the same framework of the Literature Review in the present study. In the end, the corpus of the theses contains two structures. To be more specific, twelve of them have the ILrTf[RD]C structure and eight follow the ILrM[RD]C one. However, the titles and the author names of these 20 theses are not given in the Appendices due to the ethical issues as well as the writers' concern about the confidentiality.

The size of 20 theses for the target corpus was considered sufficient and manageable. In qualitative research, purposeful sampling is usually adopted and there is no widely determined sample size on qualitative data. In related literature, the closely related study on the move structure of the whole thesis is conducted by Chen and Kuo (2012) which explored 15 M.A. theses structured in ILrMRDC format. The framework from their research was cited or adopted by other subsequent studies (e.g., Nguyen, 2014; Pieketaleyee & Bazargani, 2018) and confirmed to be applicable although new steps were found. Hence, the sample size adopted by their studies could be assumed to be adequate for the investigation of the moves and steps of the master's theses. Therefore, the present study that has collected 20 theses as the data went a step further than Chen and Kuo (2012) and the sample size was not smaller than theirs.

Furthermore, two justifications were taken into consideration on the sample size, that is, practical justification and theoretical justification (Flowerdew & Forest, 2009). From the practical perspective, involving the hand-coding of the moves and steps as well as a detailed analysis of the changes between the two different genres in question, the amount of the data should not be too large to be handled, thus the sample size of 20 was regarded to be practical. From the theoretical perspective, given that the 20 theses all belong to the same genre and the same discipline, there should be sufficient data being generated for analysis despite the small corpus size (Flowerdew & Forest, 2009). Therefore, the data of 20 theses and the corresponding thesis defense presentation slides are considered to be manageable and sufficient for a detailed analysis to accomplish the research objectives.

To build the corpus and to clean it up for research convenience, only the body part, the first chapter to the last chapter, was extracted from each thesis since the main purpose of the present study is to explore the genre transfer between the thesis and its thesis defense presentation slides which do not have Abstract and Acknowledgements that are presented in the original thesis. Therefore, these two textual elements were excluded. In addition, all the tables and figures in the body parts were removed since the visual data presentation is out of the scope of the present study. Then, the remaining parts were randomly assigned from MT01 to MT20 to preserve the confidentiality of the thesis writers.

Furthermore, for the convenience of analysis, each chapter was extracted separately to build a subcorpus, for example, MTI01-MTI20 for the Introduction chapters, MTLr01-MTLr20 for the Literature Review chapters, MTTf01-MTTf20 for Theoretical Framework chapters, MTM01-MTM20 for the Methodology chapters, MTRD01-MTRD20 for the integrated Results and Discussion chapters, and MTC01-MTC20 for the Conclusion chapters.

3.2.2 Thesis Defense Presentation Slides (PSs)

Apart from the theses, 20 sets of the corresponding thesis defense presentation slides were collected to build the second corpus. The present study regards the thesis defense presentation slides as a kind of written form (Atai & Talebzadeh, 2012; Pieketaleyee & Bazargani, 2018; Tardy, 2005), hence, the 20 sets of presentation slides were transformed into an editable file format so that their content could be analyzed manually and tagged electronically for an easy calculation of the frequencies of moves and steps. Similarly, only the body part of the presentation slides was selected to build the corpus and was coded as PS01 to PS20 which is matched with the original theses. For example, PS01 is matched with MT01 because they were produced by the same writer so that this pair could be easily compared. In addition, to clean the corpus, the references in the slide sets were removed. Furthermore, the slides were organized into several sections that were parallel to the chapters in the original theses. Therefore, each section of the presentation slides was extracted separately to form a subcorpus similar to those of the original theses, such as PSI01-PSI20 for the Introductions in the thesis defense presentation slides, PSLr01-PSLr20 for the Literature review sections, PSTf01-PSTf20 for Theoretical Framework sections, PSM01-PSM20 for the Methodology sections, PSRD01-PSRD20 for the combined Results and Discussion sections, and PSC01-PSC20 for the Conclusion sections.

3.2.3 Interview Data

To validate the findings from the textual analysis and enrich the insights on the transfer between these two genres, interviews with the supervisors and the writers were conducted as suggested by Biber et al. (2007), and Hyland (2000). The reason why the supervisors were selected for the interview is that as the direct audience of the two genres in question, the perspectives from the supervisors could provide extra insights into understanding the production of these two genres. Furthermore, the writers, as the real producers of these two genres, were interviewed so that their perspectives would add more into the comprehension of the genre transfer practice, i.e., the strategies they employed to conduct the genre transfer. The interview data from these two groups serve as a kind of triangulation for the textual analysis.

Previous pertinent studies usually select several informants to provide some ethnographic perspectives and the number of informants ranges from one to four (Bruce, 2009; Lim, 2006; Parkinton, 2017). Thus, the present study has selected two supervisors (SP1, SP2) and five thesis writers (ST1-ST5), one from each academic year, as the informants mainly based on their availability. Both of the supervisor informants are female who have been working as an M.A. supervisor for 12 years and 16 years, respectively. As for the student informants, two of them are male and three are female.

Furthermore, semi-structured interview is chosen to be conducted with the informants. The three kinds of interviews, i.e., structured interview, semi-structured interview, and unstructured interview, possess certain strengths. The semi-structured interview is chosen since it not only enables the researcher to prepare some questions based on the findings from the genre-based analysis in advance but also allows for further probing and prompting during the interview. The interview questions for the supervisors are related to the interesting results from the move analysis of the thesis and the thesis defense presentation slides, as well as about their experience in supervising their students to accomplish their theses and thesis defense in terms of the conventions or norms, difficulties, and problems as well as the expectations as the target audience.

As for the interviews with the five thesis writers, similarly, the interview questions are mainly from the textual analysis results, and a part of them is about the informants' writing experience in producing theses and thesis defense presentation slides. Besides, the strategies the writers employed when they transferred the thesis into the thesis defense presentation slides were probed during the interview.

Obtaining the consent from the informants in advance through the consent forms, both the interviews with the supervisors and the writers were conducted in Chinese, their mother tongue, to put them in a comfortable talking environment so that they could talk freely and express themselves better. The interviews with the supervisors each lasted for around 18 minutes. Moreover, the duration of the interviews with the students ranges from about 16 minutes to 28 minutes, with an average of 21 minutes per student. All the interviews were recorded with the permission from the informants. The main purposes of the interviews are to validate the findings from the textual analysis and to enrich the understanding of the genre transfer process from the authors' own perspectives. Therefore, only the related information was translated into English to help the researcher clarify the findings from the textual analysis and add some background knowledge or extra insights about the genre transfer process to the research. It should be noted that aside from these five writers selected as the interviewees, other writers (if possible) were consulted about the interesting findings found in their theses or thesis defense presentation slides.

3.3 Data Analysis

After collecting all the needed data and constructing the two main corpora (MTs and PSs), the data are ready to be analyzed to answer the proposed four research questions. In both of the corpora, the thesis titles and the names of the authors or supervisors were kept confidential to follow the ethical issues.

3.3.1 Procedures to Answer Research Question One (RQ1)

RQ1 aims to identify the moves, steps, and their structures of the whole M.A. theses written by GZU master's students in Foreign Linguistics and Applied Linguistics. After the corpus of the theses was created, their general information was presented first, especially the descriptive statistics about the length. Then, the chapter titles were analyzed and compared so that the macrostructure of the theses is to be identified in order to have an overview of the textual organizational components of the theses. After this general view of the corpus, their moves and steps were investigated manually in detail.

To find out the moves and steps of the theses, Chen and Kuo's (2012) framework for analyzing M.A. thesis, which was reviewed in detail in *Section 2.2.3.6*, was adopted by the present study. As indicated in Chapter 2, the reason for adopting their framework is twofold. On the one hand, their framework is proposed under the investigation of M.A. theses in Applied Linguistics which is similar to the focused discipline (Foreign Linguistics and Applied Linguistics) under the present study. Thus, it is assumed that their framework is relevant to the present study as well. On the other hand, their framework was applied to the exploration of TESOL M.A. theses written by Vietnamese students (Nguyen, 2014) and was confirmed to be applicable and effective in identifying the moves and steps of the theses. Although Nguyen's (2014) framework based on Chen and Kuo's (2012) is more updated, the present study prefers the adoption of the latter one. For one thing, the corpus in Chen and Kuo (2012) was built from the ProQuest Digital database which covers more nationalities of the writers. It assumes that Chinese writers may be included in their corpus. Nevertheless, the data in Nguyen's (2014) study was from writers of a single nationality, i.e., Vietnamese. Hence, the former one is considered more appropriate for the present study which focuses on the Chinese writers. For another thing, when Nguyen (2014) adopted Chen and Kuo's framework in her study, some steps of certain moves were not found in her corpus although new steps were identified. Therefore, there is a wide coverage of steps in Chen and Kuo's (2012) framework. In addition, Nguyen (2014) stated there is a cultural difference in the employment of moves and steps. It appears that one step that is adopted by this group of writers may not be found in the products of another cultural group. Thus, the present research would adopt Chen and Kuo's (2012) framework as the result of its applicability, wide nationality of the writers analyzed, and wide step coverage.

Nevertheless, based on the research objectives of the present study, several modifications are needed to make the framework more appropriate for the current research. Firstly, the main objective of the present study is to explore the genre transfer between the theses and the thesis defense presentation slides, thus, only the body part of the theses is to be examined and compared since the corresponding presentation slides do not have Abstract. Therefore, the moves and steps about the Abstract in the framework were removed. Secondly, in the original framework, Chen and Kuo (2012) added an independent move *Referring to other studies* to each chapter except for the Literature Review chapter to explicitly present the functions of the citations which is out of the scope of the present study, therefore, this independent move was removed as well. In the end, in their framework, several moves only have one step, which means that there are no options for writers to select, and its communicative function is embodied by the move already. So, it is not necessary to put only one step under a move. Thus, the only step under certain moves was excluded and merely the move was adopted to code the data.

Besides, although the framework of Chen and Kuo (2012) covers the Introduction, Literature Review, Methodology, Results, Discussion, and Conclusion chapters, the present corpus has a separate chapter called Theoretical Framework, and an integrated Results and Discussion. As for the Theoretical Framework chapter, Chen and Kuo's moves and steps (2012) of the Literature Review were utilized to analyze it since they have similar communicative purposes based on the study of Kwan (2006) and the informal interview with an experienced supervisor of GZU. As for the integrated Results and Discussion chapter, the moves and steps of the Results chapter and the Discussion chapter in the framework were combined to investigate it. This is because when comparing the moves and steps of these two chapters, it was found that they are almost the same except for one extra move in Discussion and one extra step under the move *Reporting results in Results*. Thus, it is assumed that combining the moves and steps of the two separate chapters could be sufficient to investigate the move structure of the integrated Results and Discussion chapter.

Furthermore, the modified framework was applied to the identification of the moves and steps chapter by chapter manually in the subcorpora. In the case that a text segment does not fall into any move or step of the framework, a new move or step will be assigned to it (Bunton, 2002). As for these newly found moves or steps, they will be proposed if their frequency is above 50%, following Nwogu (1997). Moreover, in identifying a move or a step, a functional approach to textual analysis was conducted, which depends on the cognitive judgment to determine the communication function of a text segment and the textual boundaries (Kwan, 2006). Hence, comprehensive and repeated reading is necessary. Then, the communicative function of each text segment was examined and coded based on the coding framework. In the situation where more than one communicative function is demonstrated in a text segment, only the salient and predominant function was coded (You & Li, 2021). Following Yang and Allison (2003), the sub-steps were not explored for the sake of an economical and explicit analysis. During the coding process, intra-coding and inter-coding were employed to improve the reliability of the analysis, details of which are provided later in *Section 3.3.5*. After checking the intercoder reliability and reaching the agreement consistency, the moves and steps were tagged electrically in the corpora for the ease of counting their frequency for further calculation and tabulation.

According to the frequency of appearance, one move or step could be categorized into three groups. From previous studies, there are two main alternatives of cut-off points to determine if a move or step is obligatory or optional. The first one is that if the frequency of the move or step is more than 60%, then it is obligatory, otherwise, it is optional (e.g., Biber et al., 2007; Dastjerdi, 2017). On the other hand, the second one indicates that only if the move or step is presented in all the text (100%), it is regarded as obligatory. It is optional if its frequency is below 60%, and those holding the frequency between 60% and 99% are considered as conventional (e.g., Kanoksilapathan, 2005; Nguyen, 2014; Nguyen & Pramoolsook, 2015). In the present research, the second alternative (Table 3.1) was adopted as it better captures the nuance of the move/step status.

Table 3.1 The Cut-off Point for Move-Step Status

Status	Cut-off point
Obligatory	100%
Conventional	60% - 99%
Optional	0% - 60%

In addition, to analyze the pattern of the moves and steps, the move-step sequence of each thesis was put into a spreadsheet (Schoeneborn, 2013) to easily identify the recurrent pattern of the moves or steps in the present corpora. Then, the recurring move-step structure of the theses produced by this group of writers was presented. It should be mentioned that the move or step sequence means the co-occurrence of more than one move or step in an order in one thesis. If this sequence appears in more than one thesis, this phenomenon is referred to as a move or step pattern. In the end, the findings of the present study were compared with Chen and Kuo's (2012) study and other pertinent studies focusing on a single chapter or chapters of theses or dissertations.

3.3.2 Procedures to Answer Research Question Two (RQ 2)

RQ 2 intends to identify the moves, steps, and their structures of the thesis defense presentation slides, which are the products of the original theses analyzed in the first research question. Similarly, the modified framework of Chen and Kuo's framework was applied to the investigation of this corpus as well. Previous studies (e.g., Atai & Talebzadeh, 2012; Pieketaleyee & Bazargani, 2018; Rowley-Jolivet, 2002; Tardy, 2005) stated that the structure of the presentation slides is influenced by that of their original written genres. Therefore, it could be expected that the framework of the structure of the original written genre, i.e., the thesis, is available for exploring the structure of their corresponding presentation slides, i.e., the thesis defense presentation slides. Besides, Pieketaleyee and Bazargani (2018) confirmed that Chen and Kuo's (2012) framework was applicable to investigate the moves and steps of the presentation slides. In addition, adopting the same framework into analyzing the theses and the corresponding thesis defense presentation slides would make the comparison between these two genres easier and the genre transfer between them in terms of the moves and steps easily identified.

Based on the framework of Chen and Kuo (2012), the texts in each slide were assigned to their corresponding move or step according to their main communicative function. After receiving a high agreement consistency, the moves and steps identified in the slides were tagged electrically in the corpus as well to calculate their frequency. Similarly, the move-step sequence of each slide set was presented in a spreadsheet to better analyze their recurrent patterns. Furthermore, the results of the moves, steps, and their structurees were discussed by referring to related previous studies. In case that there were no previous studies to be compared, then the discussion of the results was offered by the researcher herself based on the interpretations of the findings.

3.3.3 Procedures to Answer Research Question Three (RQ 3)

The aim of RQ3 is to identify the changes in terms of the moves/steps and the textual features that the writers made between the theses and the thesis defense presentation slides which could be claimed as an effect of the genre transfer.

To investigate the adoption of the moves or steps in the thesis defense presentation slides as compared with those in the original theses, the moves and steps of each pair of thesis and thesis defense presentation slides were listed in parallel table to see which ones were maintained by the writers in the presentation slides, or if there are new moves or steps were employed through the process of genre transfer. Moreover, the frequency of each move and step in both corpora was compared to see whether there was a difference in the use of certain moves or steps.

At the textual level, all the texts in the presentation slides were mapped with the same or similar texts in the original theses, hence, a constant comparison (Bremner & Costley, 2018) was conducted between the original texts in the theses on the left column and those in the corresponding slide texts on the right. Then, the two texts are to be compared to find out what kind of changes are made, i.e., the formal change, the syntactic change, and the lexical change. Each pair of the thesis and the corresponding thesis presentation slides was analyzed in detail and the changes between them in each pair were listed. After analyzing all the pairs of the theses and the corresponding slides, the recurrent changes were summarized as a list of changes which are made as a consequence of genre transfer.

3.3.4 Procedures to Answer Research Question Four (RQ 4)

RQ 4 is to find out the strategies the writers employed when transferring the theses into the thesis defense presentation slides. Based on the findings of the changes from the textual analysis in the preceding research question, corresponding strategies were identified. Drawing from the findings from previous studies (e.g., Bazerman, 2004; Devitt, 1991; Piorno, 2012; Pramoolsook, 2007; Tardy, 2011; Zhang, 2018), the actions that accomplished the changes were identified and the initial codes were assigned to them, respectively. After a constant comparison (Bremner & Costley, 2018) and investigation of the original texts and the corresponding texts, the initial codes were fine-tuned. Further, these codes were utilized as the framework of strategies to code the whole set of the slides. Moreover, the findings of the strategies were supplemented by the interviews with the writers rather than the texts themselves alone.

As for the interviews with the five thesis writers, the changes identified from the comparison between the two main corpora formed some interview questions related to what strategies the writers employed. Besides, the thesis writers were requested to share their experiences in creating the presentation slides based on their theses. The interview data, which are pertinent to the writers' experiences in preparing thesis defense presentation slides as well as their strategies of selecting content from the theses and presenting them again in the slides, were translated into English and read through to identify the strategies the students employed when creating the presentation slides. The findings from the interviews were incorporated into the findings from the textual analysis to form the final framework of strategies to code the whole data. Finally, the frequency and occurrence of each strategy were calculated. There is a difference between the frequency and the occurrence. The frequency in this research question refers to the percentage of the slide sets containing certain strategies in the total slide sets. For example, if a strategy is found in 10 out of the 20 slide sets, the frequency of this kind of strategy is 50%. On the contrary, the occurrence means the total number of certain strategy that appears in all pairs of MT and PS. One strategy would be utilized more than once in one pair. Through the frequency, it can be easily identified which strategy is used most frequently. Through the occurrence, the actual instances of one strategy are clearly shown.

3.3.5　Intra-coder Reliability and Inter-coder Agreement

To increase the reliability of the move identification, both intra-coding and inter-coding were conducted. To achieve the intra-coder reliability, the present researcher analyzed the data twice with an interval of at least four weeks. For the disagreements found in these two times of coding, a closer examination was conducted until a final category was assigned to the problematic text segments.

Furthermore, the present study mainly depends on the textual analysis, and a certain degree of subjectivity is unavoidably involved in this kind of analysis (Soler-Monreal, 2015), thus, inter-coding between more than one analyst is adopted to ensure and increase the reliability of the results. Another researcher was invited to code the data as well. The invited coder, holding a M.A. degree, has been working as an English teacher in a senior high school in China for five years. He has hosted and accomplished a research project on publicity translation based on corpus. Now, he is a member of a research team for other two research projects on English reading teaching and English listening teaching, respectively. Moreover, he has experience in corpus analysis as well as discourse analysis and is interested in genre analysis at the same time. Therefore, he could be regarded as a qualified coder of the present study.

Before the actual coding process, the invited coder was trained in terms of the definition of each move and step in the framework as well as the identification procedures to make him familiar with the framework and the coding process. Training is a general approach that enables the coder to examine the definitions of the coding protocol and to explicitly comprehend the representation of each coding category, which is necessary for achieving better inter-coder agreement (Biber et al., 2007). For the training practice, the coder and the researcher independently coded one thesis, which is randomly selected from the corpus, and the corresponding thesis defense presentation slides according to the modified framework of Chen and Kuo's (2012) framework. Then, the coding results of the moves and steps from the coder and the researcher were compared. The disagreements or discrepancies were discussed between the invited coder and the present researcher until the final agreement was reached. Then, the present researcher recoded the controversial parts.

Subsequently, the invited coder and the researcher coded 30% of the whole data independently, according to the convention of genre analysis (e.g., Liu & Buckingham, 2018), and the results between them were compared and the inter-coder agreement was calculated. The texts for the inter coder were the first 30% of the data in the corpora. For example, MTI01-MTI06 and PSI01-PSI06 were chosen to be analyzed by the inter coder. The remaining texts were analyzed by the present researcher.

As for the inter-coder agreement, two methods are usually adopted to check the agreement between the coders. One method is to use Cohen's Kappa as an index to indicate the reliability of the coding (e.g., Cotos et al., 2015; Dong & Lu, 2020; Hu & Liu, 2018) while the other one is to calculate the percentage agreement (e.g., Dastjerdi et al., 2017; Kanoksilapatham, 2005; Kwan, 2006; Soler-Monreal, 2016). According to Rau and Shih (2021), Cohen's Kappa is not appropriate for move analysis in that it requires that the units under analysis are predetermined, fixed, and independent; however, new moves are allowed to emerge and be identified during the coding process which are not predetermined and fixed. Moreover, their findings stated that only the percent agreement is valid in measuring the inter-rater or inter-coder agreement with nominal data. Therefore, the percentage agreement was adopted by the present study. The formula to calculate the percentage agreement is A/(A+D) * 100, where A is the number of agreements and D is the number of disagreements (Dastjerdi et al., 2017; Nguyen, 2014). To ensure the reliability of the results, the percentage agreement is set at 90% to indicate higher reliability (Biber et al., 2007; Kanoksilapatham, 2005; Maher & Milligan, 2019; Soler-Monreal, 2016). In addition, after the calculation of the percentage agreement, the disagreements, and the discrepancies were discussed between the invited coder and the researcher to finally reach the agreement. In the situation where the discussion did not work, a third coder with a Ph.D. and long experience of move analysis was asked to provide help in settling the analysis/coding results. Thus, in the end, all the codes were agreed between the coder and the researcher. The intra-coder and inter-coder agreement percentages in each chapter of the MT and each section of the PS are provided in the following Table 3.2.

Table 3.2　Intra-coder and Inter-coder Agreement in the MT and PS

Chapter/Section	MT Intra-coding (%)	MT Inter-coding (%)	PS Intra-coding (%)	PS Inter-coding (%)
Introduction	96.7	92.6	96.5	93.4
Literature Review	95.5	91.0	96.0	91.5
Theoretical Framework	91.5	92.2	96.7	93.1
Methodology	96.5	90.9	96.3	90.3
Results and Discussion	94.5	93.2	96.6	94.5
Conclusion	96.3	94.8	96.7	94.1

3.4　Summary

This chapter provided the detailed research design based on the research objectives and the research questions of the present study. The specific procedures to collect and analyze the data were proposed. Moreover, following the steps of the research design, a pilot study was conducted, and its findings indicated the applicability of the adopted framework for the identification of moves and steps in both genres in question. As for the transfer strategies between these two genres, the findings of the pilot study revealed that they were concerned about the moves, steps, and textual features. In addition, a preliminary framework for the identification of the transfer strategies at the textual level was created from the pilot study which will be adopted as a departure point to analyze the data in the main study.

CHAPTER 4 Results and Discussion of Moves and Steps of the Thesis

This chapter provides the results and discussion of the moves and steps identified in the corpus of the master's theses, which aims to answer the first research question of the present study proposed in Chapter 1. To make them clearer and easier to comprehend, the results and discussion are demonstrated by the macrostructure of the theses after the overview of the present corpus, that is the results and discussion of the Introduction chapters are delivered first, followed by those of the Literature Review chapters, the Theoretical Framework chapters, the Methodology chapters, the integrated Results and Discussion chapters, and the Conclusion chapters, respectively.

4.1 Overview of the Structure of the Thesis

The 20 theses (MTs) in the corpus contained 478,712 words in total, an average of 23,936 words in a single thesis. Unlike the theses from the ProQuest as in Chen and Kuo (2012) which varied enormously from 7,627 to 44,775 words, the theses in the present study showed a narrower variation, ranging from 19,151 to 34,373 words. The reason for this difference is that the guideline provided by the English Department of GZU requests the word number of the thesis in this discipline should be around 20,000 words. It indicates that there is an institutional difference in terms of the word number of the thesis.

As for the chapters of the 20 MTs, all of them contained ILrMRDC patterns (Paltridge, 2002; Swales, 2004). However, 12 of them had a separate chapter titled "Theoretical Framework" or "Theoretical Foundation" which was confirmed by the researcher's initial analysis to serve the same communicative purposes of Literature

Review. In addition, all the MTs combined the Results and the Discussion as an integrated Results and Discussion chapter. Moreover, all the 20 MTs had independent chapters, which is different from Chen and Kuo's (2012) corpus that contained embedded Literature Review in Introduction and embedded Discussion in Conclusion.

Furthermore, in terms of the headings for each chapter, all the MTs had the chapter headings of Introduction, Literature Review, and Conclusion. While for the Methodology chapter, slight variations were found, such as "Research Methodology" in two MTs and "Research Design and Methodology" in three MTs. Moreover, for the separate Theoretical framework chapter, a slightly varied heading "Theoretical Foundation" was employed in two MTs. Regarding the integrated Results and Discussion chapter, 2 out of the 20 MTs used a similar heading "Analysis and Discussion" and 8 out of them employed the topic-specific headings instead.

4.2 Findings of the Introduction Chapters

4.2.1 Overall Structure

In total, the 20 thesis Introductions (MTIs) in the subcorpus of Introduction consisted of 39,068 words, 1,953 words of a single Introduction on average, ranging from 1,186 to 3,491 words. 6 out of the 20 MTIs had a separate paragraph at the very beginning of this chapter without a heading, serving as an introductory paragraph to describe the chapter structure, 3 of which began with a sentence to reveal the overall aim of their research. Looking through their whole theses, it was found that all these six theses had an introductory paragraph at the very beginning of every chapter to demonstrate the chapter structure. Informal conversations with these writers reveal that it was their writing habit to write an introductory paragraph at the beginning of each chapter to separate the chapter heading from the section heading, and three of them stated that it was suggested by their supervisors to write in this way.

Except for the introductory paragraph, all the MTIs were organized by sections with specific headings, eight of which had subsections as well. Section headings indicate the writers' perceptions toward the function of the section and imply the moves or steps within the section (Bunton, 2002). According to Bunton (2002), they can be categorized into three types; namely, generic headings which could be utilized in any Introduction, partially generic headings which could be adopted partly to other Introductions, and topic-specific headings which refer to certain aspects of the specific research topic. In the present subcorpus, almost all the section headings were generic headings that can be used in every MTI, and only two of them were partially generic headings, for example, *Brief Introduction of X*, where *X* was a specific topic in that thesis. For the subsection headings, they are all topic-specific ones, such as *Natural and Social Situation of Guizhou* and *Present Bilingual Education Situation of Guizhou*. All the generic section headings that occurred in the subcorpus are set out in Table 4.1 in order of the appearance with their occurrences and percentage. Similar headings are grouped together to show variations of generic heading titles used by the writers.

Table 4.1   Generic Section Headings in the 20 MTIs

Section Headings	%	Section Headings	%
Research Background (16)		Research Questions (5)	25
Background of the Study (2)		Significance of the Study/Thesis (17)	100
Rationale of the Study (1)	100	Research Significance (3)	
Background and Research Problem (1)		Working definition of key terms (1)	75
Statement of the Problem (2)		Terminology (12)	
Research Objectives (15)		Definition of Key Terms (1)	
Objectives of the study (3)	100	Operational terms (1)	
Purpose of the study (2)		Layout/Organization/ Outline of the Thesis / Study (20)	100

(*Note: The number in the bracket after the heading indicates its occurrence.*)

The section heading Rationale of the Study was used in one thesis (MT04) which corresponded to the background of the research. Therefore, from the section headings, it indicates that despite the wording difference, the obligatory sections of Introductions in this particular discipline are Research Background, Research Objectives, Significance of the Study, and the Layout of the Thesis. These obligatory sections in MTIs reveal that this specific chapter presents two overall focuses found in Bunton (2002), one of which is on introducing the field and the other is on introducing the present study.

In addition, the section Terminology, in which the writers provide the operational definitions of the keywords adopted in their studies, was conventional in the present subcorpus with the frequency of 75% despite the wording difference.

4.2.2 Moves

The moves and steps identified in the 20 MTIs based on the framework of Chen and Kuo (2012) are displayed in Table 4.2, in which the total occurrence and the number of Introductions that contained each move or step are presented, as well as its frequency and status. As revealed in Table 4.2, all the three moves suggested in the framework of Chen and Kuo (2012), which were adopted from Swales' (1990, 2004) CARS models, were found in the subcorpus of MTIs.

Table 4.2 Moves Identified in the 20 MTIs

Moves	Occurrence	No. of MTIs	%	Status
Move 1 Establishing a territory	81	20	100	Obl.
Move 2 Establishing a niche	62	20	100	Obl.
Move 3 Occupying the niche	77	20	100	Obl.

(*Note: Obl.=obligatory*)

Moreover, these three moves were found to be obligatory in the present study, which is consistent with the findings of Chen and Kuo (2012), Nguyen (2014), and Zainuddin and Shaari (2021). The presence of the three moves of *Establishing a territory*, *Establishing a niche*, and *Occupying the niche* indicates that the Chinese writers in this particular discipline were also instructed and trained in a similar convention suggested by the CARS models of Swales (1990, 2004). At the same time, it confirms the wide applicability of the model despite the different cultural backgrounds of the writers.

Moreover, despite the fact that 6 out of the 20 MTIs started with Move 3 *Occupying the niche*, most of the Introductions began with Move 1 *Establishing a territory*, which is in line with the findings of Bunton (2002). It reveals that it is more conventional to start this chapter by Move 1 rather than by Move 3. Besides, the identification of Move 2 in all the Introductions in this particular discipline is in concordance with the findings of Samraj (2008) which stated that among the three disciplines of Linguistics, Philosophy, and Biology, only Introductions in Linguistics consistently had the second move to justify the study being reported. Furthermore, slightly contrary to the finding of Bunton (2002) that the majority of Introductions were closed by Move 3, all the MTIs in the present study had Move 3 at the end of the chapter, which implies that finishing the first chapter with Move 3 is a convention in the present discourse community.

When examining the move sequences, it was found that the presence of the three moves was not in the single progression of M1-M2-M3 as demonstrated in the framework. Instead, each move was cyclical in combination with another move or moves as shown in Table 4.3 below, which is consistent with the findings of Bunton (2002), Chen and Kuo (2012), Kawase (2018), and Samraj (2008).

Table 4.3 Move Sequences of the 20 MTIs

Text	Move sequences
MTI01	M1-M2-M1-M2-M1-M3-M1-M2-M1-M3-M2-M3-M1-M3
MTI02	M3-M1-M2-M3
MTI03	M1-M2-M1-M2-M1-M3-M2-M3-M2-M3-M1-M2-M1-M3-M2-M3
MTI04	M3-M2-M1-M2-M1-M3-M1-M2-M3-M1-M3-M1-M3
MTI05	M1-M2-M1-M2-M1-M3-M1-M3-M1-M2-M3-M2-M3-M1-M3
MTI06	M1-M2-M1-M3-M1-M2-M3-M1-M2-M3-M1-M2-M3-M2-M3
MTI09	M1-M2-M3-M1-M2-M3-M2-M3-M2-M3
MTI10	M1-M2-M1-M2-M3-M1-M2-M1-M3-M1-M3-M1-M3
MTI11	M3-M1-M2-M3-M1-M2-M1-M3-M1-M3-M2-M3-M1-M3
MTI12	M1-M2-M3-M1-M3-M1-M3
MTI13	M3-M1-M3-M1-M3-M1-M3-M1-M2-M3
MTI14	M1-M2-M3-M2-M3-M1-M2-M3
MTI15	M1-M2-M1-M2-M1-M2-M3-M2-M3
MTI16	M1-M2-M3-M1-M3-M1-M3-M1-M3
MTI17	M1-M2-M1-M2-M1-M2-M1-M3-M1-M3-M2-M3-M1-M2-M3-M1-M3-M2-M3
MTI18	M1-M2-M3-M1-M2-M3-M1-M2-M3
MTI19	M3-M1-M2-M3-M1-M2-M1-M2-M3-M1-M3
MTI20	M1-M2-M1-M2-M1-M2-M3-M1-M2-M1-M3

(Note: *M1* means Move 1 which contains one step or more than one step of Move 1; *M2* means Move 2 which contains one step or more than one step of Move 2; *M3* means Move 3 which contains one step or more than one step of Move 3.)

As shown, only one of the MTIs (MTI18) was produced in cycles of M1-M2-M3, whereas the rest were composed in an irregular sequence of the three moves. Therefore, no clear-cut or common move pattern for the whole Introduction chapter was identified in the present subcorpus. However, a closer investigation of the patterns of the three moves found that the majority (90%) of the Introductions contained the move progression of M1-M2-M3 that is in accordance with what was found in the corpus of Chen and Kuo (2012). Apart from the three-move progression, the patterns of M1-M2 (65%) and M1-M3 (75%) were found in most of the Introductions, indicating that the majority of the writers situated their study within the wider field when establishing a niche or announcing their research by leading the audience from the general to the specific as proposed by Dudley-Evans (1986).

Furthermore, in terms of the occurrences of the move patterns, they were recursive in nearly all the Introductions, and each contained more than two cycles of moves, which is in line with the finding of Bunton (2002). The number of move cycles ranged from two to nine, on average about five cycles in a single Introduction. Nevertheless, the number of move cycles was not correlated to the length of the text since the longest Introduction did not have the highest number of move cycles. The most frequently adopted cycle was M1-M3 (33 occurrences), in which the writers typically provided topic background or centrality claim and then proposed the objectives or significances of their studies. It was different from the findings of Bunton (2002) that in his corpus, the M1-M2 sequence was most often utilized to indicate gaps or problems from reviewing previous studies. The difference may be explained by that all the theses in the present study had a separate Literature Review chapter to demonstrate the related previous studies while part of the theses in Bunton's (2002) corpus had an embedded Literature Review in the Introductions.

4.2.3 Steps

All the MTIs in the present study were found to only consist of the moves and steps depicted in Chen and Kuo's (2012) framework. 18 out of the 24 steps under the three moves in the framework were identified, with all the four steps under Move 1 found but two steps under Move 2 and four steps under Move 3 were missing in this subcorpus.

Among all the identified steps, as shown in Table 4.4 below, S1 *Providing topic generalization/background* of Move 1 was one of the steps that had the highest frequency, which is in line with the findings of Chen and Kuo (2012) and Nguyen (2014). Slightly differently, this step was presented in every Introduction, thus it was an obligatory step in the present subcorpus. Moreover, three more steps were obligatory in the present context; namely, S1, S13, and S15 under Move 3. These four obligatory steps were in accordance with the indication from the obligatory section headings Research Background, Research Objectives, Significance of the Study, and Layout of the Thesis, as revealed previously in *Section 4.2.1*. However, when looking into the steps within each move, the preference of the steps used by the thesis writers was different.

Table 4.4 Steps Identified in the 20 MTIs

	Steps	No. of MTIs	%	Status
Move 1	S1 Providing topic generalization/ background	20	100	Obl.
	S2 Indicating centrality/importance of topic	18	90	Con.
	S3 Defining terms	7	35	Opt.
	S4 Reviewing previous research	16	80	Con.
Move 2	S1 Indicating gaps in previous research	17	85	Con.
	S2 Question-raising	0	0	/
	S3 Counter-claiming	0	0	/
	S4 Continuing/extending a tradition	2	10	Opt.
	S5 Indicating a problem/need	13	65	Con.
Move 3	S1 Indicating purposes/aims/objectives	20	100	Obl.
	S2 Indicating scope of research	7	35	Opt.
	S3 Indicating chapter/section structure	6	30	Opt.

Cont.

	Steps	No. of MTIs	%	Status
Move 3	S4 Indicating theoretical position	2	10	Opt.
	S5 Announcing research/work carried out	17	85	Con.
	S6 Describing parameters of research	0	0	/
	S7 Stating research questions/hypotheses	5	25	Opt.
	S8 Defining terms	15	75	Con.
	S9 Indicating research method	5	25	Opt.
	S10 Indicating findings results	0	0	/
	S11 Indicating models proposed	0	0	/
	S12 Indicating applications	0	0	/
	S13 Indicating value or significance	20	100	Obl.
	S14 Providing justification	6	30	Opt.
	S15 Indicating thesis structure	20	100	Obl.

(*Note: Obl.=obligatory, Con.=conventional, Opt.=optional*)

To realize Move 1, only the first step *Providing topic generalization/ background* was utilized in every single Introduction which indicates it is obligatory. Besides, S2 *Indicating centrality/importance of topic* and S4 *Reviewing previous research* were employed in most of the MTIs, which indicates they were conventional steps within Move 1. However, there was a less tendency of the writers to employ S3 *Defining terms* (35%) under this move. It may be explained that most of the thesis Introductions had a section Terminology (75%) where the writers defined certain terms in detail. The results indicate that except for S3 *Defining terms*, the other three steps were preferably utilized by the writers to accomplish Move 1 in the present discourse community. Below are the examples sharing the communicative purposes of these steps.

Excerpt 1: Move 1 Step 1

It is obvious that people acquire language and social skills together. Based on the ..., people always acquire or develop their knowledge and competence in the process of second language learning. In order to integrate into socialization, people learn to be ... consciously or unconsciously. (MTI16)

Excerpt 2: Move 1 Step 2

In English, there are large amounts of..., which is a significant part of English learning among second language learners. ... have been studied by scholars at home and abroad, including ... (MTI02)

Excerpt 3: Move 1 Step 3

Generally, a classifier is a word which pluses a numeral to modify the quantity of a noun, serving as an attribute. (MTI01)

Excerpt 4: Move 1 Step 4

Saussure (1959:113) compares language with a sheet of paper: thought is the front and the sound the back; one cannot cut the front without cutting the back at the same time; likewise in language, one can neither divide sound from thought nor thought from sound. (MTI03)

In Move 2, the majority of the MTIs used S1 *Indicating gaps in previous research*, S5 *Indicating a problem/need*, or both to establish a niche, which conforms with what has been found in Bunton (2002), Chen and Kuo (2012), and Nguyen (2014). It seems that these two steps are preferred by the writers to achieve Move 2. In addition, S4 *Continuing/ extending a tradition* was found to be optional. The examples of these three steps identified in the present subcorpus are provided below.

Excerpt 5: Move 2 Step 1

Traditional studies of ... describe the surface features of ... and scholars lack systematic researches on ... (MTI20)

Excerpt 6: Move 2 Step 4

So it is meaningful to enrich the corpus-based studies of semantic prosody of ... (MTI02)

Excerpt 7: Move 2 Step 5

However, as it is known to all that ..., and researchers cannot just put them aside and leave them alone. So that it is necessary to research the ... (MTI01)

Moreover, under Move 2, no S2 *Counter-claiming* was found, which is also the case in Chen and Kuo (2012) and Nguyen (2014). It seems that the writers hesitated to criticize the previous findings or maybe they had insufficient knowledge of this step. In addition, no S3 *Question-raising* was identified in the present subcorpus. This absence suggests that in the present discourse community, indicating a gap or a problem/need was more accepted when the writers proposed the motivation to conduct their study. It could be also explained that the writers may regard these two steps easier for them to relate their current studies with the wide field.

Furthermore, there are 15 steps in total in the framework of Chen and Kuo (2012) to achieve Move 3, but only 11 of them were identified in the present subcorpus. All the MTIs in this study utilized S1 *Indicating purposes/aims/objectives*, which is in accordance with what has been found in the Linguistics Introductions of Samraj's (2008) corpus. It reveals that this step is an obligatory step. Moreover, two more obligatory steps under this move were identified; namely, S13 *Indicating value or significance* and S15 *Indicating thesis structure*. The latter one was only found conventional in Samraj (2008). The identification of the three obligatory steps indicates that it is crucial to explicitly demonstrate the research purposes, research significance, and the thesis structure when producing MTIs in similar contexts. The examples of these three obligatory steps of Move 3 are manifested below.

Excerpt 8: Move 3 Step 1

Therefore, the present study is to explore the semantic change of ... to make up for the research gaps of semantic change for ... in English. (MTI19)

Excerpt 9: Move 3 Step 13

The study is of great significance for its theoretical contribution to ... and its practical application in writing, especially in ... (MTI08)

CHAPTER 4

Excerpt 10: Move 3 Step 15

This thesis is composed of six chapters. Chapter 1 is ... This chapter also presents ... Chapter 2 reviews ... Chapter 3 provides ... Chapter 4 constructs... Chapter 5 provides... Chapter 6 is ... (MTI06)

Apart from the obligatory steps, two conventional steps were found under Move 3. To be specific, S5 *Announcing research/work carried out* was frequently found in the MTIs, which is consistent with the findings of Kawase (2018). Furthermore, S8 *Defining terms* was found to be conventional in the MTIs by which the writers provided the operational definitions of certain terms in their studies. This step was identified in the section of Terminology, the second last section of the Introductions. These two conventional steps had the frequency of 85% and 75%, respectively, which reveals that when producing an MTI, including these two steps may make it more readable and effective. Below are the examples of these two conventional steps.

Excerpt 11: Move 3 Step 5

Firstly, the research concentrates on comparing ... This stage only analyzes the text itself, and ... (MTI13)

Excerpt 12: Move 3 Step 8

According to Xu (1992), contrastive studies (or contrastive linguistics, contrastive analysis) can be defined as... Therefore, in this paper, contrastive study serves as ..., with the aim of ... (MTI10)

The remaining six identified steps under Move 3 were optional. It is interesting to find that few research questions or hypotheses (25%) were presented in the MTIs, which is also reported in Bunton (2002). The majority of the writers demonstrated them in the later Methodology chapter in the present study. Following Bunton's (2002) claim, it seems more acceptable for at least the supervisors and external examiners of the present discourse community to put the research questions in Methodology rather than in Introduction. In addition, when research questions were proposed, they were usually enumerated as found in Bunton (2002). However, Kawase (2018) found that research questions/hypotheses in his corpus of AL(Application Linguistics) Introductions were frequently presented. Therefore, more research is required to investigate whether S7 *Stating research questions/hypotheses* is conventional or not in certain cultural contexts since the corpora of these studies are from various cultural contexts. The examples of these six optional steps are demonstrated below.

Excerpt 13: Move 3 Step 2

The study concerns on the lexical chunks related to ... used by the students. For the second research question, the author mainly focuses on the correlation between ... (MTI07)

Excerpt 14: Move 3 Step 3

This chapter mainly presents the introduction, background, purpose, and organization of the study. It begins with ... Then, the purpose and significance of the study, the research questions will be presented, and the outline of this study in the end. (MTI07)

Excerpt 15: Move 3 Step 4

The present study adopts the comparative perspective, based on the three-dimensional model of ..., which contains the analytical method of ... (MTI13)

Excerpt 16: Move 3 Step 7

There are mainly three research questions formulated for the immediate purpose of the present study:

(1) What are the ...? (2) What are the ...? (3) What is ...? (MTI03)

Excerpt 17: Move 3 Step 9

Second, for the sake of exploring ... and comparing..., the study adopts Independent-sample tests and Pearson correlation analysis on ... (MTI07)

Excerpt 18: Move 3 Step 14

For one thing, the up-to-date and massive amount of the natural language materials makes it possible to be the critical ingredients to fulfill the needs of the study. For another, ... So the genre of the raw materials for the self-built corpus in the study is argumentation. (MTI07)

As for the optional S3 *Indicating chapter/section structure*, no section structure but chapter structure was used by the writers. Six MTIs demonstrated the chapter structure at the very beginning of the chapter, similar to what had been found in Bunton (2002). It indicates that it is only in this introductory paragraph at the beginning of the chapter that this step can be used. In addition, similar to the findings of Kawase (2018), the MTIs less frequently contained S9 *Indicating research method* (25%), which might be explained that most of the writers in the present discipline tended to introduce the research method in the later Methodology chapter, as indicated by the interviews with the students. Below is one of the student informants.

ST3: *Research method will be introduced in detail in Methodology chapter later. If I provide it in Introduction chapter, it will make my thesis redundant.*

Nonetheless, four steps under Move 3 were not identified in the present subcorpus. They are S6 *Describing parameters of research*, S10 *Indicating findings/results*, S11 *Indicating models proposed*, and S12 *Indicating applications*. It seems that these four steps are not preferred by the present discourse community to present them in the Introductions. Another explanation could be that fewer experimental research approaches were adopted in the corpus of this study, which resulted in the parameters of the research appearing to be demonstrated only in experiments.

In terms of the step patterns, as revealed by Chen and Kuo (2012), the writers organized the steps within the three moves in different ways. However, one step pattern was identified to be utilized frequently in the present study. It was found that 15 out of 20 Introductions (85%) ended with the step sequence of S8 *Defining terms* and S15 *Indicating thesis structure*. This step pattern (S8-S15) suggested that the writers preferred to close the Introduction chapter by providing the working definitions of certain terms and then the thesis structure.

4.3 Findings of the Literature Review Chapters

4.3.1 Overall Structure

The 20 MTLrs consisted of 115,630 words, ranging from 2,901 to 9,063 words, with an average of 5,782 words. All the 20 MTLrs were an independent chapter, which is in disagreement with Chen and Kuo (2012) in which 4 out of 15 theses in their corpus had the Literature Review (LR) embedded in the Introduction chapter. It indicates that this chapter is preferred to be a separate chapter in the thesis writing in this discourse community to show the students' familiarity with the literature in the field. Moreover, the majority of this chapter was found to be provided in an Introduction-Body-Conclusion structure, which is in accordance with the results of Chen and Kuo (2012), Kwan (2006), Rawdhan et al. (2020), and You and Li (2021). In the Body part, several thematic sections or units were delivered. The following sections will provide the findings from the Introduction parts and Conclusions parts first, then followed by those from the Body parts that were constituted by the thematic sections.

A closer examination of the section headings of this chapter found that most of them were topic-specific headings that were only related to the content of that particular thesis and could not be replicated in other theses. However, some partially generic section headings, which can be partly replicated to other LRs, were identified, such as "Previous Studies on/of…" "Previous Studies on/of … Abroad/at Home" "Studies on …" "Studies on … Abroad/at Home", and "Comments on …", where "…" was about the specific topic of that thesis. In addition, one generic section heading, i.e., "Summary" was found.

From the section headings, it was interesting to find that almost half of the MTLrs had sections titled "Previous Studies on/of … Abroad/at Home" or "Studies on … Abroad/at Home" in which previous studies conducted by international scholars and Chinese scholars within the Chinese context were provided separately. The interviews with the two supervisor informants reveal that it is a feature of the MT written by Chinese writers. However, it is not a compulsory requirement for the writers since the main communicative purpose of the LR chapter is to review what has been conducted widely in the field. One of the supervisor informants added that it is clearer to show the research context where the study is situated if the writer separately demonstrates what has been done in that research context and those in other research contexts.

4.3.2 Introductory Texts and Concluding Texts

Among the 20 MTLrs, the majority of them (80%) began this chapter with a short paragraph serving as a brief introduction of this chapter to inform the readers of the purpose, the chapter structure, or the themes that the writer will review, which is in line with the findings of Chen and Kuo (2012), Kwan (2006), Rawdhan et al. (2020), and You and Li (2021). In addition, three of these introductory texts provided the background information of their thesis topic as a lead-in to this chapter to implicitly indicate the themes that will be reviewed. This was confirmed by these three writers that these texts were an introduction to this chapter. However, this kind of introductory text was only preferred by a small number of writers. Thus, the introductory text that aims to provide the chapter structure and the themes to be reviewed is recommended to provide when producing a MTLr.

Moreover, these introductory texts were very short and presented in only one paragraph, ranging from 42 to 228 words, averaging 86 words. This finding is consistent with You and Li (2021) that the introductory texts in M.A. thesis LRs were relatively brief. Furthermore, all the 16 introductory texts were not titled, which is similar to those in Nguyen (2014) and You and Li (2021). Nevertheless, it is in disagreement with Kwan (2006) that the majority of the introductory texts were headed with "Introduction". The difference may be caused by the length of these texts since those in Kwan (2006) were rather long. Moreover, it confirms the suggestion of You and Li (2021) that the short texts at the beginning of the LR chapter tend not to be titled "Introduction".

As for the concluding texts, it was found that 12 out of the 20 theses (60%) included them at the end of the chapter, which is similar to the findings of Kwan (2006) and You and Li (2021) that around half of their data contained concluding texts. However, the result differs from Nguyen (2014) in that about 80% of the LRs composed by Vietnamese students in her corpus had a conclusion. It indicates that the students in the present discourse community have a less tendency to include a conclusion of the LR than Vietnamese M.A. students.

The length of these 12 concluding texts varied widely, ranging from 61 to 695 words, with an average of 219 words. Compared with the introductory text, the concluding text could be longer. Moreover, it was found that 11 out of the 12 concluding texts were titled, among which ten were entitled "Summary" and one titled "Comments on Previous Studies". This finding is in line with Kwan (2006) and Nguyen (2014) that most of their data were entitled, either "Summary" or "Conclusion". However, the title "Conclusion" was not found in the present subcorpus, which suggests that "Summary" is preferred as the title in the present discourse community probably because the writers tend to differentiate this section from the final chapter, which typically uses "Conclusion" as the chapter title, according to the conversation with one of these writers.

According to Kwan (2006), the communicative purposes of the concluding texts are mainly to summarize the gist of the chapter, to restate the purposes of the review, and to display insights generated from the review. Moreover, previous studies, i.e., Kwan (2006) and Nguyen (2014), pointed out that the concluding texts are places where Move 3 *Occupying the research niche* could be identified. Therefore, the present study decided to closely investigate the moves and steps in these concluding texts. During the investigation, Move 2 was identified in these texts as well (Table 4.5), which is in accordance with the findings of Rawdhan et al. (2020) and You and Li (2021).

Table 4.5 Moves and Steps in the 12 Concluding Texts

Move/step	No. of Concluding texts	%
Move 2 Creating a research niche	9	75
S2 Gap-indicating (paucity or scarcity)	9	75
S3 Asserting confirmative claims about knowledge or research practices surveyed	2	16.7
S1 Counter-claiming (weaknesses and problems)	1	8.3
S5 Abstracting or synthesizing knowledge claims to establish a theoretical position or a theoretical framework	1	8.3
Move 3 Occupying the research niche	5	41.7

Cont.

Move/step	No. of Concluding texts	%
S3 Interpreting research design/process	4	33.3
S1 Indicating research aims, focuses, research questions or hypotheses	3	25
S2 Indicating theoretical position/theoretical framework	1	8.3

As shown in Table 4.5, Move 2 *Creating a research niche* was identified in the majority of the concluding texts, which is in line with You and Li (2021) that Move 2 occurred most in their corpus. In terms of the steps of Move 2, S2 *Gap-indicating* was the most frequently used one, which is similar to You and Li's (2021) finding as well. It suggests that when composing a conclusion to the LR chapter, apart from summarizing the themes reviewed in the chapter, it could be more effective to present Move 2 and the research gap identified from the literature review. Furthermore, Move 3 *Occupying the research niche* was found in the concluding texts as well, which is in line with the studies of Nguyen (2014), Rawdhan et al. (2020), and You and Li (2021). The frequency of Move 3 indicates that it is optional when producing the conclusions, which is similar to the findings of Nguyen (2014) and You and Li (2021). To realize Move 3, the writers usually utilized S3 *Indicating researcher design/process* to present where the data will be collected or the research approach they will use. Moreover, half of the 12 concluding texts were found to end the chapter with an advance indicator of the content in the next chapter, as shown in Excerpt 19.

Excerpt 19

*In this chapter, the author made an overview on ..., and then ....[***Summarizing the gist of the chapter****] Through the retrospect of studies on..., the author found out that the study on... is a relative new research topic, and few works have done on it[***Move 2 Step 2***]. In the next chapter, the author will provide the research design and methodology of this study* **[Advance indicator]**.

(MTLr15)

The finding of the advance indicator is consistent with Nguyen (2014) that one-third of the concluding texts in her corpus contained an advance indicator. The advance indicator prepares the readers for what will be provided in the next chapter. It was found to be optional in the present subcorpus, which reveals that the advance indicator is not necessary in the concluding texts.

4.3.3 Thematic Units

In the Body parts, 75 thematic units were found in the present subcorpus, nearly four thematic units per MTLr. The framework of Chen and Kuo (2012) was used to analyze the moves and steps in each thematic unit. To recapitulate, the previous studies utilized two approaches to present the frequency of the moves and steps. One is to count the frequency of each move/step in all the LRs (e.g., Xie, 2017), while the other is to count its frequency in all the thematic units (e.g., Kwan, 2006; Nguyen, 2014; Rawdhan et al., 2020). In the present study, both approaches were adopted but with more focus on the second one so as to better compare the findings with the previous studies.

4.3.3.1 Moves

According to the frequency of the moves/steps in the MTLrs, Move 1 *Establishing one part of the territory of one's own research* was found to be obligatory since it occurred in all the 20 MTLrs, which is in line with the finding of Xie (2017) and Chen and Kuo (2012). Moreover, it was found that 18 out of the 20 MTLrs (90%) contained Move 2 *Creating a research niche*, thus, this move was conventional in this subcorpus, which is in disagreement with Xie (2017) that Move 2 was obligatory. Moreover, Move 3 *Occupying the research niche* was identified in 14 MTLrs (70%), which indicates that this move was conventional. The above results reveal that the main part of the MTLr is primarily a place where the writers present the knowledge claims, their comprehensions, and investigations of the wide literature field, and justify the value of their study by critically evaluating the previous studies to find out the research niche.

From the perspective of the moves' frequency in the thematic units, Table 4.6 presents the individual counts of each move and the number of the units containing this move with its frequency in the 75 thematic units found in this subcorpus.

Table 4.6 Frequency Counts of the Three Moves in the Thematic Units

Move	Individual counts	No. of units with the move
Move 1	122	73(97.3%)
Move 2	77	51(68%)
Move 3	53	27(36%)

As shown in Table 4.6, Move 1 occurred with the highest frequency and it was conventional, which is in accordance with the results of Kwan (2006), Nguyen (2014), and Rawdhan et al. (2020). The high frequency and common occurrence of Move 1 indicate that in the LR chapter, M.A. students make a great effort to display their familiarity with the theory or the knowledge and the pertinent studies with their topics.

Furthermore, Move 2 was also found to be conventional, which is in line with Kwan (2006) and Nguyen (2014). When compared with Kwan's (2006) finding that Move 2 had a frequency of 95.28%, Move 2 in the present subcorpus had a lower frequency of 68%. It may be explained that doctoral students in Kwan's (2006) corpus were more capable of showing their critical thinking about the knowledge or previous studies or they were demanded to do so than M.A. students. However, after a closer examination of the distribution of Move 2, it was found that 18 out of the 20 MTLrs contained Move 2 and one MTLr presented it in the conclusion part, which reveals that M.A. students have the awareness to provide their critical evaluations in the LR chapter, but they may not have a clear idea that they should be critical in each thematic unit. Therefore, it is suggested that in future thesis writing teaching, teachers should explicitly tell the M.A. students to provide their own comprehension and evaluation in each thematic unit to make their theses more critical.

In terms of Move 3, it was found to be optional, which is in agreement with the findings of Kwan (2006), Nguyen (2014), and Rawdhan et al. (2020). This result is understandable since the research aims, questions, theoretical framework, and research design were already presented in other chapters, such as Introduction, Theoretical Framework, and Methodology. Therefore, these contents realized by Move 3 were less found in LR chapters.

Furthermore, to find out the move patterns, the move sequence in every thematic unit was closely investigated, and the results of the move combinations are presented in Table 4.7. As indicated in the table, the move patterns employed by the writers in the thematic units varied widely.

Table 4.7 Move Configurations in the Thematic Units of the 20 MTLrs

Move configuration	Examples	No. of thematic units	%
Single move			
Move 1 only	M1 alone	19	25.3
Two-move configurations			
Regular (1-2)n	1-2 1-2-1-2-1-2	27	36
Regular (1-3)n	1-3-1-3 1-3-1-3-1-3	3	4
2-3	2-3	2	2.7
1-2-1	1-2-1	2	2.7
(1-3)n-1	1-3-1 1-3-1-3-1	2	2.7
Three-move configurations			
Irregular 3-move	1-3-1-2-1-2-3 1-2-3-1-2-3-2-3	14	18.7
Regular (1-2-3)n	1-2-3 1-2-3-1-2-3	4	5.3
Regular (1-2)n-3	1-2-1-2-3	2	2.7

(*Note: N following the brackets indicates the move sequence in those brackets could be repeated n times. M1 alone means that in one cycle of the move sequence of one text, only Move 1 was used.*)

In terms of a single move as a configuration, only Move 1 was found to be utilized alone in a thematic unit, which is in disagreement with the results of Kwan (2006) and Nguyen (2014) that Move 2 or Move 3 was found in a thematic unit alone in their corpora despite with a very low frequency. Regarding the two-move configurations, Move 1 and Move 2 used together as a regular 1-2 pattern was the most frequent one. This result is similar to Kwan (2006) and Nguyen (2014), indicating that the writers have a greater tendency not only to present the knowledge or previous studies but also to provide their evaluation of the materials they just reviewed. Furthermore, the three moves were found to be combined most irregularly with a frequency of 18.7%, which conforms to the result of Nguyen (2014). However, this configuration was used far less in the present subcorpus when compared with the frequency of 42.52% found in Kwan's (2006) corpus of doctoral dissertations. This could be explained that the thematic units in the dissertation are far lengthier and more demanding in terms of the content than those in the theses, so the moves tend to be combined diversely.

4.3.3.2 Steps

To achieve the three moves identified in the LR chapters, different steps were used by the writers. Table 4.8 presents the steps employed by the writers to realize Move 1 *Establishing one part of the territory of one's own research* in the order of their frequency.

Table 4.8 Frequency Counts of Steps of Move 1 (Total Counts of Move 1=122)

Step	Individual counts	No. of instances of Move 1 with the step
S1 Surveying the non-research-related phenomena or knowledge claims	88	80(65.6%)
S3 Surveying the research-related phenomena	86	72(59.0%)
S2 Claiming centrality	37	29(23.8%)

As indicated in Table 4.8, none of these three steps was obligatory. S1 was the predominant step utilized to achieve Move 1, followed by S3, which conforms to the findings of Kwan (2006) and You and Li (2021). This reveals that writers tend to review the theories or the knowledge as well as the pertinent studies that have been conducted to establish a territory of their study. Moreover, S2 was less preferred by the writers, and it was optional. The examples of these three steps of Move 1 are displayed below.

Excerpt 20: Move 1 Step 1

Lexical ... are considered as ... Since the studies on ..., there have been many different terms defining the chunks. However, there is no widely approved term for defining ... at present. (MTLr07)

Excerpt 21: Move 1 Step 2

The previous studies on ... abroad has been lasting a few years and many research products have been harvested. (MTLr04)

Excerpt 22: Move 1 Step 3

As for the case studies, Huang and Kathleen (2001) questioned ... Moreover, Her (2012) proposed ... At the same year, Li and Walter (2012) examined ... Stephen and Laura (2015) studied ... Passer (2016) investigated ... (MTLr01)

In terms of the step patterns employed under Move 1, the steps were employed in various combinations (Table 4.9). More than half of the instances of Move 1 were realized by a single step, with S1 being the most frequent configuration of Move 1, which is in line with Kwan (2006) and Nguyen (2014).

Table 4.9 Combinations of Steps under Move 1

Step combination	No. of Move 1 with this combination	%
S1	42	34.4
S3	28	23.0
S1*S3	23	18.9
S2*S3	13	10.7
S1*S2*S3	10	8.2
S1*S2	6	4.9

(*Note: The two-step or three-step configurations do not imply any sequential order of the steps. They just indicate the co-occurrence of the steps.*)

In addition, the third common configuration was the pair of S1 and S3, which is in agreement with the findings of Chen and Kuo (2012), Nguyen (2014), and Rawdhan et al. (2020). Nevertheless, it differs from the findings by Kwan (2006) that S1 and S2 were combined more often. This indicates that the writers in the present discourse community prefer to present established knowledge or theory with different aspects of pertinent studies rather than with the indication of the significance of the theme being reviewed. Moreover, the combinations of the three steps varied extensively, which supports the claim of no predictable co-occurrence of these steps in the realization of Move 1 (Kwan, 2006).

As for the steps under Move 2, Table 4.10 displays the total occurrence of each step and the frequency of each step among the 77 instances of Move 2. It was found that S2 *Gap-indicating* was the most frequently used step to realize Move 2, which is consistent with Rawdhan et al. (2020). Nevertheless, it differs from the findings of Kwan (2006) that S1 *Counter-claiming* was the most frequently adopted one by doctoral students. This could be due to the reason that M.A. students, who are less experienced and less epistemically equipped, have a greater tendency to resort to the gaps which are academically less challenging than counter-claiming (Xie, 2017). Moreover, this result is in disagreement with Nguyen (2014) and You and Li (2021) who found the most common step of Move 2 in M.A. theses was S6 *Concluding a part of literature review and/or indicating transition to review of a different area*, and S3 *Asserting confirmative claims about knowledge or research practices surveyed*, respectively.

Table 4.10 Frequency Counts of Steps of Move 2 (Total Counts of Move 2=77)

Step	Individual counts	No. of instances of Move 2 with the step
S2 Gap-indicating	53	46 (59.7%)
S6 Concluding a part of literature review	27	26(33.8%)
S3 Asserting confirmative claims	25	23(29.9%)
S1 Counter-claiming	20	19(24.7%)
S5 Abstracting or synthesizing knowledge claims	19	8(10.4%)
S4 Asserting the relevancy	3	3(3.9%)

Furthermore, the second most adopted step of Move 2 was S6 with a frequency of 33.8%, followed by S3 with a slightly less frequency of 29.9%. This finding is also not in line with the findings of Kwan (2006), Nguyen (2014), and You and Li (2021). This marked difference in the adopted steps to realize Move 2 in different discourse communities calls for more studies to explore this phenomenon. The examples of these six steps of Move 2 are provided below.

Excerpt 23: Move 2 Step 1

CBT is applied in wide linguistic fields because of its powerful explanation. However, there are some problems in the application of CBT: ..., which results in the simplification of the diverse blending processes of ... (MTLr20)

Excerpt 24: Move 2 Step 2

However, these researches focus more attention on ..., therefore, quantitative researches are relatively rare. What's more, some researches just simply ..., while few are concerned with ... (MTLr08)

Excerpt 25: Move 2 Step 3

Those studies strongly speak for the powerful explanations and overwhelming advantages of ... and even some ... (MTLr18)

Excerpt 26: Move 2 Step 4

In fact, Nattinger & DeCarrico's classification contributes to explore a deeper understanding about ... Thus, according to the functions and forms, ... are quite clear and helpful for the author to distinguish each word group as ... (MTLr07)

Excerpt 27: Move 2 Step 5

The application studies of ... can create more value for analyzing the real contexts. Researchers have to pay much attention to the ... (MTLr13)

Excerpt 28: Move 2 Step 6

The literature reviews above reveal that studies about ... Although researches of ... are conducted in various aspects, they can be concluded as three aspects: (1) ...; (2) ...; (3) ... (MTLr17)

Moreover, the step combinations under Move 2 were investigated and the results are shown in Table 4.11 in which the step sequences that occurred more than once are displayed and those that occurred only once are categorized as "others". As indicated in the table, the steps were mostly utilized separately and accounted for around half of the realization of Move 2 (48.1%). Additionally, when the steps were adopted together, they were combined diversely with a low frequency. This corresponds with the findings of Kwan (2006) and Nguyen (2014), and it suggests that no fixed convention is established in terms of the realization of Move 2 in the present discourse community. In addition, it calls for more instruction to teach the students how to achieve Move 2 to create a research niche since this move indicates the initiation of the writer's study.

Table 4.11 Combinations of Steps under Move 2

Step combination	No. of Move 2 with this combination	%
S2	11	14.3
S5	11	14.3
S2*S6	11	14.3
S3	8	10.4
S1*S2*S6	6	7.8
S2*S3	4	5.2
S1*S2*S3	4	5.2
S6	3	3.9
S1*S2	3	3.9
S1	2	2.6
S4	2	2.6
S5*S6	2	2.6
S1*S2*S3*S6	2	2.6
Others	8	10.4

(Note: The two-step or three-step configurations do not imply any sequential order of the steps. They just indicate the co-occurrence of the steps.)

Regarding the realization of Move 3, all the four steps were identified but none of them was obligatory. As revealed in Table 4.12, the most frequently adopted step was S4 with a frequency of 37.3% in which the writers announced the adoption of terms or their definitions. This disaccords with the results of Kwan (2006), Nguyen (2014), and Rawdhan et al. (2020) that found S1 to be the most common step of Move 2. This difference indicates that the writers in the present context prefer to announce their own study by announcing the adoption of certain terms and the related definitions after reviewing the literature.

Table 4.12 Frequency Counts of Steps of Move 3 (Total Counts of Move 3=53)

Step	Individual counts	No. of instances of Move 3 with the step
S4 Interpreting terminology used in the thesis	20	20(37.3%)
S3 Indicating research design/processes	15	15(28.3%)
S2 Indicating theoretical positions/ theoretical frameworks	11	11(20.8%)
S1 Indicating research aims, focuses, research questions or hypothesis	7	7(13.2%)

In addition, the least frequent adoption of S1 to realize Move 3 in the present subcorpus may be explained that the research aims and research questions were already provided in the Introduction chapters or Methodology chapters, thus it is redundant to state them in the LR. The examples of these four steps of Move 3 are demonstrated below.

Excerpt 29: Move 3 Step 1

The general objectives of this research are to analyze ... and the ... in the context. (MTLr17)

Excerpt 30: Move 3 Step 2

In the current research, the ... are reflected by the ... The semantic preferences of ... are concluded from the ... As a result, to research the ..., the author needs to ... The first two operation models can well reflect the ... So the author refers to the first two operation models to conduct the research. (MTLr02)

Excerpt 31: Move 3 Step 3

This paper adopts the corpus-based approach as the method, which ... It is an approach for ... It is empirical and depends on both quantitative and qualitative analytical techniques (Liang et al, 2010). (MTLr11)

Excerpt 32: Move 3 Step 4

In the present study, discourse is conceptualized as a modality of social practice and it is also socially conditioned and constitutive. (MTLr13)

As for the step patterns under Move 3, all the four steps were utilized separately, so no step patterns were identified, which corresponds to the results of Chen and Kuo (2012) and Kwan (2006) that the steps of Move 3 rarely co-occur or recur. However, this is in contrast to Nguyen (2014) who found that S1 and S2 were frequently combined despite that each of them had a high frequency individually. Nevertheless, in her corpus, the combination of S1 and S2 was found in only 12.07% of the realization of Move 3, thus, it is preferred more by merely a small number of writers rather than being a convention. Similarly, in the present subcorpus, no convention was established to achieve Move 3 in the LR chapter.

4.4 Findings of the Theoretical Framework Chapters

As indicated in *Section 4.1*, 12 out of the 20 theses had a separate chapter titled Theoretical Framework (TF) after the LR chapter. This newly found chapter was considered as a part of the LR which is similar to Kwan (2006) that the chapters between Introduction and Methodology were all regarded as LR. Therefore, the same move-step framework was utilized to analyze these two chapters. Since they were separate chapters, the current study reported their findings accordingly. As revealed by the supervisor informants, the content of the TF could be presented in a single chapter or embedded in the LR chapter. Moreover, according to Kwan (2006), the LR chapter is conducted in an Introduction-Body-Conclusion structure, with several thematic units in the Body part. Therefore, it is assumed that the TF is a thematic unit of the Body part in the LR despite it being composed of sections. In other words, the sections in the TF chapter were regarded as a single thematic unit rather than several thematic units as those in the LR chapter.

4.4.1 Overall Structure

The total length of the 12 MTTfs was 32,114 words, ranging from 1,070 to 4,796 words, with an average of 2,676 words. The short length of the TF compared with the LR echoes the assumption that the TF could be considered as a thematic unit.

An examination of the section headings found that the majority of them were topic-specific ones which indicate the pertinent theories or concepts involved in the writers' theses. Despite the slight word difference, 5 out of the 12 MTTfs had a generic heading "Framework of the Present Study". The section headings of the MTTfs reveal that this chapter was mainly about the related concepts and theories which were adopted by the writers.

Furthermore, it was found that few of the MTTfs were structured as Introduction-Body-Conclusion, whereas the majority (83.3%) had an Introduction-Body structure, which is not in consonance with the results found in the LR chapters in the present study and other pertinent studies (e.g., Chen & Kuo, 2012; Nguyen, 2014). This could be attributed that the TF chapter was less lengthy than the LR chapter and mainly focused on the theoretical framework to be adopted for the study being reported, so the writers had a less tendency to summarize what had been just presented in the chapter.

As for the introductory texts found at the very beginning of all the 12 MTTfs, none of them were found to be titled "Introduction". This finding is in consonance with what was found in the LR chapters (e.g., Nguyen, 2014; You & Li, 2021). Moreover, the small size of these introductory texts also assists the assumption that short texts which inform the readers of the chapter's aims or structures at the beginning of the chapter are preferred to be untitled (You & Li, 2021).

In terms of the four concluding texts found in the present subcorpus, all of them were titled "Summary". One of them (MTTf05) also contained an advance indicator of the next chapter at the end. Furthermore, this advance indicator was found at the end of a TF text (MTTf19) without a conclusion section or paragraph. The less occurrence and frequency of the conclusion or the advance indicator reveals that summarizing a TF chapter or indicating the content of the next chapter has not been established as a norm in the current discourse community.

4.4.2 Moves

All the three moves in the LR move-step framework (Chen & Kuo, 2012) were identified in the corpus of the TF chapters. The results of these three moves are presented in Table 4.13, in which the occurrence of each move, the number of the MTTfs that contain the move, the frequency of each move among the 12 MTTfs, and the corresponding move status are provided.

Table 4.13 Moves Identified in the 12 MTTfs

Move	Occurrence	No. of MTTfs	%	Status
Move 1 Establishing one part of the territory	45	12	100	Obl.
Move 2 Creating a research niche	18	10	83.3	Con.
Move 3 Occupying the niche	34	12	100	Obl.

(*Note: Obl.=Obligatory, Con.=Conventional*)

As shown in Table 4.13, Move 1 and Move 3 were obligatory since they were identified in all of the MTTfs, while Move 2 was conventional with a frequency of 83.3%. The findings reveal that when the writers tended to have a separate chapter on Theoretical Framework, both Move 1 and Move 3 need to be presented.

Furthermore, all the three moves occurred 97 times in the 12 MTTfs. According to the occurrence of each move, 45 out of the 97 occurrences (46.4%) were found to be Move 1, and 34 (35.1%) were Move 3, whereas Move 2 accounted for the smallest proportion of the total move occurrences. It can be drawn that the communicative functions of this newly found chapter, i.e., Theoretical Framework, in the present corpus are mainly to establish the territory and to occupy the niche. To be specific, the purposes of the TF are to provide the definitions of certain terms, knowledge claims, or theories related to the writers' study and subsequently to establish the theoretical framework for their own study.

Moreover, no move pattern occurring in more than one MTTf was identified. However, the moves in the present subcorpus were cyclical in that one move was identified more than once in one MTTf, as similarly found in the LR chapters (e.g., Kwan, 2006; Nguyen, 2014). The move combinations found in the 12 MTTfs are displayed in Table 4.14.

Table 4.14 Move Combinations Identified in the 12 MTTfs

Move combination	Occurrence	No. of MTTfs	%
M1-M3	27	10	83.3
M1-M2	11	6	50.0

Cont.

Move combination	Occurrence	No. of MTTfs	%
M1-M2-M3	6	6	50.0
M2-M3	1	1	8.3

As shown in Table 4.14, the combination of M1-M3 occurred the most and was utilized in the majority of the MTTfs (83.3%). This resonates with the finding that M1-M3 accounted for most of the move occurrences as indicated in the preceding paragraphs. The second frequent move combination was M1-M2, however, it was included in merely half of the MTTfs, the same as the combination of M1-M2-M3. In addition, the combination of M2-M3 occurred only once in one MTTf.

4.4.3 Steps

In terms of the steps, there are 13 steps in total in the framework for the LR chapter (Chen & Kuo, 2012). However, not all of them were identified in the TF chapter. The steps employed to realize each move are presented in detail from Move 1 to Move 3. Table 4.15 displays the steps for the realization of Move 1 *Establishing one part of the territory*.

Table 4.15 Steps of Move 1 Identified in the 12 MTTfs

Step	Occurrence	No. of MTTfs	%	Status
S1 Surveying the non-research phenomena or knowledge claims	49	12	100	Obl.
S2 Claiming centrality	7	4	33.3	Opt.
S3 Surveying the research-related phenomena	0	0	0	/

(*Note: Obl.=Obligatory, Opt.=Optional*)

From Table 4.15, it can be seen that S1 occurred most frequently and was adopted in every MTTf which makes it an obligatory step. In addition, S2 was found to be optional with a frequency of 33.3% only. Moreover, S3 was absent in the TF chapter, which indicates that research-related previous studies are not necessary to be provided in this particular chapter. As mentioned by one of the student informants below, the TF chapter is more about the framework which will be adopted by the writers for his/her study. The results suggest that the predominant way to establish the territory in the TF chapter is to deliver the related theories or accepted knowledge that lay the theoretical foundation for the writer's study.

> ST5: *The research-related studies have been demonstrated in the Literature Review chapter already. As indicated by the chapter title, this chapter should present the information related to the adopted framework.*

As for the steps of Move 2, only three out of the six steps in the framework were identified (Table 4.16). From the table, S2, S4, and S6 were absent in the TF chapters. The most frequently used step of Move 2 was S5, but it was simply included in half of the MTTfs and thus was optional. The other two identified steps were S3 and S1, with a lower frequency of 33.3% and 16.7%, respectively. Additionally, Move 2 was conventional in the present subcorpus, yet none of these three identified steps of it was found to be conventional. The result implies that it is necessary to contain Move 2 when composing the TF chapter, however, the steps employed to achieve Move 2 have not been established as a convention.

Table 4.16 Steps of Move 2 Identified in the 12 MTTfs

Step	Occurrence	No. of MTTfs	%	Status
S1 Counter-claiming	2	2	16.7	Opt.
S2 Gap-indicating	0	0	0	/
S3 Asserting confirmative claims	6	4	33.3	Opt.
S4 Asserting relevancy of the surveyed claims	0	0	0	/
S5 Abstracting or synthesizing knowledge claims to establish a theoretical position or framework	9	6	50.0	Opt.
S6 Concluding a part of the literature review	0	0	0	/

(Note: Opt.=Optional)

Additionally, for the obligatory Move 3, all its four steps were identified in the 12 MTTfs. As shown in Table 4.17, S2 was adopted extensively frequently, and it was obligatory. The other three identified steps, i.e., S1, S3, and S4, occurred less and were utilized optionally since only two MTTfs contained S1 and merely three MTTfs employed S3 and S4. The results reveal that in the TF chapter, the writers need to present the theoretical positions or frameworks adopted in their own study to occupy

123

the niche. In other words, it is significant to inform the readers of the theoretical framework the writers are going to utilize to conduct their studies when there is a separate TF chapter.

Table 4.17 Steps of Move 3 Identified in the 12 MTTfs

Step	Occurrence	No. of TFs	%	Status
S1 Indicating research aims, focuses, research questions or hypotheses	3	2	16.7	Opt.
S2 Indicating theoretical positions/theoretical framework	23	12	100	Obl.
S3 Indicating research design/process	7	3	25.0	Opt.
S4 Interpreting terminology used in the thesis	6	3	25.0	Opt.

(*Note: Obl.=Obligatory, Opt.=Optional*)

In terms of the step patterns, no frequent step sequence or step combination was identified. To be specific, in the instances of Move 1, most of the steps were employed alone. The step combination of S1-S2 was found once in four MTTfs. In the instances of Move 2, only S4-S3 sequence was identified, and it occurred only once. Furthermore, four step sequences were in the instances of Move 3; namely, S1-S2, S2-S3, S4-S2, and S4-S3-S2. Nonetheless, all of them were only found once in the present subcorpus. The findings indicate that the writers had a less tendency to use the steps in combinations.

4.5 Findings of the Methodology Chapters

4.5.1 Overall Structure

The 20 Methodology chapters (MTMs) in the present subcorpus consisted of 41,440 words, averaging 2,072 words per MTM. The total number of words of MTMs accounted for 8.7% of the total length of the corpus, which is in disagreement with the finding of Nguyen (2014) that the words of the Methodology chapter made up 15.4% of the whole corpus. It appears that the contents related to the methodology of the study in the present discourse community tend to possess a small portion of the overall thesis compared with the Vietnamese M.A. theses. The range of the word numbers of the MTMs was from 732 words to 3,830 words, which varied considerably. This could be explained that the number of variables and the inclusion of justifications for the methods exert an influence on the length of the Methodology chapter (Lim, 2006).

Furthermore, Table 4.18 presents the generic section headings or subheadings which could be used in other MTMs. Those only utilized by one MTM are not listed in the table. It can be seen that the most frequently occurring generic heading was *Data collection*, followed by *Data analysis* and *Research questions*, which reveals that they are the main sections that need to be included in the methodology chapter. These three headings were also found in Nguyen's (2014) corpus of M.A. TESOL theses. As for the section R*esearch Questions*, as indicated in *Section 4.1*, five of the Introduction chapters contained this particular section, among which one restated the research questions in the Methodology chapter. Specifically, 15 writers presented this section only in the Methodology chapter, four writers provided it only in the Introduction chapter while one writer had it in both chapters. This result shows that it is more acceptable to display the research questions in the Methodology chapter in the present discourse community.

Table 4.18 Generic Section Headings Identified in the 20 MTMs

Generic section heading	No. of MTMs
Data collection	18
Data analysis	17
Research questions	16
Procedures to answer research question *X*	6
Data description	4
Corpus description	4
Summary	4
Instruments/Research instruments	4
Research procedures	3
Procedures of data collection	2
Procedures of data analysis	2
Participants/Research participants	2

In addition, the section or subsection heading *Procedures to answer research* question X, where X could be 1, 2, or 3 depending on the number of research questions that particular thesis had. This heading was merely found in the present subcorpus when compared with those identified in Nguyen (2014) utilized by TESOL Vietnamese students. Moreover, Data description and Corpus description were also found only in the present discourse community. It seems that the generic headings of the same chapter in a similar discipline could be diverse in different discourse communities.

4.5.2 Moves

The occurrence and frequency of each move are provided in Table 4.19. Move 1 was present in 19 out of the 20 MTMs (95%), which indicates it was a conventional move (Kanoksilapatham, 2005). This finding is in keeping with that of Mosquera and Tulud (2021) which Move 1 *Introducing the Method chapter* was conventional in their corpus with a frequency of 73.33%. Since its frequency was nearly 100%, it can be regarded as a quasi-obligatory move (Chen & Kuo, 2012). This result is similar to that of Nguyen (2014) who found Move 1 was obligatory in the TESOL theses.

Table 4.19 Moves Identified in the 20 MTMs

Move	Occurrence	No. of MTMs	%	Status
Move 1 Introducing the Method chapter	23	19	95	Con.
Move 2 Describing data collection method and procedure(s)	27	20	100	Obl.
Move 3 Delineating methods of data analysis	19	13	65	Con.
Move 4 Elucidating data analysis procedure(s)	21	20	100	Obl.
Move 5 Providing chapter summary	5	5	25	Opt.

(*Note: Obl.=Obligatory, Con.=Conventional, Opt.=Optional; the newly found move was in bold*)

Move 2 occurred most and was utilized by all the MTMs, which suggests it was an obligatory move. This finding is in congruence with those of Chen and Kuo (2012), Mosquera and Tulud (2021), and Nguyen (2014). It can be drawn that information about the data collection methods and procedures is compulsory to be provided in the Methodology chapter.

Move 3, concerning the data analysis methods, was found to be conventional with a frequency of 65%. Despite having less frequency in the present subcorpus, this result is similar to Nguyen (2014) that Move 3 was conventional and was presented in 79% of the MTMs.

In terms of Move 4, it was identified in all the Methodology chapters, thus, it was an obligatory move. This result is consistent with Mosquera and Tulud (2021) in which the move *Clarifying data analysis procedure* was obligatory. This is different from what was found in Chen and Kuo (2012) that this move occurred the least compared with the first three moves. Moreover, it is not in line with the finding of Nguyen (2014) that Move 4 was optional in her corpus. It can be drawn that the data analysis procedures are highly expected in the present discourse community, thus, the writers need to present the related content in this chapter to make this chapter more effective.

Furthermore, it should be mentioned that a new move *Providing chapter summary* was identified in the present subcorpus, in which the writers summarized what had been presented in this chapter, as shown in Excerpt 33. This move was also identified in Nguyen's (2014) corpus. Nonetheless, in disagreement with Nguyen (2014), this move was not considered a stable move or a new move since its frequency was less than 50% of the texts, according to Nwogu (1997).

Excerpt 33: Providing chapter summary

4.4 Summary

This chapter introduces the research methodology. It concentrates on the description of the collected data, and then focuses on ... Finally, data analysis ... More specifically, data description part ... Data collection part ... Data analysis .... (MTM13)

In addition, MTM19 was found to have a text segment to indicate the content of the next chapter. However, only one instance of this new text segment was identified in the MTMs, thus, it was not proposed as a new move or step.

In terms of the move patterns, as shown in Table 4.20, some moves, i.e., Move 2 and Move 3, were cyclical in one text. To illustrate, Move 2 was used four times in

MTM16, and Move 3 occurred three times in MTM07. Nevertheless, more than half of the MTMs were in a linear move sequence. This finding is consistent with that of Chen and Kuo (2012).

Table 4.20 Move Sequences of the 20 MTMs

Text	Move sequence
MTM01	M1-M2-M3-M4
MTM02	M1-M2-M3-M2-M4
MTM03	M1-M2-M4
MTM04	M1-M2-M1-M3-M4-M5
MTM05	M1-M2-M3-M4
MTM06	M1-M2-M4
MTM07	M1-M2-M3-M2-M3-M4-M3
MTM08	M1-M2-M1-M3-M2-M3-M4
MTM09	M1-M2-M3-M4-M3-M5
MTM10	M1-M3-M2-M4
MTM11	M1-M2-M4
MTM12	M1-M2-M3-M4
MTM13	M1-M2-M3-M4-M5
MTM14	M2-M4
MTM15	M1-M2-M1-M2-M4-M3-M4
MTM16	M1-M2-M1-M3-M2-M3- M2-M3-M4
MTM17	M1-M2-M4-M5
MTM18	M1-M2-M3-M2-M4
MTM19	M1-M2-M4-M5
MTM20	M1-M2-M4

Additionally, several move patterns were identified in the present subcorpus. To be specific, 4 out of the 20 MTMs (20%) were sequenced as M1-M2-M4. Three MTMs (15%) were organized by M1-M2-M3-M4. Moreover, M1-M2-M4-M5 and M1-M2-M3-M4-M5 were found in two MTMs, respectively. The results are not in accord with Nguyen (2014) that found M1-M3 was the predominant move sequence adopted by Vietnamese students in her study. In addition, these four move patterns had low frequency in the current discourse community, which suggests that there is no fixed way to present the pertinent content about the methodology in this discipline, as stated by Chen and Kuo (2012).

4.5.3 Steps

Three steps were proposed by Chen and Kuo (2012) to realize Move 1 (Table 4.21). As displayed in the table below, S1 was found to be conventional with a frequency of 80%, which is in agreement with the finding of Mosquera and Tulud (2021) that the step *Indicating the chapter/section structure* was conventional with a percentage of 73.33%. However, it is not in accordance with Nguyen (2014) that all the Method chapters started with introducing the chapter structure.

Table 4.21   Steps of Move 1 Identified in the 20 MTMs

Step	Occurrence	No. of MTMs	%	Status
S1 Indicating chapter/section structure	16	16	80	Con.
S2 Providing an overview of the study	18	16	80	Con.
S3 Indicating theory/approach	2	2	10	Opt.

(*Note: Con.=Conventional, Opt.=Optional*)

Moreover, S2 was found in 16 out of the 20 MTMs (80%) so it was conventional, which is corresponding to that of Nguyen (2014). The text segments of this step included research aims, research questions, and brief backgrounds of the writer's study as demonstrated in the Introduction chapter. However, the text segment concerning the research hypotheses was not identified in the present subcorpus, which on the other hand was found in Nguyen (2014). This could be due to that the majority of these M.A. theses were not experimental research. Nevertheless, the inclusion of research aims and research question in the Methodology chapter partly confirms the finding of Peacock (2011) in the Method section of research articles in four non-science disciplines.

Furthermore, S3 was only used by two writers and had two instances. This result is significantly different from Nguyen (2014) in which 79% of the Methodology chapters composed by Vietnamese students contained this step that reveals the theory or approach adopted by the writers. It appears that the writers in the present discourse community have a less tendency to indicate theory in the Methodology chapters. A plausible explanation is that most of the theses in the current corpus had a separate chapter, i.e., Theoretical Framework, in which the writers provided relevant information about the theories, thus, they tended to avoid repeating it in another chapter. The examples of S1, S2, and S3 are displayed below.

Excerpt 34: Move 1 Step 1

In this chapter, three research questions of the present study are manifested. Research approaches and related information of data are illustrated, containing data collection, data description and data analysis process, and so forth. (MTM01)

Excerpt 35: Move 1 Step 2

In this research, the author chooses ... and explores their ... on BNC. (MTM02)

Excerpt 36: Move 1 Step 3

While ... is a theory that analyzes the ... of language, so the present study applies this theory into researching the ... (MTM01)

In addition, in the 22 instances of Move 1, half of them used more than one step, nine of which were structured as S1-S2 (*Indicating chapter/section structure* followed by *Providing an overview of the study*), and it was identified in nine MTMs (45%). Nevertheless, this step pattern was optional, suggesting that the way to realize Move 1 was diverse.

Regarding Move 2, Table 4.22 demonstrates the steps the writers employed to realize it. It was found that S1 and S2 were adopted in all the 20 MTMs, which reveals that they were obligatory, conforming to the findings of Chen and Kuo (2012), Mosquera and Tulud (2021), and Nguyen (2014). The result demonstrates that the information about the sample or the data and about how the data were collected is important to be clearly provided to make the thesis more effective.

Table 4.22　Steps of Move 2 Identified in the 20 MTMs

Step	Occurrence	No. of MTMs	%	Status
S1 Describing the sample	40	20	100	Obl.
S2 Describing methods and steps in data collection	29	20	100	Obl.
S3 Justifying data collection procedure(s)	23	15	75	Con.

(*Note: Obl.=Obligatory, Con.=Conventional*)

Additionally, S3 was included in 15 MTMs (75%) and it was conventional. Nonetheless, this result is not in tandem with Nguyen (2014) that only 3 out of the 24 Methodology chapters (12.5%) produced by Vietnamese writers in her corpus used this step. It seems that there is a cultural variation in providing the justification of data collection procedures. Accordingly, it is suggested to elucidate the advantages of using the sample or indicate the representativity of the sample in a Chinese context when writing a Methodology chapter. The examples of these three steps of Move 2 are manifested below.

Excerpt 37: Move 2 Step 1

Data needed in this study are ... and they can be directly collected from ..., a 706,000-word novel constituting a closed corpus. (MTM03)

Excerpt 38: Move 2 Step 2

During the process of data collection, the author chose conversations ... The speakers of conversations are all anonymous in this study. They are replaced by speaker A, B, C, and so on ... At the first step, the writer borrowed ... then the writer selected ... Among these conversations, the writer selected ... At last, the author obtained ... as the research data. (MTM15)

Excerpt 39: Move 2 Step 3

As one of the most famous ..., ... not only exposes ... but also reflects ... Because this novel was ..., the pervasive... in this classic novel makes it the most appropriate for the present study. (MTM03)

Moreover, as indicated in Table 4.19, 27 instances of Move 2 were found. Among them, 24 instances included more than one step, and two step patterns were identified. They were the sequence of S1-S3-S1-S2 found in three MTMs (15%), and the sequence of S1-S3-S2 found in two MTMs (10%). Both of these two step patterns were optional, which reveals that there is no established way to describe the data collection method and procedures. It may be because the data collection methods employed in each thesis are different and the elements to be demonstrated are, thus, varied.

Table 4.23 sets out the occurrence and frequency of the steps under Move 3. The most frequently adopted step was S1 which presents the research design; however, it was optional.

Table 4.23 Steps of Move 3 Identified in the 20 MTMs

Step	Occurrence	No. of MTMs	%	Status
S1 Presenting an overview of the design	12	11	55	Opt.
S2 Explaining specific methods of data analysis	6	4	20	Opt.
S3 Explaining variables and variable measurement	1	1	5	Opt.
S4 Justifying the methods of measuring variables or data analysis	0	0	0	/

(*Note: Opt.=Optional*)

This result is not consistent with the findings of Mosquera and Tulud (2021) that *Pointing out the research design used in the study* was obligatory in their corpus. Moreover, it is not in line with Nguyen (2014) who found this step was absent. In addition, S2 *Explaining specific methods of data analysis* was merely found in four MTMs, so it was optional. However, this step was found to be conventional in Nguyen (2014). One possible reason is that the writers in the present subcorpus tended to present the detailed data analysis procedures where the data analysis methods were implied, which was confirmed by the student informants as well, as shown below.

> ST1: *When the detailed data analysis procedures are demonstrated, the readers can have a clue what specific methods will be used in the present study. If you only mention the name of the method, the readers will not comprehend how you will analyze your data.*

Moreover, only one instance of S3 *Explaining variables and variable measurement* was found and S4 was absent in the present subcorpus. This result is in line with the finding of Nguyen (2014). It could be explained that the studies in the present discourse community were mainly corpus-based, thus content about the variables was less presented. Furthermore, a closer examination of the 19 instances of Move 3 found that the steps under this move were all used individually. Therefore, no step pattern was identified in the realization of this move. The examples of S1, S2, and S3 of Move 3 are provided below.

Excerpt 40: Move 3 Step 1

Considering the fact that ... is both multi-functional and context-dependent, the research employs a corpus-based method together with discourse analysis. On the one hand, the quantitative analysis is ..., and a comparison of ... will be made afterward. On the other hand, the qualitative analysis is ... Therefore, the combined quantitative and qualitative analysis adopted by this thesis ..., which allows for ... (MTM08)

Excerpt 41: Move 3 Step 2

After ..., and the self-built corpus are collected, the researcher is able to conduct data analysis. ... For the process of analyzing the second research question, the ... is applied. ... In the study, statistics analysis such as descriptive statistics and correlation analysis are used in data analysis. (MTM07)

Excerpt 42: Move 3 Step 3

According to ..., there are many potential elements such as gender, family background, and so on, which are related to ... The background information should be involved in the questionnaire from item A1 to A12 (see also Appendix 1 part A). It aims to know the background information ... (MTM16)

In terms of the realization of Move 4, as displayed in Table 4.24, it was found that S1 was a compulsory step utilized by all the writers, which is similar to the finding of Mosquera and Tulud (2021) that *Pointing out the steps in data analysis* was present in 90% of the texts. Nevertheless, this finding is totally different from Nguyen's (2014) in which S1 was only identified in one text. It can be inferred that the steps the writers took to analyze the data in chronological order were emphasized by the present discourse community, thus, it was established as a convention.

Table 4.24 Steps of Move 4 Identified in the 20 MTMs

Step	Occurrence	No. of MTMs	%	Status
S1 Relating (or recounting) data analysis procedure(s)	23	20	100	Obl.
S2 Justifying the data analysis procedure(s)	1	1	5	Opt.
S3 Previewing results	3	2	10	Opt.

(*Note: Obl.=Obligatory, Opt.=Optional*)

Furthermore, S2 was found to be optional, which is in accordance with those of Mosquera and Tulud (2021) and Nguyen (2014). In addition, S3 was also found to be optional. However, this is not consistent with Lim (2006) that this step was the most common in the Management RA method sections. It could be due to the different conventions of various disciplines and genre types. Additionally, the less frequency of S3 could be explained that there is a Results and Discussion chapter where the writers can present their results. Thus, they tended not to provide the preliminary results in this Methodology chapter in order to make their writing succinct, as mentioned by the student informant ST4 below. Moreover, the examples of these three steps of Move 4 are displayed below.

> ST4: *Methodology chapter is about the research method and the specific procedures about it. It is not appropriate to present the results here. Instead, the results should be provided in the Results and Discussion chapter.*

Excerpt 43: Move 4 Step 1

Two research questions have been answered one by one in this study because the second question is more convenient to solve with the settlement of the first question. The detailed analyses procedures are stated as follows: ... (MTM17)

Excerpt 44: Move 4 Step 2

The reason for discussing the top ten ... in this study is ... To be more specifically, the differences between ... appear to be obvious, which makes it more typical than the top eleven to twenty or twenty to thirty. (MTM07)

Excerpt 45: Move 4 Step 3

According to observation on these linguistic data, the author found out that ... can be manifested through lexical level, sentential level, and non-verbal symbols ... In different levels, there are different representations of ... (MTM15)

Finally, in the 21 instances of Move 4, only one writer employed more than one step to achieve this move. Thus, no step pattern was found under Move 4 in the current subcorpus. It seems that the writer preferred to adopt a single step to realize Move 4 despite three steps being available.

4.6 Findings of the Integrated Results and Discussion Chapters

4.6.1 Overall Structure

As revealed in *Section 3.2.1*, no single Results chapter or Discussion chapter was found in the present corpus. All the writers combined them as a single chapter, which is not in congruence with Chen and Kuo (2012) that five Discussion chapters out of the 15 international theses were embedded in the Results or the Conclusion. Moreover, it is not in consonance with Nguyen (2014) who found around half of her corpus had separate Results chapter and Discussion chapter. The interviews with the supervisors demonstrate that the Results chapter and the Discussion chapter could be either combined or separated, depending on the amount of the content. Moreover, one of the supervisor informants claimed that the combination of the Results and Discussion could make the report of the results and the pertinent discussion more closely related. The results indicate that it is more appropriate to combine these two chapters when the amount of the content in Discussion is much less than that of the Results.

The 20 integrated Results and Discussion chapters (MTRDs) were 222,846 words in total, with an average of 11,142 words per MTRD. The shortest one consisted of 5,670 words while the longest one contained 15,614 words. This chapter was the largest one compared with the other chapters whose total number accounted for 46.6% of the whole corpus of theses.

In terms of the section headings of these integrated chapters, it was found that nearly all of them were content-specific ones which were only related to that particular topic, except two MTRDs that had generic section headings titled "Answers to the First Research Question" or "Answers to Research Question 1". This result suggests that topic-related section headings are more appropriate and more acceptable for the integrated Results and Discussion chapters in the present discourse community.

4.6.2 Moves

As demonstrated in *Section 3.3.1*, the frameworks in Chen and Kuo (2012) were for the single Results chapter and the Discussion chapter, with no framework for the integrated Results and Discussion chapter. Therefore, following Nguyen (2014), the present study combined the two separate frameworks for the move/step identification of these integrated chapters, which is displayed in Table 4.25. To make the combined framework more adaptable to the present study, one modification was conducted. To be specific, the first step of Move 1 in Results chapter was *Providing background information or how results are presented*, and the counterpart in the Discussion chapter was *Providing background information (such as purpose, design, research questions/ hypotheses, etc.) or how discussions are presented*. When combining these two steps, it becomes *Providing background information or how the chapter is presented*. However, it contains two different communicative functions, so the present researcher decided to split this step into two (S1 and S2 under Move 1), as shown in Table 4.25.

Table 4.25 Combined Move-Step Framework for the Integrated Results and Discussion Chapters of M.A. theses

Move	Step
Move 1 Introducing the Result-Discussion chapter	S1 Providing background information (such as purpose, design, research questions/ hypotheses, etc.)
	S2 Indicating how the chapter is presented
	S3 Indicating methods used or statistical procedure applied
Move 2 Reporting results	S1 Locating graphics
	S2 Reporting major findings
Move 3 Commenting on results	S1 Interpreting results
	S2 Comparing results with literature
	S3 Evaluating results (including strengths, limitations, generations, etc. of results)
	S4 Accounting for results (giving reasons)
Move 4 Summarizing results	/
Move 5 Summarizing the study	/
Move 6 Evaluating the study	S1 Indicating limitations of the study
	S2 Indicating significance/advantage of the study
Move 7 Deductions from the (research) study	S1 Recommending further research
	S2 Drawing pedagogic implications
	S3 Making suggestions

This combined framework was then adopted to identify the moves and steps in the 20 integrated Results and Discussion chapters in the present subcorpus. Table 4.26 demonstrates the results of the moves identified in the present subcorpus in which the total occurrences of each move, the number of the MTRDs containing this move, and the corresponding percentage of the MTRDs are delivered.

Table 4.26 Moves Identified in the 20 MTRDs

Move	Occurrence	No. of MTRDs	%	Status
Move 1 Introducing the Result-Discussion chapter	301	20	100	Obl.
Move 2 Reporting results	478	20	100	Obl.
Move 3 Commenting on results	178	20	100	Obl.
Move 4 Summarizing results	103	19	95	Con.
Move 5 Summarizing the study	0	0	0	/
Move 6 Evaluating the study	0	0	0	/
Move 7 Deductions from the (research) study	9	6	30	Opt.
Move 8 Providing chapter summary and/or next chapter introduction	9	9	45	Opt.

(Note: The newly identified move is in bold; Obl.=Obligatory, Con.=Conventional, Opt.=Optional)

As shown in Table 4.26, the first three moves were all found obligatory since they were observed in every MTRD. This finding is in agreement with that of Nguyen (2014). In other words, these three moves are necessary when composing an integrated Results and Discussion. Moreover, a further investigation of the occurrences found that M2 *Reporting results* had the highest occurrences followed by M1 *Introducing the Results-Discussion chapter*, which indicates that the main communicative purposes of the integrated Results and Discussion chapter were to introduce this chapter and report what have been found. This result is not consistent with the study of Dastjerdi et al. (2017) that *Stating results* followed by *Stating comments on the results* had the most instances in the M.A. theses from social science disciplines in a Malaysian university. Furthermore, it is against the claim of Kanoksilapatham (2005) that the main communicative functions of a Results and Discussion section in the RA are objectively presenting the results and subjectively commenting on them at the same time. It appears that the writers in the present discourse community were not quite clear about the communicative purposes of this particular chapter, which was confirmed by the interviews with the supervisors, thus, more instruction on how to compose this chapter, i.e., how to comment on the results, is suggested to be included in the future writing courses. The interviews with the students point out that some of them had insufficient knowledge or experience in terms of how to comment on the results and they considered that answering the research questions was enough, as revealed by the student informant ST1 below. Therefore, the results indicate that the future instruction of thesis writing should pay more attention to the methods of discussing and commenting on the results to better equip the students for their writing of the discussion part.

> ST1: *Actually, I don't know how to comment on the results. I thought that I got the answers to the research questions I proposed in Chapter 1, and it was enough.*

In addition, Move 4 *Summarizing results* was identified in 19 MTRDs (95%) with 103 occurrences. It indicates that Move 4 was conventional in the present subcorpus, which is in line with that of Nodoushan and Khakbaz (2011). Additionally, it is in consonance with Chen and Kuo's (2012) finding that *Making conclusions of results* was identified in 80% of the Discussion chapters composed by international writers. Nevertheless, this move was found to be optional with a far less frequency of 45.5% in Nguyen's (2014) corpus. This finding implies that the writers in the present discourse community tended to summarize several specific results after a lengthy presentation of the results, which could be reader-friendly for such a long chapter.

Furthermore, Move 5 *Summarizing the study*, and Move 6 *Evaluating the study* were not found in the 20 MTRDs, which is similar to Nguyen (2014) who observed an absence of Move 5 and a very low frequency of Move 6 in the TESOL M.A. theses written by Vietnamese students. Nonetheless, it is in disagreement with that of Nodoushan and Khakbaz (2011) who found these two moves were conventional in the single Discussion chapters produced by Iranian EFL students. The result demonstrates that these two moves may be not the main communicative functions of an integrated Results and Discussion.

Moreover, Move 7 *Deductions from the study* was identified in six MTRDs, thus it was optional. This finding is in accordance with that of Nguyen (2014). However, it is not in congruence with Nodoushan and Khakbaz (2011) in which Move 7 was found to be obligatory in EFL M.A. theses written by Iranian writers. It seems that the adoption of Move 7 is varied in different discourse communities.

Additionally, a new move, i.e., Move 8 *Providing chapter summary and/or next chapter introduction*, was identified in the present subcorpus. Chapter summary was observed at the end of five MTRDs and the next chapter introduction in one MTRD, the remaining three contained both. Since the frequency of this move was lower than 50%, it was not a stable move, according to Nwogu (1997).

In terms of the move patterns, all the MTRDs started with Move 1, however, no specific move sequence was found in more than one MTRD. The number of move instances varied extensively in the present subcorpus, ranging from 16 instances to 105 instances, with an average of 54 instances per MTRD, which reveals that certain moves were employed cyclically. This finding is similar to that of Hopkins and Dudley-Evans' (1988) study on the Discussion of the RA and thesis in which they found there "was clearly cyclical patterning in the writer's choice of moves". Table 4.27 provides the move configurations observed at least in 20% of the subcorpus which is listed in the order of their occurrences.

Table 4.27 Move Patterns in the 20 MTRDs

Move configuration	Examples	Occurrence	No. of MTRDs	%
(M1-M2)*n*-M3	1-2-3 12-1-2-1-2-3	80	18	90
M2	Move 2 alone	53	19	95
(M1-M2)*n*-M4	1-2-4 1-2-1-2-4	44	15	75
(M2-M3)*n*	2-3-2-3 2-3-2-3-2-3	42	15	75
(M2-M4)*n*	2-4 2-4-2-4	29	14	70
M3	Move 3 alone	6	5	20
(M1-M2)*n*	1-2-1-2 1-2-1-2-1-2	6	5	20

(Note: N following the brackets indicates the move sequence in those brackets could be repeated n times. Move 2 alone means that in one cycle of the move sequence of one text, only Move 2 was used. So does Move 3 alone.)

From the table above, it can be seen that (M1-M2)*n*-M3 was widely utilized by the writers, which had the highest occurrence of 80 instances. In this way, the writers introduced the chapter and then provided the results, two of which may be repeated, and then ended by commenting on the result. It indicates that the writers have the awareness to give their personal comments on the result, however, they just select certain results to discuss rather than commenting on every result they found in their study.

Furthermore, Move 2 alone was employed frequently as well, with 53 instances in 19 MTRDs. It reveals that the writers simply presented what they had found from their research and did not attempt to provide subjective comments on the results. This finding suggests that the writers in the present discourse community need more instruction on how to provide comments on the results.

Other frequent move configurations were (M1-M2)*n*-M4 and (M2-M3)*n*, which had similar occurrences and frequencies, followed by (M2-M4)*n* identified in 14 MTRDs with 29 occurrences. It is interesting to find out that Move 3 was used alone as a cycle in 6 instances. A closer examination revealed that five of them followed Move 4 in which the writers commented on the conclusion of the results, and the remaining one, i.e., MTRD09, followed Move 7 *Deductions from the research*.

In a nutshell, there were no fixed move patterns identified in a whole MTRD. Moreover, the move sequence as in the framework from Move 1 to Move 7 was not observed in the present subcorpus. Instead, the moves were combined in diverse ways. The results indicate that the first four moves were frequently adopted in various combinations.

4.6.3 Steps

In the combined framework of Results and Discussion, except for Move 4 *Summarizing results* and Move 5 *Summarizing the study* whose communicative functions have been realized only at the move level, the other five moves each had several step options for the writers to select. The findings of the steps of these five moves were presented in this section according to each move. Table 4.28 illustrates the defailed results of the steps of Move 1.

Table 4.28 Steps of Move 1 Identified in the 20 MTRDs

Step	Occurrence	No. of MTRDs	%	Status
S1 Providing background information	212	20	100	Obl.
S2 Indicating chapter purposes and/or structure	23	20	100	Obl.
S3 Indicating methods used or statistical procedure applied	114	20	100	Obl.

(*Note: Obl.=Obligatory; The modified step was in italics.*)

It should be mentioned that the second step in the original framework was *Indicating how the chapter is presented*, as indicated in Table 4.25 in *Section 4.6.2*. Nevertheless, during the data coding process, it was found that the chapter purposes were provided in some MTRDs, thus, the current researcher decided to expand this step into *Indicating chapter purposes and/or structure* to capture the full communicative functions, as shown in Excerpt 46 below.

Excerpt 46

This chapter concerns on the analysis and discussion of ... It is organized into three sections. The first section deals with the first research question with the help of ... Then, according to ..., the second section aims to ... The last section reports the results of ... (MTRD07)

As Table 4.28 shows, S1 *Providing background information* was identified in all the 20 MTRDs so it was found to be obligatory. This result is slightly different from Nguyen (2014) that S1 was conventional in her corpus. It appears that more importance is attached to providing background information on the present discourse community. This can be also seen in the wide occurrences of S1 with 212 instances, which echoes that of Hopkins and Dudley-Evans (1988) who found Background information can appear at any point of the cycles identified in the Discussion of the thesis. Moreover, the frequent occurrence of S1 is in tandem with Nodoushan and Khakbaz (2011) that the Discussion of Iranian theses took much effort to provide background information. This could be caused by the writers' concern about the validity of their research findings, so they rely heavily on the background information to make the findings more convincing and reliable, which was confirmed by the interviews with the students as well who pointed out that they were not confident in their own words, so they tried to validate their findings by providing much background information, as demonstrated by one of the student informants below. Nevertheless, this may result in the mixture of the communicative functions of "Literature Review" and "Discussion" (Nodoushan & Khakbaz, 2011).

> ST2: *I thought that if I only present the results, the readers may not understand what the results refer to if they haven't read my Literature Review chapter. What's more, I am not confident whether my interpretation is appropriate or not. So, I decided to add background information to help me.*

Furthermore, S2 *Indicating the chapter purposes/structure* was also found to be obligatory, which is similar to those of Dastjerdi et al. (2017) who found Structure of section obligatory in the integrated Results and Discussion of the theses from social sciences, and Nguyen (2014) who found *Indicating how the chapter is presented* was compulsory in the Results-Discussion chapters of TESOL theses. This result implies that providing chapter purposes or structure is necessary for the larger combined Results and Discussion.

In addition, S3 *Indicating methods used or statistical procedure applied* was observed in all the MTRDs, which indicates its obligatory status. This finding is in congruence with Dastjerdi et al. (2017) that *Listing procedures/methodological techniques* was found obligatory in the theses from social sciences. Nonetheless, it is not in agreement with those of Chen and Kuo (2012) and Nguyen (2014) in which S3 was found to be conventional in their corpora. It can be drawn that providing the information related to how the writers get the results is valued in the present discourse community. It seems that the writers try to emphasize the validity of their findings, as revealed by Dastjerdi et al. (2017). The examples of these three steps of Move 1 are demonstrated below.

Excerpt 47: Move 1 Step 1

Using critical or aggressive words refers to ... These words make people ... (MTRD04)

Excerpt 48: Move 1 Step 2

Through an insightful investigation into ..., data analysis and analysis of ... are illustrated in this chapter. (MTRD06)

Excerpt 49: Move 1 Step 3

According to the function of KWIC in Concordance, the researcher finds out the specific chunks with the help of context lines. (MTRD07)

In terms of the step patterns under Move 1, the majority of the instances of Move 1 contained merely one step, either S1 or S3. A few instances had the step combinations of S1-S2, S1-S3, or S1-S2-S3, which were usually identified at the beginning of the chapter. The results demonstrate that there is no fixed step pattern to realize Move 1 and the realization of Move 1 is mainly achieved by a single step.

As for the steps of Move 2, it should be pointed out that, similar to Nguyen (2014) who found a new step *Section structure*, this step was also identified in the present subcorpus. Nevertheless, the current study observed that section purposes were provided in some text segments as well. Therefore, the new step *Section structure* found by Nguyen (2014) was expanded to *Indicating section purposes/structure* in the current subcorpus, as shown in Excerpt 50 below.

Excerpt 50

The following part of this section will introduce some specific sub-categories of ... which contribute to the credibility appeals. (MTRD08)

Table 4.29 illustrates the detailed results of the steps of Move 2. It can be seen that the new step S1 was identified in 90% of the MTRDs, which can be proposed as a new and stable step according to the criteria (higher than 50%) of Nwogu (1997). S1 was found to be conventional in the present subcorpus, which is not in line with Nguyen (2014) that Section structure was optional in her corpus. The result indicates that the writers in the current discourse community have a greater tendency to inform the readers of the purposes or the structure of the section in advance in order to guide the readers through the lengthy texts.

Table 4.29 Steps of Move 2 Identified in the 20 MTRDs

Step	Occurrence	No. of MTRDs	%	Status
S1 Indicating section purposes /structure	70	18	90	Con.
S2 Locating graphics	148	18	90	Con.
S3 Reporting major findings	544	20	100	Obl.

(*Note: Con.=Conventional, Obl.=Obligatory; The modified step was in italics.*)

Moreover, S2 *Locating graphics*, as displayed in Excerpt 51, was also found to be conventional with 148 instances. This result is in accordance with that of Chen and Kuo (2012) in which *Locating graphics* was conventional with a frequency of 80% in the Results chapters of the international theses. Nevertheless, it is not consistent with Nguyen (2014) that this step was obligatory in her corpus. Additionally, it is different from the finding of Dastjerdi et al. (2017) that the step *Pointer* whose function was to inform the reader the location of the data being discussed was found to be obligatory in the integrated Results and Discussion of the social science theses. The difference may be explained that some writers in the present subcorpus indicated the location of the graphics implicitly, as shown in Excerpt 52 below.

Excerpt 51: Move 2 Step 2

Therefore, the following table shows the detailed information of the distribution of ... (MTRD08)

Excerpt 52：

According to the proportion in the table, *the cohesive function of ellipsis is the most frequently used in the first category and ... (MTRD17)*

Furthermore, S3 *Reporting major findings*, as indicated in Excerpt 53, was the most frequently employed step in Move 2 with 544 instances and was observed in each of the MTRDs. This finding is in keeping with that of Nguyen (2014). In addition, it echoes Dastjerdi et al. (2017) that a similar step *Substantiating results* was found to be obligatory in the integrated Results and Discussion chapters in their corpus. It can be inferred that reporting major findings is one of the main communicative purposes of this combined chapter.

Excerpt 53: Move 2 Step 3

There are up to 107 significant collocates of ... in BNC and the total co-occur frequencies of ... is 3,684, among which ... are the most frequently employed collocates of ... with frequencies of 343. (MTRD02)

In terms of the step patterns under Move 2, the top six step sequences are listed in Table 4.30. The total account of Move 2 instances was 478, as indicated in Table 4.26 in the preceding part. According to Table 4.30, it can be seen that the writers tended to use S3 *Reporting major findings* alone to realize Move 2. Nonetheless, the step sequence of S2-S3 (*Locating graphics* followed by *Reporting major findings*) was found to be frequently utilized as in the step patterns of S3-(S2-S3)*n* and (S2-S3)*n*. The high frequency of the S2-S3 step pattern is in congruence with those of Chen and Kuo (2012) found in the Results chapter and Nguyen (2014) found in the combined Results and Discussion chapter. Moreover, this finding resonates with Brett (1994) that the pattern *Pointer→Statement of finding→Substantiation of finding* was the most frequent pattern in the Results section of sociology articles. This finding reflects that the location of the graphics is essential when reporting the results from them.

Table 4.30 Step Patterns under Move 2 in the 20 MTRDs

Step pattern	Examples	Occurrence	No. of MTRDs	%
S3	S3 alone	307	20	100
S3-(S2-S3)*n*	S3-S2-S3 S3-S2-S3-S2-S3	44	15	75
(S2-S3)*n*	S2-S3 S2-S3-S2-S3	45	12	60
S1	S1 alone	19	9	45
S2	S2 alone	10	6	30

As for the steps under Move 3 *Commenting on results,* as shown in Table 4.31, it was found that S1 *Interpreting results* was frequently adopted by the writers to realize Move 3 and it was conventional in the present subcorpus. This finding is in consonance with Chen and Kuo (2012) who found *Interpreting results* was conventional in both the single Results chapter and the Discussion chapter. However, this is not in line with those of Nguyen (2014) who found this step was obligatory in her corpus, and of Dastjerti et al. (2017) who identified a similar step *Making generalizations/ interpretations of results* that was obligatory in the combined Results and Discussion chapters. This result suggests that *Interpreting results* was not a necessary step to comment on the results in the present discourse community.

Table 4.31   Steps of Move 3 Identified in the 20 MTRDs

Step	Occurrence	No. of MTRDs	%	Status
S1 Interpreting results	117	16	80	Con.
S2 Comparing results with literature	10	7	35	Opt.
S3 Evaluating results	0	0	0	/
S4 Accounting for results (giving reason)	63	16	80	Con.

(*Note: Con.=Conventional, Opt.=Optional*)

In addition, S2 *Comparing results with literature* was identified in the seven MTRDs (35%), which reveals it was an optional step. This is not consistent with Nguyen (2014) in which S2 was conventional with a far higher frequency of 63.6%. The interviews with the students reveal that some of them thought that this chapter was about their own results, so they did not realize they needed to compare with those of others, as mentioned by one of the student informants below. The result demonstrates that the writers in the present discourse community may lack the awareness to compare their own results with other related studies to situate their study in the wider field. Hence, in the future writing courses, comparing findings with previous studies need to be emphasized.

SS1: *I thought this chapter was about my own results. Thus, I didn't realize that I needed to compare them with those of previous studies.*

Furthermore, similar to Nguyen (2014) that only one instance of S3 was found, S3 was not observed in the present subcorpus. This suggests that *Evaluating results*, which aims to display the strengths, limitations, generalizations of the results, might be too demanding for M.A. students to provide. This was verified by the interviews with the supervisors. Additionally, the interviews with the students reveal that they were not aware that evaluating the results could be one way to comment on the results. Instead, they regarded that the section "Limitations of the Study" in the Conclusion chapter was the proper place to evaluate the whole research, including the results, as demonstrated by one of the student informants below. It is, therefore, suggested that the future thesis writing instruction could add this step, i.e., *Evaluating results*, to the options for the students to comment on the results.

> SS2: *I haven't saw the evaluation of results in the Results and Discussion chapter before. Instead, I prefer to evaluate my study in the Limitation of the Study in the Conclusion chapter.*

The last step S4 *Accounting for results* was found to be conventional, which is in agreement with that of Nguyen (2014). Nevertheless, it is contrary to the study of Dastjerdi et al. (2017) in which a similar step *Explaining the results* was identified to be obligatory in their corpus of combined Result-Discussion chapters of social science theses in a Malaysian university. The difference may be caused by the convention variations in different institutions. The examples of S1, S2, and S4 of Move 3 found in the present subcorpus are displayed below.

Excerpt 54: Move 3 Step 1

   This indicates that the students tend to choose those familiar and fixed chunks that they have learned in ... (MTRD07)

Excerpt 55: Move 3 Step 2

   In this ..., it is consistent with Swales' CARS model in that ... frequently follows ... and illustrates that ... (MTRD09)

Excerpt 56: Move 3 Step 4

   The reasons accounting for the syntactic function changes are various. First, ... Moreover, ... Second, ... As for the weakening of attribute function, the reason is that ... (MTRD01)

In terms of the step patterns of Move 3, it was revealed that in the 178 instances of Move 3, only nine instances of the combination of S1 and S4 were identified in five MTRDs. The result demonstrates that although there were four step options, most writers tended to employ one step, either S1 or S4, to realize Move 3.

As for the steps for Move 4 and Move 5, since there is no step option for these two moves, no discussion on them is available. Additionally, although there are two steps under Move 6, no discussion was provided as Move 6 was absent in the current subcorpus as revealed in Table 4.25 in *Section 4.6.2*. Table 4.32 lists the steps of Move 7 that were identified in the 20 MTRDs.

Table 4.32 Steps of Move 7 Identified in the 20 MTRDs

Step	Occurrence	No. of MTRDs	%	Status
S1 Recommending further research	2	2	10	Opt.
S2 Drawing pedagogical implications	3	2	10	Opt.
S3 Making suggestions	4	4	20	Opt.

(*Note: Opt.=Optional*)

It can be seen from Table 4.32 that all the three steps under Move 7 were optional, which is similar to Nguyen (2014) who found these steps absent or optional in her corpus. In addition, it corresponds to the study of Dastjerti et al. (2017) that found *Suggesting further research* was absent in the integrated Results and Discussion chapters. The reason why these steps had a low frequency is that they are not the main communicative purposes of this chapter. Instead, they were found to be presented in the last chapter, i.e., the Conclusion, as revealed later in *Section 4.6*. Furthermore, since a few instances of Move 7 were observed and all of them only contained one step, thus, no step pattern was identified under this move. The examples of these three steps of Move 7 are provided below.

Excerpt 57: Move 7 Step 1

   Nevertheless, every ... has its feature that should be analyzed separately in future research. (MTRD19)

Excerpt 58: Move 7 Step 2

Based on ..., not only can teachers even educators help them how to learn English well but also they should pay more special attention to minority students' trilingual learning. (MTRD16)

Excerpt 59: Move 7 Step 3

In order to create a good image of the schools, writers or editors of ... should pay special attention to ... of their discourse, so it is of great significance for them to use ... In particular, they need to take into account ... as well as ... (MTRD08)

4.7 Findings of the Conclusion Chapters

4.7.1 Overall Structure

The total length of the 20 thesis Conclusions (MTCs) was 26,936 words, with an average of 1,347 words per MTC. The number of words in each text varied widely from 794 words to 2,340 words. All the MTCs were a single chapter themselves, which is consistent with those M.A. theses in Nguyen (2014). Nevertheless, this is different from Bunton (2005) in which a small number of the Ph.D. conclusion chapters were found in two chapters or the last section of a final chapter in a range of disciplines. The difference may be caused by the difference between M.A. and Ph.D. or the disciplines.

Furthermore, all the 20 MTCs were titled "Conclusion", except for two MTCs being "Conclusions". This result is not in line with those of Bunton (2005) and Nguyen (2014) that the title of this chapter varied considerably. It appears that the communicative purposes of the last chapter in the present discourse community are more straightforward since the titles entailed the role of the chapter in the writers' opinion (Bunton, 2005).

Moreover, all the chapters were divided into sections, which is not in agreement with Bunton (2005) that around half of his corpus was presented as a whole. Table 4.33 lists the section headings employed in the present subcorpus, and similar ones were grouped by their shared communicative functions.

Table 4.33 Generic Section Headings Identified in the 20 MTCs

Generic section heading	No. of MTCs
Major Findings (11) Major Research Findings (3) Findings (2) Major Findings of the Present Study/the Study (2) Research Findings (1) Main Findings (1)	20
Limitations (8) Limitations of the Present Study/the Study (5) Limitations of the Present Research/the Research (3) Limitations of the Research (1)	16
Suggestions for Further Study/Research (15) Recommendations for Further Research (1)	16
Implications (10) Implications of the Present Study/the Study (2) Pedagogical Implications (1)	13
Limitations and Suggestions (2) Limitations and Suggestions for Further Study (1) Limitations and Implications for Further Study (1)	4

(*Note:* The number in the bracket after the heading indicates its occurrence.)

It can be seen that all the section headings were generic ones indicating the section's functions and were applicable to other MTCs. The various section headings support Bunton (2005) who found diverse section heading patterns in the humanities and social sciences dissertation Conclusion chapters. Despite the wording difference, a closer examination of these section headings reveals that the concluding chapters mainly achieved four communicative functions, i.e., providing major findings, implications, limitations, and suggestions for future studies. This finding is not in line with Nguyen's (2014) that chapter introduction and chapter summary were demonstrated in the section headings. It seems that these two communicative functions are not preferred by the writers in the present discourse community.

It should be mentioned that four of the MTCs had the section headings of *Limitations* and *Suggestions for Further Study* being combined as one. The consultation with these four writers pointed out that their suggestions for more studies were generated from and corresponding to the limitations of their own research, thus, they tended to integrate these two sections.

4.7.2 Moves

Table 4.34 provides the occurrence and frequency of each move identified in the 20 MTCs. It can be seen that 16 out of the 20 MTCs (80%) contained Move 1, which suggests it was a conventional move. This finding is consistent with that of Nguyen (2014). It is likely that introducing the chapter at the beginning of the MTC would more cater to the expectation of the audience.

Table 4.34 Moves Identified in the 20 MTCs

Move	Occurrence	No. of MTCs	%	Status
Move 1 Introducing the Conclusions chapter	16	16	80	Con.
Move 2 Summarizing the study	20	20	100	Obl.
Move 3 Evaluating the study	24	20	100	Obl.
Move 4 Deductions from the study	24	20	100	Obl.

(*Note: Obl.=Obligatory, Con.=Conventional*)

Moreover, Move 2, as shown in Excerpt 61, was found in every MTC, and it was obligatory, which is consistent with Chen and Kuo (2012) that *Summarizing the study* briefly was obligatory in their corpus. Nevertheless, this move was found to be conventional in Nguyen (2014). The result reveals that this move is significant in the present discourse community.

Excerpt 60: Move 1

This chapter is the conclusion of the thesis, which mainly concludes ... and ... Then, the suggestions for further researches are introduced as well ... At last, the conclusion of suggestions is demonstrated for future studies... (MTC13)

Excerpt 61: Move 2

The following are the main findings of this research. Firstly, ... Secondly, ... Thirdly, ... Except for the above findings, the author has discovered a new finding ... (MTC01)

In addition, Move 3 was found to be obligatory as well in the current subcorpus. This was not in accordance with Nguyen (2014) who found Move 3 was conventional in her corpus. The finding demonstrates that evaluation of the writer's own study is also important when concluding a thesis in the present context.

Furthermore, all the MTCs were found to include Move 4, which indicates its status as obligatory. This result is in keeping with that of Nguyen (2014). It is suggested that deductions from the writer's own study were valued by the present discourse community, thus the writers are recommended to relate their studies to the field or the reality.

In a nutshell, all the last three moves were obligatory while the first move was conventional. The high occurrences and frequencies of the last three moves support the claim of Chen and Kuo (2012) that the communicative purposes of the thesis Conclusion are mainly characterized by Moves 2, 3, and 4. This finding also echoes that of Yang and Allison (2003) who found *Summarizing the study*, *Evaluating the study*, and *Deductions from the study* were the most commonly utilized moves in the RA Conclusion sections.

Additionally, Table 4.35 presents the move sequence of each MTC in which several move patterns were identified. It can be seen that the majority of the MTC was produced in a linear way, except for five MTCs that had Move 3 or Move 4 recycled (e.g., MTC02, MTC05, MTC07, MTC09, and MTC16). The linear structure found in the present subcorpus is in consonance with those of Chen and Kuo (2012), Nguyen (2014), and Yang and Allison (2003). The findings indicate that Conclusion chapter has a clear structure.

Table 4.35 Move Sequences of the 20 MTCs

Text	Move sequence	Text	Move sequence
MTC01	M1-M2-M3-M4	MTC11	M1-M2-M3-M4
MTC02	M1-M2-M4-M3-M4	MTC12	M2-M3-M4
MTC03	M1-M2-M3-M4	MTC13	M1-M2-M3-M4
MTC04	M1-M2-M3-M4	MTC14	M1-M2-M3-M4
MTC05	M1-M3-M2-M3-M4	MTC15	M2-M3-M4
MTC06	M2-M3-M4	MTC16	M1-M3-M2-M3-M4-M3-M4
MTC07	M1-M2-M4-M3-M4	MTC17	M1-M2-M3-M4
MTC08	M1-M2-M3-M4	MTC18	M2-M3-M4

Cont.

Text	Move sequence	Text	Move sequence
MTC09	M1-M2-M3-M4-M3-M4	MTC19	M1-M2-M3-M4
MTC10	M1-M2-M3-M4	MTC20	M1-M2-M3-M4

In terms of the move patterns, as shown in Table 4.35, 11 out of the 20 MTCs were sequenced by M1-M2-M3-M4, the same as the move progression in the framework. Moreover, the move sequence M2-M3-M4 was found in four MTCs and M1-M2-M4-M3-M4 in two MTCs. The remaining three were in an irregular move order. Nevertheless, no matter in what move order, they all ended with Move 4. It can be inferred from the results that there is a greater tendency for the writers to organize their Conclusion chapters in a predictable way by introducing it first, briefly summarizing the study next, then moving to evaluate the study, and ending with the deductions from it.

4.7.3 Steps

As indicated in the framework of Chen and Kuo (2012), there is no step option under Move 1 and Move 2. Therefore, this section mainly presented the results of the steps in Move 3 and Move 4. Table 4.36 provides the steps of Move 3 identified in the 20 MTCs first.

Table 4.36 Steps of Move 3 Identified in the 20 MTCs

Step	Occurrence	No. of MTCs	%	Status
S1 Indicating significance/advantage	14	11	55	Opt.
S2 Indicating limitations	20	20	100	Obl.
S3 Evaluating methodology	0	0	0	/

(Note: Obl.=Obligatory, Opt.=Optional)

As displayed in Table 4.36, S1 was employed by 11 MTCs and it was found to be optional. This is in agreement with the findings of Nguyen (2014). It can be reasonable since there was already one section revealing the research significance in the Introduction chapter as indicated in *Section 4.1*. Moreover, S2 was contained in every MTC, thus obligatory, which is not in line with those of Chen and Kuo (2012) and Nguyen (2014) who found providing the limitations of the study was conventional rather than compulsory. In addition, similar to Nguyen (2014), S3 was not identified in the present subcorpus, which suggests that evaluating the study methodology was not expected in the current discourse community. It can be drawn from the results that when evaluating the writer's study, it is necessary for them to state the limitations of their study to make their thesis more effective. The examples of S1 and S2 of Move 3 identified in the current subcorpus are demonstrated below.

Excerpt 62: Move 3 Step 1

Firstly, in this study, ... is no longer regarded as ... but as ... From the perspective of ..., the present study has investigated ... and built modified models to reveal ... Secondly, this study offers a new perspective to interpret ... Instead of the interpretation of the ... from phonetic metaphor or semantic metaphor, this study provides a new perspective to explain that ... (MTC20)

Excerpt 63: Move 3 Step 2

First, the linguistic data collected are limited in ... And the quantity of the research data, which are total 60 ..., is somewhat limited. (MTC14)

Furthermore, in the 24 instances of Move 3, most of them merely contained one step, either S1 or S2. However, in nine MTCs, these two steps were used in combination and a sequence of S1-S2. It seems that providing both the advantages and the limitations of the study could be one way to evaluate one's study. The low frequency of the step patterns also corresponds to Yang and Allison's (2003) study that Conclusion sections in RAs tended to be structured linearly. Table 4.37 provides the steps of Move 4 identified in the 20 MTCs.

Table 4.37　Steps of Move 4 Identified in the 20 MTCs

Step	Occurrence	No. of MTCs	%	Status
S1 Recommending further research	20	20	100	Obl.
S2 Drawing pedagogical implications	3	3	15	Opt.
S3 Making suggestions	2	2	10	Opt.

(Note: Obl.=Obligatory, Opt.=Optional)

CHAPTER 4

Regarding the steps under Move 4, as displayed in Table 4.37, S1 was found in all the 20 MTCs, thus, it was obligatory. This finding is not in accordance with Chen and Kuo (2012) and Nguyen (2014) in which *Recommending further research* was conventional in their corpora. Apart from S1, S2 was found to be optional in the present subcorpus with a very low frequency, which is also not consistent with the findings of these previous two studies that S2 had a wider occurrence (13 occurrences in 11 Conclusions) and S2 was conventional with a high frequency of 92%, respectively. It is interesting that 13 MTCs had a section heading containing the keyword "Implications" ("Implications" in 12 MTCs and "Pedagogical Implications" in one MTC), as revealed in the preceding *Section 4.6.1*. However, most of them provided the significance or the advantage of the writer's study rather than drawing pedagogical implications. One possible reason could be that the writers' studies were not very related to teaching and learning. Another possible explanation is that recommending future studies was easier for the writers to present which can correspond to the limitations of their study. As for S3 *Making suggestions*, it was optional with a low frequency of 10%. This finding is in congruence with that of Nguyen (2014). The overall results of the Move 4 steps demonstrate that the main deduction from the writers' studies was recommendations for further research in the present discourse community. The examples of these three steps of Move 4 are displayed below.

Excerpt 64: Move 4 Step 1

In this research, the author just chose ..., so in the future study, the research object can be enlarged to ... In another way, the further study can choose ... (MTC01)

Excerpt 65: Move 4 Step 2

The research finds that high proficient students have a better ... than low proficient ones, and ... has a positive correlation with ... So, in this part, some pedagogical implications are made for teaching and learning, aiming at improving students' English writing proficiency. (MTC07)

Excerpt 66: Move 4 Step 3

Governments can make full use of the current results to make suitable plans and ... So the government can make some specific ... This also reminds researchers that ..., who must take practicable measures to ... (MTC16)

Moreover, a closer investigation of the step sequences in the 24 instances of Move 4 found that almost all the instances only utilized one step under Move 4, except for one instance that had the combination of S2 and S3. Therefore, no step pattern was identified in the steps of Move 4. This finding indicates that the writers tended to use merely one step to realize Move 4.

4.8 Summary

In this chapter, the detailed results and the related discussion of the rhetorical structure of the master's theses have been demonstrated according to the macrostructure of the thesis. To be specific, the overall structure, the moves, and the steps found in each chapter of the master's thesis are delineated separately. Moreover, through the reporting of the major findings in terms of the rhetorical structure, the discussion on the employment of the moves and the steps is also provided. The next chapter will deliver the results and discussion of the moves and steps identified in the corresponding thesis defense presentation slides.

CHAPTER 5 Results and Discussion of Moves and Steps of the Thesis Defense Presentation Slides

The present chapter presents the results and discussion of the move analysis of the thesis defense presentation slides, which is organized according to the sections of this particular genre. After the overview of the thesis defense presentation slides, it starts with the results and discussion of the Introduction section, followed by those in the Literature Review section, the Theoretical Framework section, the Methodology section, the integrated Results and Discussion section, and the Conclusion section, respectively. In addition, the overall structure, the moves, and the steps of each section of the thesis defense presentation slides are demonstrated in detail.

5.1 Overview of the Structure of the Thesis Defense Presentation Slides

The corpus of the corresponding thesis defense presentation slides contains 538 slides in total, ranging from 14 to 40 slides in one slide set and about 27 slides on average. When comparing the number of slides with the length of the original theses, it was found that there was no correlation between them. To be specific, the longest thesis was not presented in a much greater number of slides. Table 5.1 below presents the detailed results of types of slide found in the 20 Thesis Defense Presentation.

Table 5.1 Types of Slides in the 20 Thesis Defense Presentation Slide Sets

Type of slide	No. of slides	%
Scriptural	437	81.2
Numerical	26	4.8
Graphical	25	4.6
Figurative	5	0.9
Scripto-numerical	24	4.5
Scripto-graphical	20	3.7
Figuro-script	1	0.2
Total	538	~100

The slides were presented in different types based on the typology of Rowley-Jolivet (2002). It should be noticed that the photos or icons used as the decoration and the template were not counted since they were not used to reveal the content of the original thesis or the oral commentary. As shown in Table 5.1 below, the majority of the slides (81.2%) fell into the Scriptural category (e.g., texts), which is similar to the findings of Azizifar et al. (2014) that M.A. students in Applied Linguistics mostly utilized scriptural slides to present their theses during the defense session. Besides, it was also in agreement with the results found in Atai and Talebzadeh (2012), Diani (2015), and Zapletalová (2014), which explored the Applied Linguistics conference presentation slides. This may be determined by the nature of the soft fields which are predominated by verbal and linguistic systems other than other semiotic systems. Other types of slides were also identified, such as Graphical slides (e.g., graphics, diagrams), Figurative slides (e.g., photographs), and Numerical slides (e.g., numerical tables). However, they were in a much lesser proportion compared with the Scriptural type.

In line with Atai and Talebzadeh (2012), hybrid slides were found in the present corpus, such as Scripto-numerical slides which contained a numerical table as well as some sentences or phrases alongside to interpret it. Moreover, in conformity with their study, the frequently utilized hybrid slides by the writers were Scripto-graphical and Scripto-numerical ones. It indicates that in this discipline, texts, graphics, and tables with numbers were used more than photos in the slides to report the theses.

Apart from the types of the slides, some characteristics of the slides were identified in the present study. All the 20 slide sets began with a slide demonstrating the title of the original theses. In this "title slide", called by Atai and Talebzadeh (2012), the English title of the thesis was found in 12 slide sets, while both the English title and its Chinese version were identified in the remaining eight slide sets, which are similar to the cover page of their original theses.

In the present corpus, except for one title slide that merely demonstrated the thesis title, 19 title slides were found to include other kinds of information as well, such as the students' names, the supervisors' names, the date of the thesis defense, and the discipline name. To be specific, the majority of the title slides (75%) included both the names of the student and the supervisor(s) under the thesis title in a smaller font size, seven of which were shown in Chinese. Moreover, only the name of the writer, without the name of the supervisor(s), was found in four instances of the title slides and one of them was in Chinese. In addition, the discipline name, and the date of the thesis defense were found in five title slides and in three title slides, respectively. Besides, the student ID number, and the event name "M.A. Thesis Defense at XX University in the Year 2017" in Chinese were identified in two title slides and in one title slide, respectively.

From the texts demonstrated in the title slides, they suggest that the English title of the original thesis is obligatory in this slide, while the name of the student, the name of the supervisor(s), and the Chinese title of the thesis are conventional. Furthermore, other extra information provided in this slide was found optional, such as the discipline name, date of the thesis defense, student ID number, and the event name. Besides, demonstrating these texts in Chinese other than the thesis title was also found optional.

In the second slide of nearly all the presentations, contents or outlines were presented to indicate the plan of the oral presentation. However, three of them were found to demonstrate the chapter headings of the original thesis rather than the outline of the presentation, which reveals that these writers tended to misunderstand the function of the outline in the slide with the contents of the original theses, or maybe they deliberately showed the audience that their theses were organized into different chapters.

Furthermore, almost all the slide sets (95%) had a single slide at the end to show gratitude to the audience, one of which had it preceding the References rather than in the last slide. In this "Thank You" slide called by Atai and Talebzadeh (2012), various words or phrases were used, ranging from "Thanks" (3), "Thank you" (9), "Thank you very much" (1), "Thanks for your listening" (1), "Thank you for your attention" (1), "Thank you for your kind suggestions" (1), and "Thank you for your patience and suggestions" (1). Besides, two of them also included the Chinese version of "thank you" or "welcome all the teachers to criticize", which is explicitly used to show the humble attitude of the writer. Moreover, two of the slide sets ended only in Chinese in this "Thank You" slide to express gratitude or welcome the committee members to give comments. Apart from the expression of gratitude, the student's name, the affiliation, and the date of the thesis defense were also added by one writer in this slide. In another "Thank You" slide, the discipline name and the names of the student and the supervisor were included. To conclude, in the "Thank You" slide, expressing gratitude is conventional, but the words employed to express it are various, and using or adding Chinese versions of it are optional.

In terms of the background and the design, diverse templates were utilized either provided by Microsoft PowerPoint or downloaded from the Internet. Three of the writers added the logo and the name of the university into the template, one of which showed the motto of the university in the template as well.

As for the body part of the slide sets, the units in the rhetorical structure of the thesis defense presentation slides were examined based on those of the theses, which include Introduction, Literature Review, Theoretical Framework, Methodology, Results and Discussion, and Conclusion. According to the content and the slide headings, the macrostructure of the thesis defense presentation slides was identified, with confirmation from the writers whenever there was a difficulty in distinguishing which part the slide belongs to.

As shown in Table 5.2 below, the macrostructure of the thesis defense presentation slides was organized in various ways. It indicates that there is not a norm or a fixed or required convention for the writers to design the thesis defense presentation slides in the present discourse community, thus, the writers seem to produce them mainly according to their knowledge or own understanding and past experience of seeing the slides in previous presentations. All the slide sets demonstrated the content from the thesis chapters of Introduction as well as Results and Discussion, which indicates these two chapters were obligatory in the defense session. Moreover, the majority of the slide sets also included the content from Methodology (80%) and Conclusion (85%). This result reveals that the content from these two chapters of the original thesis is conventional to be presented in the corresponding slides. On the other hand, less than half of the presentations included the content from the Literature Review chapter (40%) and the Theoretical Framework chapter (40%), demonstrating that they are optional to be selected from the theses to reappear in the slides.

Table 5.2 Macrostructure of the 20 Thesis Defense Presentation Slide Sets

Macrostructure	No. of PSs	%
I-Lr-M-R&D-C	5	25
I-R&D-C	2	10
I-Tf-R&D-C	2	10
I-Tf-M-R&D-C	2	10
I-Lr-Tf-M-R&D-C	2	10
I-M-R&D	2	10
I-M-R&D-C	1	5
I-Tf-M-R&D	1	5
I-Lr-Tf-M-R&D	1	5
I-Lr-M-R&D-Rc-C	1	5
I-Lr-M-R&D-C-Rc	1	5
Total	20	100

(Note: I=Introduction, Lr=Literature Review, Tf=Theoretical Framework; M=Methodology, RD=Results and Discussion, C=Conclusion, Rc=Reviewer's Comments and Revision)

Apart from the content selected from the thesis, it was found that two of the presentations had several slides to demonstrate the comments from the anonymous reviewers and their revisions based on the comments, which was typical in the slides rather than in the thesis. Interviews with these two writers reveal that the intention for them to display this content was to show that their theses were already reviewed by the anonymous experts and to show their positive reaction to the comments in order to increase the possibility of passing their thesis defense. The lower frequency of demonstrating reviewers' comments and the corresponding revisions found in the present corpus was because only 10% of the theses will be randomly selected by the department to be reviewed anonymously by the experts outside of the province of the present research context GZU each year as mentioned in *Section 1.1.3*.

The main chapters from the theses found to be present in the thesis defense presentation slides were Introduction, Methodology, Results and Discussion, and Conclusion. It is different from the findings of Pieketaleyee and Bazargani (2018) that five chapters of the M.A. theses (Introduction, Literature Review, Methodology, Results, and Discussion) were presented in the slides during the defense session. In the present corpus, there was less tendency of the writers to include the content from the Literature Review chapter in the slides. It might be caused by the time limitation of the defense session so the writers attach more importance to announcing their research rather than to showing the research field. However, the content from the Conclusion chapter was presented in nearly all of the presentations, while it was absent in the corpus of Pieketaleyee and Bazargani (2018) which was produced by Iranian M.A. students. It appears that the macrostructure of the presentation slides may be varied in different cultural contexts.

5.2 Findings on the Introduction Sections

5.2.1 Overall Structure

The slides presenting the corresponding content from the original Thesis Introduction in each presentation ranged from two slides to six slides, on average 3.5 slides in one PSI.

It is known that theses are organized by chapters and sections or subsections under each chapter, while the slide sets are composed of a sequence of slides. Furthermore, except for the first title slide and the last Thank You slide, the slides in between usually have a heading or subheading, then the body text, which is the default layout setting of PowerPoint (Atai & Talebzadeh, 2012; Green, 2021), but the writers can change the layout by themselves. For example, the writers can delete the heading of the slide to contain only the body part of the slide. A common feature of the thesis defense presentation slides is the prevalence of the slide headings which play a significant role in guiding the audience through the content presented in that specific slide. All the writers in the present corpus demonstrated the content from the original MTIs into the corresponding PSIs. 11 out of the 20 PSIs transferred the chapter heading "Introduction" of the original MTIs into the slides as a slide heading as well, which was used in a single slide as the boundary device, at the top of every single slide or only at the first slide that demonstrates the content from the original MTIs. However, one writer utilized the word "Introduction" to demonstrate the research background rather than to imply the whole introductory part from the thesis. In addition, one writer employed the word "Why" to demonstrate the content from the thesis Introduction. In those that utilized "Introduction" as a slide heading at the top of each slide that contained the MTI content, section headings from the MTIs were adopted as the slide subheadings.

Most of the slide headings or subheadings were the generic section headings from the theses. According to the sequence of the headings used, half of the PSIs (50%) had the slide heading "Research Background" or "Background" to direct the audience to the items that indicate the research background. Other utilized headings were "Motivation" "Rationale" "Rationale of the Study" "Research Orientation" and "Basis for the Selected Topic", all of which were not found in the original MTIs.

18 out of the 20 PSIs had a slide heading to indicate the research objectives, such as "Research Objectives" "Objectives of the Study" "Purpose" or "Objectives". Besides, a majority of the PSIs (75%) had one slide titled "Research Questions" to reveal the proposed research questions in the thesis. In addition, headings that demonstrated the research significance were used in eight of the PSIs, such as, "Significance of the Study" and "Significance". Moreover, two PSIs were found to have "Terminology" as a slide heading and one PSI had "Layout of the Thesis" to finish this introductory section of the PSI.

From the slide headings, it was found that research background, research objectives, and research questions were the mostly presented content in the corresponding PSIs. Moreover, it reveals that the writers regarded the three parts as the most important information necessary to be demonstrated in the defense session to introduce their research.

5.2.2 Moves

The identified moves are shown in Table 5.3 below based on the framework of Chen and Kuo (2012). The total number of PSIs, in which the specific move or step was identified, and the related frequency were revealed as well. As shown, all the three moves of *Establishing a territory*, *Establishing a niche*, and *Occupying the niche* were found in the PSIs. According to the frequency, Move 1 was conventional as it was presented in the majority of the presentation slides (80%) which is in line with the findings of Pieketaleyee and Bazargani (2018). It indicates that it is necessary to introduce the audience with certain information about the field at the beginning of the defense session. Nevertheless, Move 1 was found to be obligatory in the Applied Linguistic conference presentation slides in Atai and Talebzadeh (2012) and Diani (2015). This may be because there is a wider range of audiences at the conference and the presenters intend to provide certain background information to make the audiences familiar with their topics.

Table 5.3 Moves Identified in the 20 PSIs

Moves	No. of PSIs	%	Status
Move 1 Establishing a territory	16	80	Con.
Move 2 Establishing a niche	11	55	Opt.
Move 3 Occupying the niche	20	100	Obl.

(*Note: Obl.=obligatory, Con.=conventional, Opt.=optional*)

Furthermore, Move 2 had a frequency of 55% which implies it was optional in the present study, while it was obligatory in Pieketaleyee and Bazargani's (2018) study of TEFL thesis defense presentation slides produced by Iranian M.A. students. When comparing the results with those identified in the conference presentation slides, differences were found as well. The finding of Move 2 being optional in the present study is in accordance with that of Diani's (2015) which has a lower frequency of

12.5%. Nonetheless, it disagrees with the result in Atai and Talebzadeh (2012) that Move 2 was conventional in their corpus. The slides in Diani (2015) were produced by native and non-native English speakers, whereas those in Atai and Talebzadeh (2012) were produced exclusively by Iranian linguists. Therefore, it seems that the adoption of Move 2 in the presentation slides may be various in different discourse communities.

Moreover, the main purpose of the thesis defense presentation is to report one's own research. Hence, Move 3 was unsurprisingly found being employed in all the presentations, which indicates it was an obligatory move. It is in conformity with the results of Pieketaleyee and Bazargani (2018). In addition, it is in agreement with the finding of Diani (2015) that Move 3 was obligatory in the conference presentation slides. Besides, Move 3 had a high frequency of 87.5% in Atai and Talebzadeh (2012). The result reveals that occupying the niche is significant and necessary when presenting a research report.

In terms of the move sequence, the three moves were in single progression in the majority of the presentations as shown in Table 5.4 below, except one of the presentations (PSI18) that had a recursive Move 1, and five of them had a recursive Move 3. This finding is contrary to the results found in the original thesis Introductions that the moves are cyclical (e.g., Bunton, 2002; Chen & Kuo, 2012; Kawase, 2018).

Table 5.4 Move Sequences of the 20 PSIs

Text	Move sequence	Text	Move sequence
PSI1	M1-M3	PSI11	M3-M2-M3
PSI2	M1-M2-M3	PSI12	M3
PSI3	M1-M2-M3	PSI13	M1-M3
PSI4	M1-M3	PSI14	M3-M1-M3
PSI5	M1-M2-M3	PSI15	M3-M1-M2-M3
PSI6	M2-M3	PSI16	M3-M1-M3
PSI7	M3	PSI17	M1-M3
PSI8	M1-M3	PSI18	M1-M2-M1-M3
PSI9	M1-M2-M3	PSI19	M3-M1-M2-M3
PSI10	M1-M2-M3	PSI20	M1-M2-M3

As indicated in Table 5.4, two of the slide sets (PSI7, PSI12) only utilized Move 3 to introduce their research, so the introduction of the presentation was all about the writers' own research. The identified move patterns in the present corpus were M1-M3 and M1-M2-M3, with the frequency of 35% and 40%, respectively. The move progression in the framework of Chen and Kuo (2012) as M1-M2-M3 was employed more in the present corpus, which suggests that the presentation of the thesis Introduction in the slides also conforms to the convention proposed by Swales' CARS models (1990, 2004) for research articles.

5.2.3 Steps

As the second layer of the rhetorical structure, the steps of the slides have received less attention which saw that only one previous study has touched upon it, i.e., Pieketaleyee and Bazargani (2018). Therefore, the present researcher endeavors to offer her own discussion by keeping the discussion of moves which have more previous studies to support as a guiding frame. The step results are presented in terms of the overall findings from the frequency of the steps, the employment of the steps under each move, and the step sequences.

The steps in the PSIs were found only to have those proposed in the framework of Chen and Kuo (2012). However, about half of the steps were not identified in the present corpus (Table 5.5). It is different from Pieketaleyee and Bazargani (2018) that found only 4 out of the 24 steps were absent in their corpus. It should be noticed that the step *Defining terms* appears in both Move 1 and Move 3, but their communicative functions are different. The one under Move 1 is concerned with the wide research field (Bunton, 2002), whereas the one under Move 3 is to offer the operational definitions of some terms used in the writer's own study. There were instances of defining terms found in two slide sets, which were presented under the title "Terminology", thus, they were regarded to belong to Move 3.

Table 5.5 Steps Identified in the 20 PSIs

	Steps	No. of PSIs	%	Status
Move 1	S1 Providing topic generalization/ background	14	70	Con.
	S2 Indicating centrality/importance of topic	5	25	Opt.
	S3 Defining terms	0	0	/
	S4 Reviewing previous research	4	20	Opt.

Cont.

	Steps	No. of PSIs	%	Status
Move 2	S1 Indicating gaps in previous research	11	55	Opt.
	S2 Question-raising	0	0	/
	S3 Counter-claiming	0	0	/
	S4 Continuing/extending a tradition	0	0	/
	S5 Indicating a problem/need	0	0	/
Move 3	S1 Indicating purposes/aims/objectives	18	90	Con.
	S2 Indicating scope of research	1	5	Opt.
	S3 Indicating chapter/section structure	3	15	Opt.
	S4 Indicating theoretical position	2	10	Opt.
	S5 Announcing research/work carried out	2	10	Opt.
	S6 Describing parameters of research	0	0	/
	S7 Stating research questions/hypotheses	15	75	Con.
	S8 Defining terms	2	10	Opt.
	S9 Indicating research method	1	5	Opt.
	S10 Indicating findings/results	0	0	/
	S11 Indicating models proposed	0	0	/
	S12 Indicating applications	0	0	/
	S13 Indicating value or significance	8	40	Opt.
	S14 Providing justification	0	0	/
	S15 Indicating thesis structure	3	15	Opt.

(*Note: Obl.=obligatory, Con.=conventional, Opt.=optional*)

Among all the steps found in the PSIs, S1 *Indicating purposes/aims/objectives* of Move 3 had the highest frequency (90%). It suggests that the writers considered the research objectives of their own research the most significant when introducing their study during the thesis defense. Other frequently utilized steps are S7 *Stating research questions/hypotheses* (75%) of Move 3 and S1 *Providing topic generalization/ background* (70%) of Move 1. These three steps are the only conventional steps in the PSIs in the present corpus. No obligatory steps were identified. It indicates that there is no convention for students to produce the presentation slides, thus, the steps in the slide sets are varied among the writers.

In the realization of Move 1, S1 *Providing topic generalization/background* was most frequently employed, which is similar to the result of Pieketaleyee and Bazargani (2018). It indicates that background information is conventional to be presented in the thesis defense. Moreover, few of the slide sets contained S2 *Indicating centrality/ importance* of topic (25%) and S4 *Reviewing previous research* (20%), which reveals that the content related to these two steps is not necessary to be demonstrated again in the slides when facing a live audience. Besides, no S3 *Defining terms* step was found in the present subcorpus. It is understandable that the target audience, i.e., the committee members, is experts who already have knowledge about the research field, so there is no need to waste the limited presentation time on presenting this aspect.

Move 2 was optional in the present study, while when it was utilized, only S1 *Indicating gaps in previous research* was employed to realize it. In other words, all the PSIs which had Move 2 only employed S1 to indicate the niche. The other four steps were not identified in the realization of Move 2. This is in disagreement with the results of Pieketaleyee and Bazargani (2018) that S5 *Indicating a problem/need* was found in all the presentations to be an obligatory step, meanwhile, S2 *Question-raising* and S3 *Counter-claiming* were also found in their corpus. The interviews with the writers reveal that they considered the research gap as the strongest motivation for their research because it underscores the value of their research. As for the research need, some of the writers stated that where there is a research gap, there is a research need, as indicated by one of the student informants below. Hence, the need is not necessary to be demonstrated explicitly and it can be delivered orally during the presentation.

> SS2: *The research gap indicates a research need at the same time. Moreover, the research gap can explicitly manifest the value of my study, thus, I prefer to present it in the slides.*

Among the 15 steps under Move 3, only two steps, S1 *Indicating purposes/aims/ objectives* and S7 *Stating research questions/hypotheses*, were found with a high frequency, 90% and 75%, respectively, which reveals that they were conventional steps. This result suggests that during the presentation, it is better to include the research aims and research questions in the slides. A closer examination of the presence of research questions showed that those without research questions in the introductory part placed them in the later part of the presentations, such as in the Methodology part, except one writer who did not explicitly state the research questions in the slides. Besides these two steps, eight out of the 20 PSIs (40%) employed S13 *Indicating value or significance*, but it was just an optional step in the present subcorpus. However, it was a conventional step with a frequency of 94% in Pieketaleyee and Bazargani (2018). This may be explained that the presentation time for the writers in the current research is limited (within 15 minutes), while the time is longer in Pieketaleyee and Bazargani (2018) because the writers were given 15 to 25 minutes. Thus, the writers in the present subcorpus tended to give less attention to the research significance compared with the research objectives and questions which implicitly indicated the research values.

Furthermore, under Move 3, few PSIs included S8 *Defining terms* (10%) and S15 *Indicating thesis structure* (15%). It should be mentioned that two of the three PSIs had a single slide demonstrating the chapter headings of the thesis rather than the outline for the presentation, thus both were coded as *Indicating thesis structure*. In addition, no S12 *Indicating applications* step was identified. Nevertheless, these three steps were conventional in the corpus of Pieketaleyee and Bazargani (2018) which was produced by Iranian M.A. students. It seems that writers in the present discourse community presented less content in the Introduction slides than their Iranian counterparts. It may be because the writers in the current study mainly produced the slides based on their own understanding and observation of the seniors, whereas the Iranian writers might have a convention to conform to present their thesis in the defense session.

A noteworthy finding was that S3 *Indicating chapter/section structure* was identified in four PSIs. These four PSIs utilized a single slide as a boundary device to reveal the outline of the introductory part of the slides. For example, as shown in Figure 5.1, "Introduction" was placed in the middle of a single slide to signal the beginning of presenting the related content. Under the word "Introduction" "Research Background" "Research Objectives", and "Research Questions" were listed in a smaller font size to indicate the outline of this part, which guided the audience about the structure of this part. It suggests that in the present subcorpus, a single slide as a boundary device is preferred when indicating the chapter structure in the slide sets.

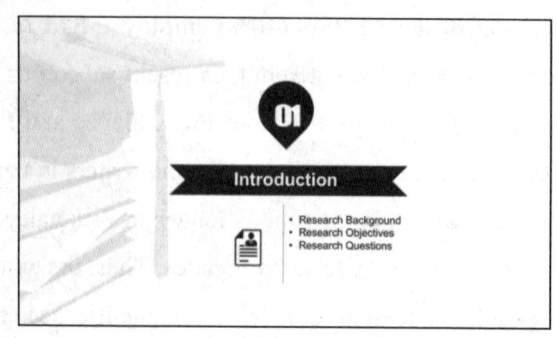

Figure 5.1   Example of the Step *Indicating Chapter/Section Structure* (PSI19_S3)

As for the step patterns, the majority of the slide sets only had one step within Move 1 and Move 3. More steps were found under Move 3. However, only one step sequence was identified under Move 3 in more than half of the PSIs (60%), that is S1-S7, which indicated that when these two steps were utilized, S1 *Indicating purposes/aims/objectives* always preceded S7 *Stating research questions/hypotheses*.

5.3   Findings on the Literature Review Sections

5.3.1   Overall Structure

As indicated in *Section 3.4.3*, only 8 out of the 20 thesis defense presentation slide sets included a section of Literature Review (PSLr). This result is inconsistent with the study of Pieketaleyee and Bazargani (2018) in which all the 50 thesis defense presentation slide sets composed by Iranian M.A. students had the Literature Review sections. The difference may be caused by the cultural variation or the various conventions in different institutions. It demonstrates that this section is optional to be included in the thesis defense presentation slides in the present discourse community.

There were a total of 25 slides, averaging around three slides per PSLr. The number of slides in every PSLr varied largely, ranging from one to six. The examination of the slide headings found that all PSLrs but one utilized the same chapter title "Literature Review" as the slide heading to indicate the content of this chapter. One PSLr contained only one slide and was entitled "Review of Previous Researches".

These same or similar section headings as those in the original theses made it clear to extract this section out of other sections. No other generic slide headings were found in the present subcorpus.

The seven PSLrs which had the heading "Literature Review" utilized it in different ways. Firstly, three PSLrs employed "Literature Review" as the slide heading for every slide in the related slide sets, one of which added the keyword of the theme that indicated the content in that particular slide, as demonstrated in Figure 5.2 below. Secondly, as shown in Figure 5.3 below, the heading "Literature Review" was adopted as a boundary device in two PSLrs, one of which did not have additional slide headings in the following slides while the other one had other specific slide headings in the remaining slides, such as "Previous Studies on Language Attitude" and "Related Theories". Finally, two PSLr only had the slide heading in the first slide of the slide set, whereas the other slides only demonstrated the content without a slide heading.

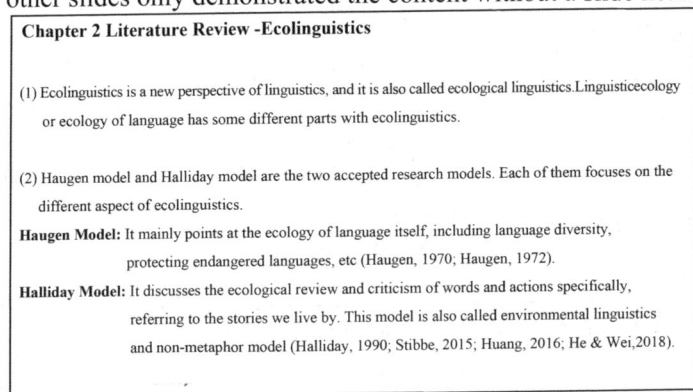

Chapter 2 Literature Review -Ecolinguistics

(1) Ecolinguistics is a new perspective of linguistics, and it is also called ecological linguistics.Linguisticecology or ecology of language has some different parts with ecolinguistics.

(2) Haugen model and Halliday model are the two accepted research models. Each of them focuses on the different aspect of ecolinguistics.

Haugen Model: It mainly points at the ecology of language itself, including language diversity, protecting endangered languages, etc (Haugen, 1970; Haugen, 1972).

Halliday Model: It discusses the ecological review and criticism of words and actions specifically, referring to the stories we live by. This model is also called environmental linguistics and non-metaphor model (Halliday, 1990; Stibbe, 2015; Huang, 2016; He & Wei,2018).

Figure 5.2   Example of Adding a Keyword to the Slide Heading (PSLr13)

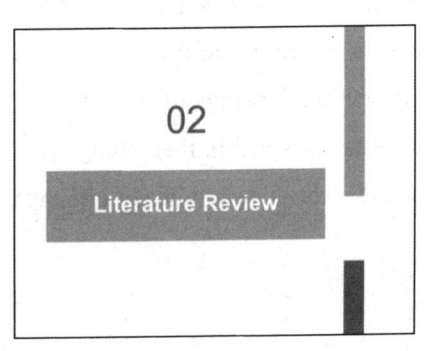

Figure 5.3   Example of Using Heading as a Boundary Device (PSLr08)

5.3.2 Moves

The same framework for analyzing the thesis LR proposed by Chen and Kuo (2012) was adopted to identify the moves and steps of the eight PSLrs. It should be pointed out that in the original thesis LRs, the Introduction-Body-Conclusion configuration was identified, and the move/step was analyzed in each thematic unit in the Body parts. Nonetheless, in the corresponding PSLrs, it was hard to find out the thematic units in a clearly demonstrated manner like in the thesis. Following Pieketaleyee and Bazargani (2018), the present study therefore regarded the PSLr as a whole unit, and the Introduction as well as the Conclusion as two moves. Table 5.6 below presents the detailed results of the moves found in the eight PSLrs.

Table 5.6 Moves Identified in the 8 PSLrs

Move	Occurrence	No. of PSLrs	%	Status
Introduction	5	5	62.5	Con.
Move 1 Establishing one part of the territory of one's own research	11	5	62.5	Con.
Move 2 Creating a research niche	4	3	37.5	Opt.
Move 3 Occupying the research niche	5	4	50	Opt.
Conclusion	0	0	0	/

(*Note: Con.=Conventional, Opt.=Optional*)

The Introduction move was observed in five out of the eight PSLrs with a frequency of 62.5%, which suggests it was a conventional move in the present subcorpus. Among these five PSLrs, three PSLrs only provided the outline of the Literature Review, i.e., the section headings of this chapter from the original thesis, to indicate the themes had been reviewed in their study. The Introduction move in the other two PSLrs was observed in the slide serving as a boundary device, as displayed in Figure 5.4 below.

> **Literature Review**
> - Previous Studies onLanguage Attitude
> - Previous Studies on Attitude and Language Use
> - Related Theories
> - Theoretical Framework

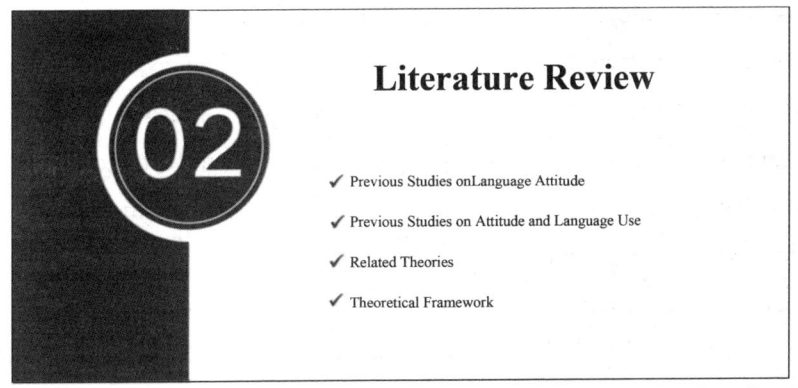

Figure 5.4 Example of the Introduction Move Found at the Boundary Device in the Slide

The finding of *Introduction* being conventional is not consistent with that of Pieketaleyee and Bazargani (2018) in which this move was merely identified in 20% of their corpus. The difference could be ascribed to the corpus size as the current study only has eight PSLrs while there were 50 PowerPoint presentations in Pieketaleyee and Bazargani's (2018) study. Another possible explanation could be that the writers deemed indicating the organization or the themes being reviewed in their studies was essential for the audience to clearly understand the content of this section. The interviews with the two supervisor informants, who were the target audience of the thesis defense presentation slides, found different perspectives related to this advance introduction of the section structure. One of the informants regarded that it was not necessary to provide the section outline except for the whole outline at the beginning of the presentation. The other informant shared an opinion that it was good to have this section introduction since it made the organization clearer for the audience to have an advance overview and comprehension of this section. These insights demonstrate that the audience have different opinions on the section introduction. Further studies, thus, are needed to investigate if the advance introduction of the section is necessary to be provided in the slides from the audience's perspective.

Furthermore, Move 1 *Establishing one part of the territory* was identified to be conventional with a frequency of 62.5%. Then, Move 2 and Move 3 were optional with a frequency of 37.5% and 50%, respectively. These results are in congruence with those in Pieketaleyee and Bazargani (2018). It can be inferred that the writers prefer to establish the territory rather than to create a niche and occupy the niche when demonstrating the literature review content in the slides. It can be understandable that creating a niche and occupying the niche were found to be optional since these two moves might be also found in other sections, such as the Introduction section, Theoretical Framework section, and the Methodology section.

In addition, the *Conclusion* move, which aims to provide a summary of the themes being reviewed, was found absent in the present subcorpus. This result is similar to Pieketaleyee and Bazargani (2018) in which this move was optional with a pretty low frequency of 15%. This could be attributed to the characteristic of the presentation slide genre that is delivered to a live audience with a commentary in which the writers could briefly conclude what had been just reviewed. Moreover, the Literature Review section in the thesis defense presentation slides was rather brief and succinct, thus, it is not necessary to provide a summary of the content in around three slides. Table 5.7 presents the move sequences of the 8 PSLrs.

Table 5.7　Move Sequences of the 8 PSLrs

Text	Move sequence	Text	Move sequence
PSLr03	Introduction	PSLr10	Introduction
PSLr07	M1-M3	PSLr12	Introduction-M1-M2-M3
PSLr08	Introduction	PSLr13	M1-M3-M1-M3-M1
PSLr09	M1-M2-M1-M3	PSLr16	Introduction-M1-M2-M1-M2-M1

In terms of the move pattern, no frequently employed move sequence was identified. As indicated in Table 5.7 above, three PSLrs merely contained the *Introduction* move to demonstrate what themes had been reviewed in the original theses. Additionally, only two PSLrs, i.e., PSLr07 and PSLr12, had a linear move sequence. The remaining three PSLrs were observed to use Move 1, Move 2, or Move 3 cyclically. The investigation of the move sequence reveals that no convention has been established to present the Literature Review section in the thesis defense presentation slides in the present discourse community. It could be because this section is not considered to be compulsory to be presented during the defense session. It is also probably because the content of this section is not what the audience expected, thus, only a few writers included it in the presentation. However, the interviews with the supervisors demonstrate that they held a view that this Literature Review section is essential to be provided in the slides since it is the place in which the writers situated their research. Nevertheless, they also mentioned that the writers need to summarize or synthesize the most influential pertinent studies rather than listing every reference in the slides, as mentioned by one of the supervisor informants below.

> SP1: *The Literature Review section is necessary to be provided in the student's slides to make their thesis being completely presented. However, the student needs to synthesize what have been conducted before and present the most related ones rather than listing all the references.*

These results indicate that there is an information gap between the supervisors and the students in terms of what should be included in the thesis defense presentation slides. Therefore, further research is necessary to probe more perspectives from the audience in order to assist the students to compose the thesis defense presentation slides more efficiently.

5.3.3 Steps

Except for the *Introduction* move and the *Conclusion* move, the other three moves contained step options. Table 5.8 provides the results of the steps under Move 1 *Establishing one part of the territory*. It can be seen that S1 was observed in five PSLrs (62.5%), indicating it was a conventional step. This result accords with that of Pieketaleyee and Bazargani (2018), so it appears that providing theoretical information or knowledge is important for the writers to establish the territory in this particular genre.

Table 5.8 Steps of Move 1 Identified in the 8 PSLrs

Step	Occurrence	No. of PSLrs	%	Status
S1 Surveying the non-research-related phenomena or knowledge claim	7	5	62.5	Con.
S2 Claiming centrality	0	0	0	/
S3 Surveying the research-related phenomena	4	3	37.5	Opt.

(*Note: Con.=Conventional, Opt.=Optional*)

Moreover, S2 *Claiming centrality* was not identified in the present subcorpus, which is in disagreement with Pieketaleyee and Bazargani's (2018) study in which S2 had a frequency of 75% in their corpus. It seems that the writers in the current discourse community had a less tendency to claim the importance of the theme. It might be because the writers think it is not vital to be explicitly presented in the slides giving their limited space since it can be delivered by the commentary. Besides, the centrality of the theme could have already been claimed in the preceding Introduction section of the slides.

Furthermore, S3 *Surveying the research-related phenomena* was found to be optional with a frequency of 37.5%, which is far less than that of Pieketaleyee and Bazargani (2018) in which S3 was conventional with a frequency of 80%. This difference may be attributed to the varied presentation time given to the students. Only 15 minutes at maximum were assigned to each student in the current context, whereas 15 to 25 minutes were provided by the writers in Pieketaleyee and Bazargani's (2018) study. Therefore, the specific studies conducted previously which could occupy a certain amount of time to describe were not popularly presented in the present subcopus.

To sum up, to realize Move 1 in the slides, the writers preferred to show their familiarity with the theories or concepts rather than summarize the related findings from previous studies. Additionally, merely a few instances of Move 1 were identified in this subcorpus, thus, no step pattern under Move 1 was observed.

In terms of the steps for the realization of Move 2 *Creating a research niche* that only had three instances, merely S2 and S5 were identified with a frequency of 37.5% and 12.5%, respectively, as indicated in Table 5.9 below. It reveals that when presenting the content to create a research niche, the writers tended to state the gap found in the field. The other four steps were absent in the present subcorpus, which might be ascribed to the small size of the subcorpus. It can be drawn that all the steps were optional, which is similar to the findings of Pieketaleyee and Bazargani (2018). Moreover, these steps were found to be used separately rather than in combination, thus, no step pattern under Move 2 was identified.

Table 5.9 Steps of Move 2 Identified in the 8 PSLrs

Step	Occurrence	No. of PSLrs	%	Status
S1 Counter-claiming	0	0	0	/
S2 Gap-indicating	3	3	37.5	Opt.
S3 Asserting confirmative claims	0	0	0	/
S4 Asserting the relevancy of the surveyed claims	0	0	0	/
S5 Abstracting or synthesizing knowledge claims	1	1	12.5	Opt.
S6 Concluding a part of	0	0	0	/

(*Note: Opt.=Optional*)

As for the steps employed to realize Move 3 *Occupying the research niche*, Table 5.10 lists the detailed results. It was found that S1 was absent, and the remaining three steps were used with a relatively low frequency of 25%, 12.5%, and 12.5%, respectively. Similar to Pieketaleyee and Bazargani (2018), all the steps were observed to be optional. In addition, no step pattern under Move 3 was identified as only five instances of Move 3 were found among which the step was used separately.

Table 5.10 Steps of Move 3 Identified in the 8 PSLrs

Step	Occurrence	No. of PSLrs	%	Status
S1 Indicating research aims, focuses, research questions or hypotheses	0	0	0	/
S2 Indicating theoretical positions/theoretical framework	2	2	25.0	Opt.
S3 Indicating research design/processes	1	1	12.5	Opt.
S4 Interpreting terminology used in the thesis	2	1	12.5	Opt.

(*Note: Opt.=Optional*)

In a nutshell, among the 13 steps of these three moves, all but one was optional in the present subcorpus. Moreover, only one step was conventional. In addition, no fixed step pattern was identified to provide the Literature Review content in the slides. It can be inferred that the Literature Review section received less attention in the present discourse community, so no convention or norm has been established yet.

5.4 Findings on the Theoretical Framework Sections

5.4.1 Overall Structure

Only 8 out of the 20 thesis defense presentation slide sets contained a Theoretical Framework section (PSTf) which is a place where the writers provide the pertinent theories or knowledge claims and then establish the theoretical framework for their own research accordingly. This indicates that providing information related to the theoretical framework is not the main communicative purpose during the defense session. It is in consonance with Hu and Liu's (2018) study of three-minute thesis presentations, a similar genre of thesis defense presentation, in which *Framework*, aiming to demonstrate a theoretical position or framework serving as a basis for the writer's research, was an optional move.

These 8 PSTfs consisted of 19 slides in total, ranging from one to four slides with an average of two slides per PSTf. In terms of the slide headings, it was found that all but one of the PSTfs employed "Theoretical Framework" as the slide heading. To be specific, five PSTfs had "Theoretical Framework" as the heading for every slide in this section. One PSTf used the same slide heading but added a concrete theme as a subheading, for example, "Chapter 3 Theoretical Framework—Analytical Model of EDA in This Thesis" in PSTf13. Moreover, one PSTf had this heading in a single slide as a boundary device, then followed by two slides entitled "Theoretical Framework of the Present Study" and "Classification of Chinese Borrowings", respectively. The rest employed a similar slide heading, i.e., "Theoretical Foundation", as a boundary device as well, followed by three slides without a heading.

5.4.2 Moves

Similar to the move/step identification in the Theoretical Framework chapters in the original theses, the framework for Literature Review proposed by Chen and Kuo (2012) was adopted to analyze the Theoretical Framework sections in the slides.

Furthermore, according to Kwan (2006), the Literature Review chapter was configured as Introduction-Body-Conclusion, with several thematic units in the Body part. Nevertheless, the same as the investigation of the Theoretical Framework chapter in the original thesis, this section in the slides was considered as a whole thematic unit and thus the identification of its moves and steps was conducted accordingly.

During the data coding process, it was challenging to identify the communicative function of certain slides since no linguistic signal was provided in the slides. To illustrate, as indicated in Figure 5.5 below, the content in the slide could function as an introduction to the theory or as an indication of the theoretical framework adopted by that study. To solve this uncertainty, the present researcher either identified the original text in the thesis to see which move it belongs to or consulted the actual writer about its real communicative function.

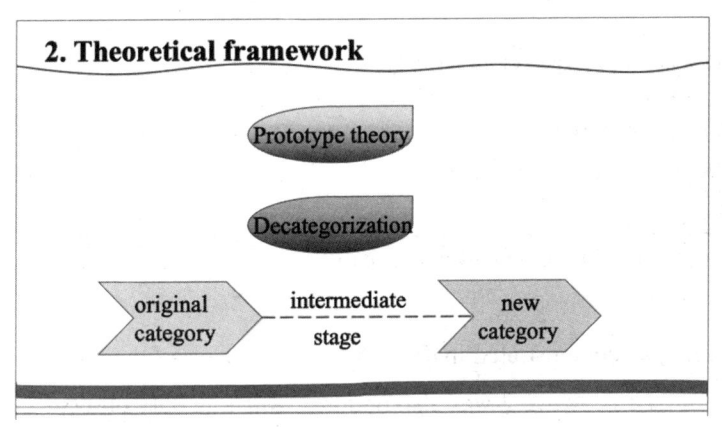

Figure 5.5   Example of Uncertainty of the Move Identification (PSTf01_S1)

Table 5.11 below provides the moves observed in the present subcorpus. It was interesting that one instance of *Introduction* move was identified, as displayed in Figure 5.6 below. This writer informed us what was to be presented in the following slides in this section in a smaller font under the section heading. Nonetheless, it might not be expected by the audience since merely two slides were included in this section and it could be easy for the audience to comprehend already.

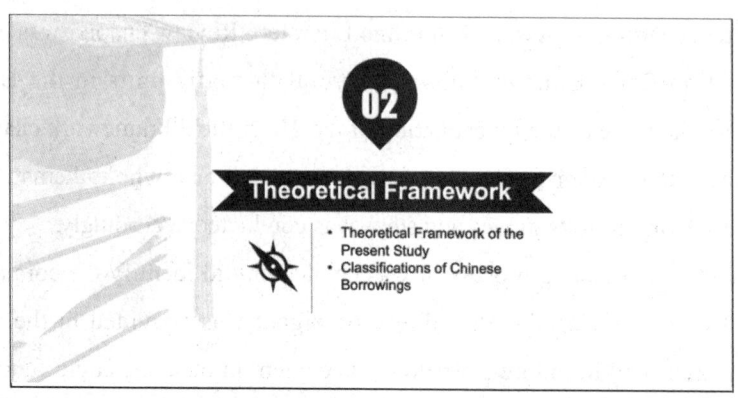

Figure 5.6 Example of Introduction Move in the Slide (PSTf19_S1)

Table 5.11 Moves Identified in the 8 PSTfs

Move	Occurrence	No. of PSTfs	%	Status
Introduction	1	1	12.5	Opt.
Move 1 Establishing one part of the territory of one's own research	3	3	37.5	Opt.
Move 2 Creating a research niche	1	1	12.5	Opt.
Move 3 Occupying the research niche	9	8	100	Obl.
Conclusion	0	0	0	/

(*Note: Opt.=Optional, Obl.=Obligatory*)

In addition, as demonstrated in Table 5.11, Move 1 was found to be optional with a frequency of 37.5%. Move 2 was also optional as it was only observed in one PSTf. Moreover, Move 3 was identified in all the PSTfs, indicating it was an obligatory move. The results show that the predominant communicative purpose of this Theoretical Framework section in the slides was to announce one's own study and reveal how the writer occupied the research niche.

Furthermore, in line with what was found in the LR section in the slides, the *Conclusion* move was absent in the present subcorpus, which is understandable since only around two slides were included in this section. It can be inferred that *Conclusion* is not appropriate to be provided if the content is brief and succinct in the slides.

In terms of the move pattern, four PSTfs contained more than one move, but all of them were structured differently. Therefore, no frequently adopted move pattern was identified to demonstrate the Theoretical Framework section in the slides.

5.4.3 Steps

Among the 13 steps under Move 1 to Move 3, only three steps were identified in this subcorpus, thus, the current researcher listed all the three steps in one table rather than provided them separately according to each move. As shown in Table 5.12, one step under each move was observed.

Table 5.12 Steps Identified in the 8 PSTfs

Step	Occurrence	No. of PSTfs	%	Status
M1S1 Surveying the non-research-related phenomena	3	3	37.5	Opt.
M2S1 Counter-claiming	1	1	12.5	Opt.
M3S2 Indicating theoretical position/theoretical framework	9	8	100	Obl.

(*Note: Opt.=Optional, Obl.=Obligatory*)

In the instances of Move 1 *Establishing the territory*, as revealed in Table 5.12, only S1 *Surveying the non-research-related phenomena* was identified with a rather low frequency of 37.5%, giving it the optional status in the subcorpus. The other two steps under Move 1, i.e., *Claiming centrality* and *Surveying the research-related phenomena*, were not found in the slides, which suggests that they were not the communicative functions of the PSTfs.

As for the instance of Move 2 *Creating a research niche*, it was realized by S1 *Counter-claiming* and it was optional as only one instance was observed. This result reveals that Move 2 and its related steps were not expected by the audience in this Theoretical Framework section. It could be explained that the research niche may be provided in the Literature Review section already.

In terms of the instances of Move 3 *Occupying the research niche*, only S2 *Indicating theoretical position/theoretical framework* was identified, which occurred in all the eight PSTfs, thus the obligatory status. This finding reveals that in the Theoretical Framework sections, indicating the framework that serves as a theoretical basis of the study is an essential option to occupy the research niche. Therefore, it is suggested that the writers need to explicitly provide the theoretical framework they adopted for their study when they include a Theoretical Framework section in the slides.

To conclude, only one step, i.e., *Indicating theoretical position/theoretical framework* was found obligatory in this subcorpus, whereas the remaining steps were optional with a far lower frequency. It demonstrates that the main communicative purpose of this section in the slides is to show the theoretical framework adopted by the writers to conduct their study, as revealed by the section heading "Theoretical Framework".

5.5 Findings on the Methodology Sections

5.5.1 Overall Structure

In the pool of the 20 thesis defense presentation slide sets, 16 of them (80%) contained a Methodology section (PSM), which is in congruence with the finding of Hu and Liu's (2018) study on three-minute thesis presentation that the *Methods* move was identified in around 83 % of the presentations. The result reveals that when presenting a thesis to an audience for a defense presentation, how the research was conducted is a vital part to be provided.

Among these 16 PSMs, it was found that one PSM (PSM11) mixed a part of the Methodology section with the Results and Discussion section even if it had a single slide as a boundary device to indicate these two sections, thus, there was a certain overlap between these two sections, which makes it possess a parallel structure of PSM1-PSRD1-PSM2-PSRD2-PSM3-PSRD3. Therefore, the present researcher decided to report this case separately because its unique structure deserves to be elaborated in detail, which will be delivered in *Section 5.5.4* later. The findings of the remaining 15 PSMs are reported in this section.

These 15 PSMs contained 58 slides in total, averaging nearly four slides per PSM. The number of slides in each PSM varied widely from 1 to 11. From the examination of the slide headings, it was found that 10 PSMs clearly demonstrated the section boundary from other sections. Among them, eight PSMs had the section heading "Methodology", two of which were in a single slide serving as a boundary device. Moreover, two PSMs utilized "Research Methodology" instead. It should be mentioned that two PSMs used the section heading and the specific theme of the slide at the same time, such as "Methodology-Corpus Description" and "Chapter 4 Research Methodology-Data Description" in PSM03 and PSM13, respectively. The remaining five PSMs were not observed to have this section heading. Instead, they used specific slide heading merely indicating the content of that slide which can be inferred to belong to the Methodology section, such as "Data Collection" "Data analysis", and other slide headings related to methodology.

The slide headings employed in these 15 PSMs varied extensively. The most frequently used slide heading was "Data Collection" which was found in seven PSMs. Moreover, "Research Questions" was observed in three PSMs, and "Data Analysis" was identified in two PSMs. Other slide headings that were only utilized by a single PSM were not listed in the present study. From the results of the slide headings, it seems that the majority of the writers tended to inform the audience of the information related to the data collection in their studies.

5.5.2 Moves

Chen and Kuo's (2012) framework for thesis Methodology chapters was adopted to identify the moves and steps of the Methodology sections in the slides. Table 5.13 displays the results of the moves identified in the 15 PSMs that had a clear boundary. All the four moves in the framework were observed in the subcorpus. Move 1 was optional as only five out of the 15 PSMs utilized it. It is understandable since a small number of slides, i.e., only around four slides, were employed to provide this section.

Table 5.13 Moves Identified in the 15 PSMs

Move	Occurrence	No. of PSMs	%	Status
Move 1 Introducing the Method chapter	6	5	33.3	Opt.

Cont.

Move	Occurrence	No. of PSMs	%	Status
Move 2 Describing data collection method and procedure(s)	15	14	93.3	Con.
Move 3 Delineating methods of data analysis	5	5	33.3	Opt.
Move 4 Elucidating data analysis procedure(s)	9	9	60.0	Con.

(*Note: Opt.=Optional, Con.=Conventional*)

Furthermore, Move 2 *Describing data collection methods and procedure(s)* was found in almost all the PSMs, which indicates that it was a conventional move to demonstrate the Methodology section in the slides. This finding is in congruence with that of Atai and Talebzadeh's (2012) study on the conference presentation slides that 15 out of the 16 slide sets contained the move *Describing data collection procedure(s)* in their corpus. It can be drawn that information on how the data was collected is an essential part to be provided in the slides pertaining to the Methodology section of a research report.

Moreover, Move 3 *Delineating methods of data analysis* was observed to be optional in the present subcorpus with a frequency of 33.3%, whereas Move 4 *Elucidating data analysis procedure(s)* was conventional since it was identified in 60% of the PSMs. Both moves were related to data analysis, but the writers preferred to demonstrate the procedures rather than the methods they used to analyze the data. This could be explained that the data analysis methods were implied in the procedures of the data analysis, thus, given the limited time of the presentation, the writers tended to provide more about the data analysis procedures. This was confirmed by the interviews with the students who shared that the time was so limited that they preferred to provide the procedures which were more important and embodied the methods of the data analysis as well. The conventional status of Move 4 found in the present subcorpus is not in agreement with the study of another similar genre, i.e., conference presentation slides, by Atai and Talebzadeh (2012) who found that the move *Elucidating data analysis procedure(s)* was optional with a frequency of 43.75%. This difference may be explained that during the defense session, the students tended to manifest the data analysis procedures with the aim of showing the reliability of their results to the examiners. Thus, the data analysis procedures are suggested to be provided in the PSM to be more effective in the present discourse community.

In a nutshell, Move 1 and Move 3 were optional to be presented in the PSM in the slides, while Move 2 and Move 4 were conventional. These results show that the predominant communicative purposes of the PSM are to demonstrate the procedures of the data collection and data analysis during the thesis defense presentation.

In terms of the move pattern, this section was found to be structured linearly without moves being utilized cyclically, except for Move 2 which was observed twice in PSM16, as demonstrated in Table 5.14 below. However, the move sequence was not in the progression from Move 1 to Move 4 as suggested in the framework. To be specific, six PSMs only contained a single move, such as Move 2 alone in five PSMs and Move 4 alone in one PSM, respectively. In addition, merely two PSMs included all the four moves, i.e., PSM04 and PSM10, but the moves were not in the order from Move 1 to Move 4.

Table 5.14 Move Sequences in the 15 PSMs

Text	Move sequence	Text	Move sequence
PSM01	M2	PSM10	M1-M3-M2-M4
PSM02	M2-M4	PSM12	M2-M3
PSM03	M2	PSM13	M2-M4
PSM04	M2-M1-M3-M4	PSM14	M2
PSM05	M2	PSM15	M2-M4
PSM07	M2-M4-M3	PSM16	M1-M2-M1-M2-M3
PSM08	M1-M2-M4	PSM20	M4
PSM09	M1-M2-M4		

From the move sequence, two move patterns were identified. The move pattern of M2-M4 was observed in three PSMs. Additionally, M1-M2-M4 was found in two PSMs. Nevertheless, the frequencies of these two move patterns were rather low, indicating that no fixed convention was established to organize the Methodology section in the thesis defense presentation slides.

5.5.3 Steps

The steps found under Move 1 are provided in Table 5.15 below. It can be seen that all the three steps of Move1 were optional in the present subcorpus. S2 *Providing an overview of the study* was found in more instances than the other two steps. It was mainly employed to demonstrate the research questions of the writer's study. Move 1 was optional, and so did the steps under it. The results reveal that the section structure, the overview of the study, and the theory were not necessary to be provided in the slides related to the Methodology section during the defense. This section was relatively short; hence, its structure was clear. In addition, the overview of the study and the theory may be already provided in the preceding Introduction section or the Theoretical Framework section.

Table 5.15 Steps of Move 1 Identified in the 15 PSMs

Step	Occurrence	No. of PSMs	%	Status
S1 Indicating chapter/section structure	1	1	6.7	Opt.
S2 Providing an overview of the study	4	4	26.7	Opt.
S3 Indicating theory/approach	1	1	6.7	Opt.

(*Note: Opt.=Optional*)

Moreover, the steps under Move 2 are listed in Table 5.16, from which it can be seen that S1 was found to be conventional as it occurred in 11 out of the 15 PSMs. This finding is in line with that found in the conference presentation slides in Atai and Talebzadeh's (2012) study in which *Describing the sample* was identified in 15 of the 16 conference presentation slide sets (93.75%), so it was conventional as well. It indicates that the information about the sample is significant when describing the method and procedures of the data collection.

Table 5.16 Steps of Move 2 Identified in the 15 PSMs

Step	Occurrence	No. of PSMs	%	Status
S1 Describing the sample	11	11	73.3	Con.
S2 Describing methods and steps in data collection	10	9	60.0	Con.
S3 Justifying data collection procedure(s)	0	0	0	/

(*Note: Con.=Conventional*)

Furthermore, S2 was identified in nine PSMs (60%), thus, it was conventional in the present subcorpus. This result suggests that the data collection steps or methods were what was expected by the audience in the current discourse community. Hence, it is suggested to plainly present the data collection procedures in the slides to increase the comprehension of the audience.

In addition, S3 *Justifying data collection procedure(s)* was found to be absent in these PSMs. The reason might be that the justification of the procedures could be delivered orally and simultaneously when presenting the content of S2 *Describing methods and steps in data collection*, thus, it was not necessary to be provided in the slide on account of the limited presentation time and the limited space of a single slide.

The steps of Move 2 were found to be employed in combinations in some instances. To illustrate, the step pattern of S1-S2 was identified in seven PSMs (46.7%). However, since the frequency of this step pattern was relatively low, it demonstrates that the realization of Move 2 was varied and there was no established way to organize it in the present discourse community

As for the steps under Move 3 which was found to be optional in the present subcorpus, all of them were identified to be optional in the 15 PSMs, as shown in Table 5.17 below. To be specific, S1 and S2 were each found in two PSMs, while S3 was only observed in one PSM and S4 was absent. The far lower frequency of S3 in the present subcorpus is contrary to the finding of Atai and Talebzadeh (2012) that *Explaining methods of measuring variables*, a similar step to S3 was identified in 13 out of the 16 conference presentation slide sets (81.25%), indicating this step was conventional in their corpus. This difference may be attributed to the fact that most of the studies in the current corpus were corpus-based studies rather than experimental ones that involved the measurement of the variables. It can be inferred that the research approach or research design of the study exerts an influence on the selection of the steps, thus, future studies on the genre analysis of the thesis defense presentation slides that are based on different research approaches are suggested.

Table 5.17 Steps of Move 3 Identified in the 15 PSMs

Step	Occurrence	No. of PSMs	%	Status
S1 Presenting an overview of the design	2	2	13.3	Opt.
S2 Explaining specific method(s) of data analysis	2	2	13.3	Opt.
S3 Explaining variables and variable measurement	1	1	6.7	Opt.
S4 Justifying the methods of measuring variables or data analysis	0	0	0	/

(*Note: Opt.=Optional*)

As for the steps under Move 4 *Elucidating data analysis procedure(s)*, only one step among its three steps in the framework was identified in the present subcorpus. As displayed in Table 5.18, S1 *Relating data analysis procedure(s)* was found to be conventional with a frequency of 60%. The other two steps were not identified in these PSMs. It reveals that to realize Move 4 in the slides, the steps of data analysis are the most vital information that needs to be provided.

Table 5.18 Steps of Move 4 Identified in the 15 PSMs

Step	Occurrence	No. of PSMs	%	Status
S1 Relating (or recounting) data analysis procedure(s)	9	9	60	Con.
S2 Justifying the data analysis procedure(s)	0	0	0	/
S3 Previewing results	0	0	0	/

(*Note: Con.=Conventional*)

To summarize, among the 13 steps in the framework, no compulsory step was identified in the PSMs. Nevertheless, three steps were found to be conventional, i.e., *Describing the sample, Describing methods and steps in data collection*, and *Relating data analysis procedures*, which, in turn, imply the main communicative purposes of the PSM. The remaining steps were all optional.

5.6 Findings on the Integrated Results and Discussion Sections

5.6.1 Overall Structure

In the 20 thesis defense presentation slide sets, all of them were observed to have an integrated Results and Discussion section (PSRD). Nonetheless, as stated in *Section 5.4.1*, one thesis defense presentation slide set (PS11) had a recurrent structure of PSM-PSRD, thus, it will be reported separately in *Section 5.5.4* later. Hence, the following texts report the results from the 19 ordinary PSRDs first.

The categorization of this integrated Results and Discussion (RD) section was found to be challenging since the writers mixed some contents drawn from the RD chapter and the Conclusion chapter in the slides. As Yang and Allison (2003) claimed that the Results, Discussion, and Conclusion in research articles can overlap, it was found that certain parts of the Conclusion chapter overlapped with a RD chapter in the present subcorpus as these two chapters both have the communicative function of summarizing the results even though they have other particular communicative functions. This overlap was reflected in the production of the RD section in the thesis defense presentation slides. The Conclusion chapter of the original thesis had a section titled "Major Findings" to summarize and highlight the main results of the study. This section was found to be relocated from the Conclusion section and was combined with the RD section in some instances, such as in PSRD09 and PSRD16. Thus, it was difficult to decide to which section of the slides the content from "Major Findings" in the original thesis belongs. After a closer examination of all the slide sets in the corpus and the consultation with several writers, it was decided to classify the content from the Major Findings to the RD section if there is a Conclusion section with a clear boundary in the end when Results and Major Findings are combined. It will be categorized as the Conclusion section if it is put in the last part of the slide set and no other contents from the Conclusion chapter in the original thesis are observed at the end of the slide set.

The total number of slides in these 19 PSRDs was 205, averaging around 11 slides per PSRD. The number of slides in each PSRD varied considerably, ranging from 3 slides to 25 slides, which was caused by the number of contents the writers selected to display in the slides.

The examination of the slide headings found that six PSRDs utilized "Results and Discussion" to start this section or across the slides in the whole section. Moreover, "Analysis and Discussion" "Results and Major Findings", and "Major Findings" were observed in two PSRDs, respectively. Other generic slide headings, such as "Findings" and "Analyses", were also found in the present subcorpus.

5.6.2 Moves

The combined framework for the integrated Results and Discussion chapter in the thesis, which was adapted from Chen and Kuo (2012), was adopted to identify the moves and steps employed in the 19 PSRDs. Table 5.19 displays the results of the moves observed in the present subcorpus. It can be seen that no obligatory move was found in the PSRDs. Move 1 had 30 instances in these 19 PSRDs, which demonstrates that it was employed recursively by some writers, while it was only adopted in 12 PSRDs, indicating it was a conventional move. The writers provided certain preparatory information in this move for the audience to facilitate the comprehension of the results of their study. This result is not in line with that of Atai and Talebzadeh's (2012) study on the conference presentation slides in which the move *Preparatory Information* was only found in 3 out of the 16 slide sets in their corpus, thus it was optional. The difference may be caused by the different writers of these two genres, as the M.A. students in the present subcorpus were less experienced than the researchers in their corpus. It seems that the writers who were less experienced, i.e., the M.A. students, tended to demonstrate more preparatory information in the slides.

Table 5.19 Moves Identified in the 19 PSRDs

Move	Occurrence	No. of PSRDs	%	Status
Move 1 Introducing the Results-Discussion chapter	30	12	63.2	Con.
Move 2 Reporting results	38	17	89.5	Con.
Move 3 Commenting on results	3	2	10.5	Opt.
Move 4 Summarizing results	4	4	21.1	Opt.
Move 5 Summarizing the study	0	0	0	/
Move 6 Evaluating the study	0	0	0	/

Cont.

Move	Occurrence	No. of PSRDs	%	Status
Move 7 Deductions from the study	0	0	0	/

(*Note: Con.=Conventional, Opt.=Optional*)

Furthermore, Move 2 *Reporting results* was identified in the majority of the PSRDs with a high frequency of 89.5%, thus, it was conventional. This result is similar to the finding of Atai and Talebzadeh (2012) that the move *Reporting results* was obligatory in the Results section of the conference presentation slides. It reveals that presenting the main results is an essential component when composing a PSRD.

In addition, Move 3 *Commenting on results* was identified as an optional move in the present subcorpus with a far lower frequency of 10.5%, which is in agreement with Atai and Talebzadeh (2012) who found *Commenting on results* optional in the Results section conference presentation slides. It is interesting that this move, the main communicative purpose in a RA Discussion section as claimed by Yang and Allison (2003), was found considerably less than Move 2 *Reporting results*, which is the main communicative function of a Results section, in the PSRD whose contents were from the combined Results and Discussion chapters in the original theses. It can be assumed that Move 2 and Move 3 have a similar frequency in a PSRD, however, the slides tend to present Move 2 much more than Move 3, which makes this section more like a Results section rather than a Results and Discussion section. It supports the claim of Atai and Talebzadeh (2012) that writers in Applied Linguistics have less tendency to assign their restricted time and space of presentations to Discussion.

Moreover, Move 4 *Summarizing results* was found in four PSRDs (21.1%), indicating it was an optional move in the present subcorpus, which reveals that making a summary of the results presented in the preceding slides was not preferred by the writers in the current discourse community. Hence, summarizing the results in the production of a PSRD is not suggested.

The last three moves, i.e., *Summarizing the study, Evaluation the study*, and *Deductions from the study*, were not identified in the PSRDs, which shows that these three moves are not the communicative functions of a PSRD. A possible reason could be that they are preferred to be displayed in the Conclusion section since these three moves were identified in that section. Table 5.20 presents the move sequenves of the 19 PSRDs.

Table 5.20 Move Sequence of the 19 PSRDs

Text	Move sequence	Text	Move sequence
PSRD01	M1-M2-M1-M2-M1-M2-M1-M2	PSRD12	M2
PSRD02	M2-M4	PSRD13	M1
PSRD03	M2	PSRD14	M1-M2
PSRD04	M2-M1-M2-M4-M2	PSRD15	M2
PSRD05	M1-M2-M1-M2-M1-M2-M1-M2-M1-M2-M1-M2-M1	PSRD16	M2-M3-M2-M4
PSRD06	M1-M2-M1-M2-M1-M2-M1-M2	PSRD17	M2
PSRD07	M2-M3-M2-M1-M2-M1-M2-M3	PSRD18	M1-M2-M1-M2-M1-M2
PSRD08	M1	PSRD19	M1-M2
PSRD09	M2	PSRD20	M1-M2-M1-M2
PSRD10	M1-M2-M4-M1-M2		

In terms of the move pattern, as can be seen in Table 5.20, seven PSRDs only employed one move, thus no move sequence was observed among them. In the remaining 12 PSRDs that utilized more than one move, a move pattern of (M1-M2)n was identified in six of them, such as in PSRD01 and PSRD14. Nevertheless, this move pattern only had a low frequency of 31.6%. Hence, it appears that no convention has been established to compose the RD section in the slides in the present discourse community.

5.6.3 Steps

As demonstrated in the preceding section, only four moves, i.e., Moves 1, 2, 3, and 4, were identified in the present subcorpus. Moreover, there is no step option for Move 4 *Summarizing results*, thus, this section mainly reports the results of the steps under Move 1, Move 2, and Move 3.

As demonstrated in Table 5.21, all the three steps of Move 1 were identified in the PSRDs, however, they were all found to be optional. For S1 *Providing background information*, the writers usually utilized it to inform the audience of the research questions or the theoretical information that helped them understand the related results. It was identified in merely six PSRDs even if it had the highest occurrence of 19 instances. It indicates that S1 was used cyclically only by certain writers, so it seems that this step was not preferred or expected by the present discourse community since the audience, i.e., the examiners, are experts. Moreover, the optional status of S2 which shows the structure of the RD section was within expectation, given the limited presentation time. In addition, the low frequency of S3 *Indicating methods used or statistical procedure applied* was understandable since its related content could be presented in the Methodology section already and the writers tended not to repeat it in the RD section.

Table 5.21 Steps of Move 1 Identified in the 19 PSRDs

Step	Occurrence	No. of PSRDs	%	Status
S1 Providing background information	19	6	31.6	Opt.
S2 Indicating chapter purposes and/or structure	2	2	10.5	Opt.
S3 Indicating methods used or statistical procedure applied	9	7	36.8	Opt.

(*Note: Opt.=Optional*)

As for the steps under Move 2 *Reporting results*, only S2 *Reporting major findings* was identified with a high frequency of 89.5%, whereas the other step, S1 *Locating graphics*, was absent in the present subcorpus, as indicated in Table 5.22. It demonstrates that the realization of Move 2 predominantly relied on presenting the major findings. The absence of *Locating graphics* could be ascribed to the nature of the slides in which the graphics can be displayed clearly, and the commentary of the graphics is delivered orally simultaneously, thus, the guideline of the location of the graphics is not necessary to be shown in the slides.

Table 5.22 Steps of Move 2 Identified in the 19 PSRDs

Step	Occurrence	No. of PSRDs	%	Status
S1 Locating graphics	0	0	0	/
S2 Reporting major findings	38	17	89.5	Con.

(*Note: Con.=Conventional*)

As for the steps under Move 3 *Commenting on results*, as can be seen in Table 5.23, only one out of the four steps was observed, i.e., S1 *Interpreting results*. Nonetheless, S1 was optional since only two writers employed it. The results reveal that all the steps of Move 3, including Move 3 itself, were not necessary to be provided in the slides.

Table 5.23 Steps of Move 3 Identified in the 19 PSRDs

Step	Occurrence	No. of PSRDs	%	Status
S1 Interpreting results	3	2	10.5	Opt.
S2 Comparing results with literature	0	0	0	/
S3 Evaluating results	0	0	0	/
S4 Accounting for results	0	0	0	/

(*Note: Opt.=Optional*)

In terms of the step pattern, two step sequences were identified in more than one PSRD. To be specific, the step sequence of M1S1-M2S2 (*Providing background information* followed by *Reporting major findings*) was observed in six PSRDs (31.6%), and the step sequence of M1S3-M2S2 (*Indicating methods used or statistical procedure applied* followed by *Reporting major findings*) in five PSRDs (26.3%). The frequencies of these two step patterns were rather low, which implies that these step patterns are not common and thus the PSRD section was produced in various ways in the present discourse community.

5.6.4 A Special Case of PSMRD11

As indicated earlier in *Section 5.5.2*, PS11 had an overlap with the Methodology section and the Results and Discussion section(PSMRD), which was assigned as PSMRD11, thus, it was investigated separately in this section with the frameworks for the Methodology section and the integrated Results and Discussion section, respectively.

PS11 divided its content into three main parts "Why" "How" and "What" which corresponded to the Introduction, Methodology, and Results and Discussion chapters in the thesis. However, a closer examination of the Methodology section found that the last slide was connected with the first slide of the Results and Discussion section, and then three cycles of PSM-PSRD were formed based on the three research questions of that study.

PSMRD11 consisted of 22 slides in total. The Methodology section started with a single slide as a boundary device, as revealed in Figure 5.7 below, in which the outline of this section was also demonstrated. Then, the following five slides (Slide 2 to Slide 6) were all related to Move 2 *Describing data collection method and procedure(s)*. In this move, S1 *Describing the sample* and S2 *Describing methods and steps in data collection* were identified in a sequence of S1-S2-S1-S2.

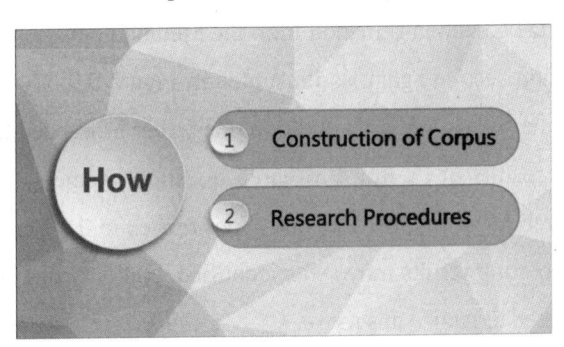

Figure 5.7 The First Slide in PSMRD11

Subsequently, the following two slides (Slide 7 and Slide 8) demonstrated the content pertinent to Move 4 *Elucidating data analysis procedure(s)*, with a mixture of Move 1 *Introducing the Method chapter*, as displayed in Figure 5.8 below.

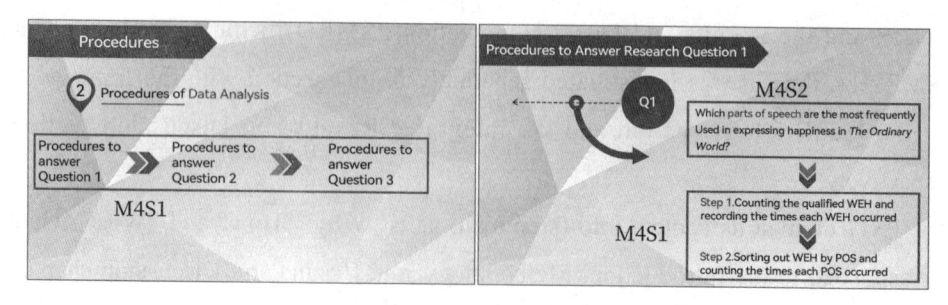

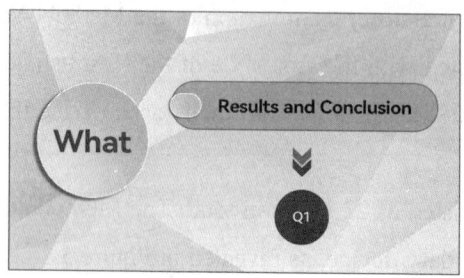

Figure 5.8　Slide 7 to Slide 9 in PSMRD11

Then, Slide 9 obviously signaled the beginning of the Results and Discussion section. Nevertheless, utilizing three slides to show the results of the first research question, this writer turned to provide certain information from the Methodology section, followed by the Results and Discussion section again, as illustrated in Figure 5.9. Then, after three slides about the results of the second research question, the writer proceeded to the data analysis procedures and the results of the third research question by the same structure as the preceding two research questions. For the nine slides related to the Results and Discussion section, only the Reporting results move was identified, and only one step, i.e., *Reporting major findings* was used to realize this move.

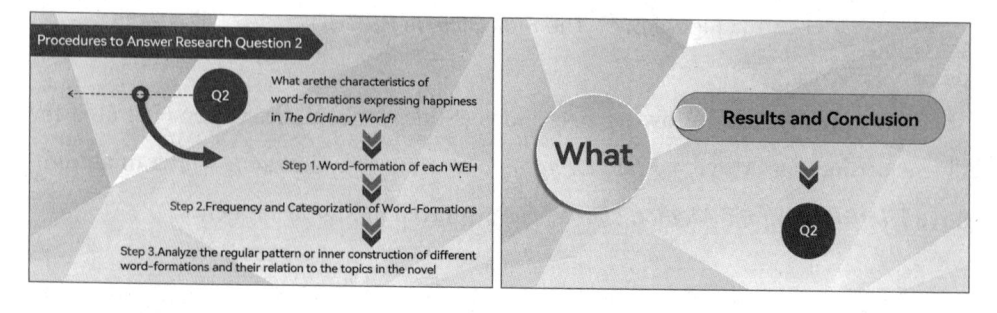

Figure 5.9　Slide 13 and Slide 14 in PSMRD11

It can be seen that PSMRD11 presented the steps of data analysis and the corresponding results based on the research questions in a parallel structure rather than providing all the related information of the methodology first and then moving to the whole results and discussion. The conversation with the writer of PSM11 reveals that the reason why she employed this structure was that it may be clearer to inform the audience of the methods and the corresponding results in her study. It seems that the writer tried to reduce the memory workload for the audience since the procedures to answer each research question might be different, so the audience needs to memorize all the data analysis procedures first and match them with the results.

To sum up, as the Methodology section involved the information on how the research questions were to be answered and the Results and Discussion section provided the answers to the research questions, these two sections could be overlapped to a certain extent. Since the frequency of this kind of organization was very low, it indicates that this unique or even innovative structure was not preferred by the majority of the writers in the present discourse community. However, its presence in the present corpus can point out that it is allowed in this discourse community. It will be interesting to find out if this unique organization can set an example for the other writers to follow or not.

5.7 Findings on the Conclusion Sections

5.7.1 Overall Structure

This subcorpus contained 17 Conclusion sections of the thesis defense presentation slides (PSCs). These 17 PSCs were made up of 41 slides in total, ranging from one to six slides, averaging about three slides per PSC. The length of the PSCs was relatively short compared with that of the PSRDs.

The examination of the slide headings found that the most frequently used generic one was "Conclusion(s)" which occurred in 11 PSCs, followed by "Major Findings" in five PSCs and "Limitations and Suggestions" in three PSCs. Other generic slide headings identified in this subcorpus were "Suggestions for further research"

"Limitations" "Implication" "Major Findings of the Study", and "Limitations of the Study". The slide headings reveal that this section in the slides was primarily utilized to highlight the major findings of the writers' studies and to present the limitations of their studies and suggestions.

5.7.2 Moves

The framework proposed by Chen and Kuo (2012) for the thesis Conclusion chapter was employed to analyze the moves and steps of the PSCs.

All the four moves in the framework were observed in the present subcorpus. The detailed results are provided in Table 5.24 below. It can be seen that no obligatory move was found among these 17 PSCs. Move 1 was found to be optional since only four PSCs employed it. It can be explained that the introduction of this section could be addressed orally by the writers during the presentation.

Table 5.24 Moves Identified in the 17 PSCs

Move	Occurrence	No. of PSCs	%	Status
Move 1 Introducing the Conclusions chapter	4	4	23.5	Opt.
Move 2 Summarizing the study	12	12	70.6	Con.
Move 3 Evaluating the study	7	7	58.3	Opt.
Move 4 Deductions from the study	5	5	29.4	Opt.

(*Note: Opt.=Optional, Con.=Conventional*)

Furthermore, Move 2 was identified in 12 PSCs (70.6%), thus, it was a conventional move in the current subcorpus. This demonstrates that it is better for the writers to summarize their study in the Conclusion section to make it more effective in the present discourse community.

Moreover, Move 3 was found to be optional with a frequency of 58.3%. This finding is congruent with that of Atai and Talebzadeh (2012) in which *Evaluating the study* was identified in 43.75% of their corpus of conference presentation slides in Applied Linguistics. It manifests that the writer's own evaluation of the study is not necessarily provided in the slides.

In addition, Move 4 *Deduction from the study* was also identified to be optional with a lower frequency of 29.4%, whereas it was observed to be conventional in the study of Atai and Talebzadeh (2012). It is probably because there is wider coverage of the audience of the conference, including the M.A. students, who may be looking for a new idea for their further study or who may pay attention to the practical application of the writer's research, thus, the writers of the conference presentation slides tended to explicitly display it to the audience. It indicates that the deductions from the writer's study were less valued in the present discourse community and the writers had less tendency to exhibit them in the slides when facing an audience, i.e., the committee members, who are more experienced than themselves.

To conclude, in the Conclusion section of the slides, only one move, i.e., *Summarizing the study*, was found to be conventional. It can be drawn that the predominant communicative purpose of this section in the slides is to provide a summary of the writer's study.

In terms of the move pattern, most of the PSCs merely contained one move, as manifested in Table 5.25 below. To be specific, seven PSCs used only Move 2 *Summarizing the study*, two utilized M1 *Introducing the Conclusion chapter*, and one included M3 *Evaluating the study*. This finding shows that to the majority of the writer, a PSC just contains a single communicative purpose, that is to summarize their study by emphasizing the main findings.

Table 5.25 Move Sequences in the 17 PSCs

Text	Move sequence	Text	Move sequence
PSC01	M2	PSC13	M2-M3-M4
PSC05	M2	PSC14	M2
PSC06	M2	PSC15	M2-M3-M4
PSC07	M2-M3	PSC16	M1-M3-M4
PSC08	M1	PSC17	M3
PSC09	M3-M4	PSC18	M2
PSC10	M1	PSC19	M1-M2
PSC11	M2	PSC20	M2
PSC12	M2-M3-M4		

As for the remaining seven PSCs that employed more than one move, a move sequence of M2-M3-M4 was found in three of them. Nevertheless, the frequency of this move pattern was not high, thus, it appears that it is not preferred by the writers in the current discourse community.

5.7.3 Steps

For the steps found in the present subcorpus, as only Move 3 and Move 4 contain step options, this section mainly demonstrates the results of the steps of these two moves. Table 5.26 displays the results of the steps observed under Move 3 *Evaluating the study*, from which it can be seen that S1 was found in only two PSCs (11.8%), suggesting it was an optional step. The optional status of S1 may be because the research significance could be presented in the Introduction section at the beginning as well, thus, the writers tended not to repeat it.

Table 5.26   Steps of Move 3 Identified in the 17 PSCs

Step	Occurrence	No. of PSCs	%	Status
S1 Indicating significance/advantage	2	2	11.8	Opt.
S2 Indicating limitations	7	7	58.3	Opt.
S3 Evaluating methodology	0	0	0	/

(*Note: Opt.=Optional*)

Furthermore, S2 *Indicating limitations* was identified to be optional as well with a rather higher frequency of 58.3% compared with that of S1. Additionally, S3 *Evaluating methodology* was not observed among these PSCs. It indicates that the writers preferred to state the limitations when they evaluated their study in the slides.

Table 5.27 sets out the steps of Move 4 *Deductions from the study* found in the present subcorpus. Among the three step options of Move 4, the writers only employed S1 *Recommending further research* to realize it. Nonetheless, S1 was identified to be optional with a low frequency of 29.4%, which is similar to the finding of Diani (2015) that the step Recommendation was observed in 7.14% of her corpus. This reveals that suggestions for further studies were not expected by the audience during the thesis defense.

Table 5.27 Steps of Move 4 Identified in the 17 PSCs

Step	Occurrence	No. of PSCs	%	Status
S1 Recommending further research	5	5	29.4	Opt.
S2 Drawing pedagogical implications	0	0	0	/
S3 Making suggestions	0	0	0	/

(Note: Opt.=Optional)

In terms of the step pattern, the step sequence of M3S2-M4S1 (*Indicating limitations* followed by *Recommending further research*) was found in four PSCs (23.5%). In addition, the step sequence of M3S1-M3S2 (*Indicating significance/advantage* followed by *Indicating limitations*) was identified in two PSCs. The frequencies of these two step patterns were comparatively low, thus, they were not preferred by most of the writers in the present discourse community.

5.8 Summary

This chapter delineated the results and discussions of the second research question concerning the rhetorical structure of the thesis defense presentation slides in terms of their moves and steps according to each section of the slides. The overall structure, the moves, and the steps of that particular section were depicted, respectively. Along with the moves and steps, their sequences were also investigated to identify the patterns used by the writers in the present discourse community. The next chapter will demonstrate the results and discussion related to the changes and strategies as an effect of genre transfer from the thesis to the corresponding thesis defense presentation slides.

CHAPTER 6 Results and Discussion of Changes and Transfer Strategies From the Thesis to the Corresponding Thesis Defense Presentation Slides

This chapter demonstrates the results found by the constant comparison of the theses and the corresponding thesis defense presentation slides in terms of the changes and the transfer strategies through the transfer between these two closely related genres. At the same time, the discussions are also conducted on how the theses were transferred to the corresponding thesis defense presentation slides. The changes and the transfer strategies are presented in the sequence of the components in the macrostructure of the thesis, i.e., Introduction, Literature Review, Theoretical Framework, Methodology, Integrated Results and Discussion, and Conclusion. Moreover, within each section, the changes and the transfer strategies are pointed out and discussed at the levels of the overall structures, moves, steps, and the textual features.

6.1 The Introduction Pair

The creation of the thesis defense presentation slides is mainly based on the content and the texts from the original theses. However, although having similar target audiences, these two genres are different in format and style, especially the slides which are in digital media and are displayed with oral commentary during the presentation. The following paragraphs present the changes between the thesis Introductions (MTIs) and the Introductions in the corresponding thesis defense presentation slides (PSIs) in terms of the overall structure, moves, steps, and textual features, which can be claimed to be a collection effect of genre transfer.

6.1.1 Changes and Transfer Strategies of the Overall Structure

In the original theses, all of them had the first chapter titled "Introduction". However, when being transferred into the PSIs, only 11 out of the 20 PSIs had the chapter heading "Introduction" of the original MTIs as the slide heading. Among the eleven PSIs, four of them placed the chapter title "Introduction" in a single slide serving as a boundary device, while four showed it at the top of every single slide. Besides, the other three PSIs merely had it at the top of the body texts of the first slide. Moreover, one presentation utilized "Why" as the heading, rather than "Introduction", to cover the aspects selected by the writer from the original MTI. The remaining eight PSIs did not have the chapter heading "Introduction" as the slide heading. Instead, they directly began with the section heading from the original MTIs, such as "Research Background". Therefore, the transfer of the chapter title indicates that the structure of the thesis defense presentation slides is not consistent with that of the original theses.

Except for using the chapter heading as the slide heading, section headings of the MTIs were also found to be employed as the slide headings. However, certain changes and modifications as an effect of genre transfer were identified in the slides. In the original thesis, the content of the "Introduction" chapter was organized into sections and subsections. Most of the MTIs were only structured by sections, such as "1.1 Research Background" and "1.2 Research Objectives". Nevertheless, seven out of the 20 MTIs had subsections under certain sections, for example, "1.1.1 Natural and Social Situation of Guizhou" under "1.1 Research Background". When being transferred into the slides, only the section headings of MTIs were identified in the PSIs. None of the subsection headings of MTIs were found in the slides, revealing that elaborate detail is not necessary to be presented in the slides.

16 out of the 20 MTIs started with the section "Research Background". However, only seven PSIs transferred it into the slides as the slide heading. One PSI utilized the short version "Background" instead and two PSIs omitted it. The section heading "Research Background" of the other six MTIs had been changed when transferred into the slides. Two PSIs changed it into "Rationale" and one used "Rationale of the

Study" as the heading instead. Besides, two altered it as "Research Orientation" and "Motivation", respectively. It is interesting to find that one PSI employed "Introduction" as the slide heading to present the content about "Background", "Deficiencies of previous studies", and "Present study", and then followed by a slide with the heading of "Research Objectives" to show the research purposes which is also the content of "Present study". The informal interview with the writer reveals that he used the heading "Introduction" to pack all the basic information of his research and prepared the slides according to the flow of his speech in the defense session rather than the structure of the original thesis. It seems that there are two ways to organize the PS; one is to follow the structure of the original thesis, and the other is to comply with the flow of the speaker's speech.

Furthermore, two MTIs began with the section heading "Background of the Study", a similar heading "Research Background". Nevertheless, in the corresponding slides, one PSI omitted it and its related content, while the other one modified it as "Research Background". The other two MTIs had different headings for their first section, titled "Rationale of the Study" and "Background and Research Problem", respectively. The first one was found in the corresponding PSI the same as "Rationale of the Study". However, the other one was changed to "Basis for the selected topic" in the slide which was colloquial and was not identified in any of the original theses.

The next frequently transferred section heading of MTIs was "Research Objectives". In the original MTIs, fifteen of them used the section heading "Research Objectives". In the corresponding PSIs, most of them remained the same. Nevertheless, one PSI shortened it to "Objectives" in the slide and one PSI incorporated it into the body texts of the slide as one of the itemized lists. Besides, two PSIs did not present the content from this section of MTI, thus the heading "Research Objectives" was not found in these two PSIs. The consultation of these two writers indicates that the reason why they did not present the content of research objectives is that the research questions correspond to the research objectives, thus they selected research questions which embody the objectives to be presented in the slides due to the time limitation. In addition, three of the original MTIs used a similar section heading "Objectives of the Study" to embody the content related to research purposes. When presenting in the corresponding PSIs, one of the PSIs changed it into "Research Objectives". Moreover, another heading "Purposes of the Study" was used in two of the original MTIs. Nonetheless, one corresponding PSI utilized the same heading while the other one shortened it to "Purpose".

Furthermore, the section heading "Research Questions" in MTIs was found as a frequently used slide heading in the PSIs. In the original MTIs, only five of them had a section to demonstrate the content concerning research questions, four of which used the section heading "Research Questions" and one employed "Research Questions of the Present Study" instead. All the five section headings were transferred into the corresponding PSIs as "Research Questions" serving as a slide heading. However, it was found that 10 more PSIs had the slide heading "Research Questions" while it was not identified in their original MTIs, which was relocated from the Methodology chapter of the original theses. It can be assumed that certain texts were relocated from other chapters of the original theses into the PSIs as well.

In addition, the section headings indicating research significances in the MTIs were also found to be transferred into some of the corresponding PSIs and similarly, certain changes and modifications were identified. In the original MTIs, 16 of them used the heading "Significance of the Study". However, only six corresponding PSIs included the content from this section and three of which shortened this section heading to "Significance". Besides, two MTIs used "Significance of the Research" as the section heading, while in the corresponding PSIs, one omitted the content of this section, and the other one incorporated the heading as an introductory phrase of one itemized list in the slide. The other two MTIs utilized "Research Significance" as the section heading but only one of the corresponding PSIs transferred it as the slide heading.

Other identified slide headings from the original MTIs were "Terminology" in two PSIs and "Layout of the Thesis" in one PSI. It reveals that the contents from these two sections in most of the original MTIs were rarely transferred into the corresponding PSIs and were regarded as insignificant information during the defense session.

The comparison of the headings indicates that there is a greater tendency of the writers to use the original section headings as the slide headings or subheadings when preparing the slides. Moreover, the omission of the section headings from the MTIs in the corresponding PSIs indicates the omission of the related content at the same time, except for the content from the section of "Research Background" which was under another heading or without heading in the slides. It should be mentioned that when the chapter title "Introduction" and the section headings such as "Research Background" were both transferred in a single slide, the former one served as the slide heading while the latter one served as the slide subheading.

Furthermore, several possible transfer strategies were identified in some instances in terms of the headings. The first strategy is to shorten the headings from the original MTIs as the slide headings. For example, the writers tended to shorten "Significance of the Study" to "Significance". The second strategy is to utilize a similar version of the section heading from the MTIs as the slide headings. To illustrate, the heading "Objectives of the Study" of the MTIs was modified to "Research Objectives" in some instances of the PSIs. The third strategy is to employ a new heading to emphasize the communicative purpose of the texts in the slides. This strategy was found especially in the slide presenting the content from the "Research Background" section of the MTIs. The identified heading substitutes were "Motivation", "Rationale", and "Basis for the selected topic", which were found acceptable during the thesis defense presentations. These changes and modifications of the headings indicate that there is more freedom for writers to present the content from the theses during the defense session.

6.1.2　Changes and Transfer Strategies of the Moves

As mentioned before, all the three moves in the framework of Chen and Kuo (2012) were found in both the subcorpora of thesis Introductions and Introduction sections of the slide sets. However, some changes were identified when comparing the move frequency between them, as shown in Table 6.1 below. It can be seen that the three moves in the original MTIs were all obligatory, being employed in every single thesis. Nevertheless, only Move 3 was found to be obligatory in the corresponding PSIs.

As for Move 1, most of the writers retained it through the transfer to the corresponding PSIs. However, it became a conventional move as an impact of genre transfer. Moreover, only around half of the writers decided to present Move 2 in the slides. As a result, it was optional in the PSIs rather than obligatory as found in the original MTIs.

Table 6.1 Move Frequency in the 20 Pairs of MTIs and PSIs

Move	% (MTIs)	%(PSIs)
Move 1 Establishing a territory	100	80
Move 2 Establishing a niche	100	55
Move 3 Occupying the niche	100	100

Moreover, regarding the move sequence, except for two PSIs which only used one move, the moves in the other PSIs were almost in a single progression, such as in the sequences of M1-M3, M2-M3, and M1-M2-M3. Only one PSI was found to have a recursive Move 1, which led to a move sequence of M1-M2-M1-M3. The move sequences found in the PSIs were different from those in the original MTIs which had longer move sequences and cyclical move patterns in a single MTI. This change may largely be caused by the time limitation of the defense session, in which only 15 minutes were given to the writers so only the important aspects were selected by the writers to present, and elaboration or repetition of information was avoided.

The strategy the writers frequently employed at the move level was the omission of Move 1 and Move 2, especially Move 2. Interviews with the writer informants revealed that there was no guideline or instruction for preparing thesis defense presentation slides. Most of them studied the thesis defense presentation slides of seniors or peers and then imitated the model of the slides they studied or prepared the slides based on the structure of the original thesis. As for the moves, most of them had no knowledge of the CARS models by Swales (1990, 2004). Therefore, when they prepared the slides, they selected what they considered the most important that needed to be explicitly shown in the slides for the audience. For them, announcing their own research outweighed providing the field and indicating the niche to be occupied in the thesis defense session. Hence, only Move 3 was found obligatory in their thesis defense presentation slides.

6.1.3　Changes and Transfer Strategies of the Steps

There are four steps under Move 1 in the framework of Chen and Kuo (2012). All these four steps were identified in the MTIs, while only three of them were found in the PSIs. As shown in Table 6.2, the most obvious change was the absence of *Defining terms* in the slides. Moreover, the frequency of the steps *Indicating centrality/importance of topic* and *Reviewing previous research* greatly decreased to 25% and 20%, respectively, both of which were changed from conventional into optional steps. In addition, six of the PSIs omitted the step *Providing topic generalization/background*, so this step was downranked from obligatory to a conventional step.

Table 6.2　Step Frequency under Move 1 in the 20 Pairs of MTIs and PSIs

Steps	%(MTIs)	%(PSIs)
S1 Providing topic generalization/background	100	70
S2 Indicating centrality/importance of topic	90	25
S3 Defining terms	35	0
S4 Reviewing previous research	80	20

In terms of the step sequence under Move 1, in the original MTIs, the steps were recursive as they occurred more than once in a single MTI. For example, S1 occurred 81 times among the 20 MTIs. Nonetheless, these Move 1 steps only occurred once in each of the corresponding PSIs when being transferred. Moreover, 19 out of the 20 original MTIs utilized more than one step to fulfill Move 1. However, when transferred into the slides, eight out of the 19 PSIs only used S1 to realize Move 1. In addition, four corresponding PSIs even omitted Move 1, thus no step under this move was identified in them.

Under Move 2, there were five steps to realize it according to Chen and Kuo's (2012) framework. Three of these steps were identified in the original MTIs, while only one of them was found in the corresponding slides. As indicated in Table 6.3, S2 *Question-raising* and S3 *Counter-claiming* were not used in the realization of Move 2 in both subcorpora. The most noteworthy change was the absence of S5 *Indicating a problem/need*, which was a conventional step in the theses, while it was entirely omitted in the slides. Moreover, the optional S4 *Continuing/extending a tradition identified in the theses* was not employed at all in the slides as well. In addition, the only step S1 *Indicating gaps in previous research* that occurred in the corpus of the corresponding PSIs was optional rather than conventional as in the corpus of the original MTIs.

Table 6.3 Step Frequency under Move 2 in the 20 Pairs of MTIs and PSIs

Steps	%(MTIs)	%(PSIs)
S1 Indicating gaps in previous research	85	55
S2 Question-raising	0	0
S3 Counter-claiming	0	0
S4 Continuing/extending a tradition	10	0
S5 Indicating a problem/need	65	0

Furthermore, according to the step occurrence, the steps under Move 2 were recursive in most of the original MTIs. Besides, more than half of them utilized two steps in this move, i.e., S1 *Indicating gaps in previous research* and S5 *Indicating a problem/need*. However, only one single step was used in the corresponding PSIs. A closer examination of the selection of the steps found that, among the 11 PSIs which contained S1, nine of their original MTIs adopted both S1 and S5. However, only the former step was selected to be presented in the slides. It seems that the writers tended to regard the gaps in the previous studies as the stronger motivation for their research when facing a live audience. This was confirmed by the interviews with the writers. They regarded that the research gap highlighted their research value better so they preferred to present the gap and they might mention the research need orally during the presentation.

Moreover, it was interesting to find that in MTI02, S4 *Continuing/extending a tradition* was employed to achieve Move 2. Nevertheless, in the corresponding PSI02, the step was changed to S1 *Indicating gaps in previous research*. The conversation with this writer reveals that he had no idea about the moves/steps and he just imitated one senior's slides which contained S1.

To realize Move 3, fifteen steps are set out in the framework of Chen and Kuo (2012). In both subcorpora, the identified steps within this move only consist of those in the framework. It was found that the steps not identified in the original MTIs were not mentioned in the corresponding PSIs (Table 6.4). Similarly, most of the optional steps in the theses remained optional in the presentation slides, such as S2 *Indicating scope of research*, S3 *Indicating chapter/section structure*, S4 *Indicating theoretical position*, and S9 *Indicating research method*. However, the optional step S14 *Providing justification in the theses* was excluded when transferred into the presentation slides.

Table 6.4 Step Frequency under Move 3 in the 20 Pairs of MTIs and PSIs

Steps	%(MTIs)	%(PSIs)
S1 Indicating purposes/aims/objectives	100	90
S2 Indicating scope of research	35	5
S3 Indicating chapter/section structure	30	15
S4 Indicating theoretical position	10	10
S5 Announcing research/work carried out	85	10
S6 Describing parameters of research	0	0
S7 Stating research questions/hypotheses	25	75
S8 Defining terms	75	10
S9 Indicating research method	25	5
S10 Indicating findings/results	0	0
S11 Indicating models proposed	0	0
S12 Indicating applications	0	0
S13 Indicating value or significance	100	40
S14 Providing justification	30	0
S15 Indicating thesis structure	100	15

The status of the steps was changed after the genre transfer. It was noteworthy that the optional step S7 *Stating research questions/hypotheses* had a low frequency of 25% in the theses. Nevertheless, it became a conventional step with a high frequency of 75% in the presentation slides. In the theses, research questions were mainly proposed in the Methodology chapter instead of in the Introduction, while in the presentation slides, they were moved into the Introductions. It should be mentioned that in two instances of the corresponding thesis defense presentation slides, the content of the Methodology chapter from the original theses was not found and only the content of research questions was presented in the slides, thus it was difficult to recognize whether the content of research questions belongs to the Introduction part or not. However, the interviews with the writers confirmed that it belongs to the Introduction part of the slides. Moreover, the interviewees revealed that there were two reasons why the writers moved the content of research questions into the Introduction part of the slides. On one hand, the writers just imitated the seniors' model they studied which had "Research Questions" in the Introduction part. On the other hand, the writers did not follow the structure of the original theses, but instead, they prepared the slides based on their own understanding. Moreover, they claimed that the research questions guided their analysis and discussion to find out the answers, thus it was better to put them at the beginning to make the audience clearer about the study they conducted.

Furthermore, apart from the changes of the optional steps in the original MTIs, the conventional steps were also found to have certain changes when being transferred into the slides. The conventional steps in the original MTIs were all shifted into optional steps in the corresponding PSIs. In the MTIs, the conventional steps, S5 *Announcing research/work carried out* and S8 *Defining terms* had high frequencies with 85% and 75%, respectively, while they were optional steps in the PSIs with frequencies of only 10%. It could be explained that the target audience was experts in certain fields, and they had already read through the writers' theses before the thesis defense, therefore, the writers may assume that it was unnecessary to spend the limited time explaining the terms. Moreover, what they have done about their research may be delivered orally during the presentation or be implicitly demonstrated in other parts, such as Methodology, Results, and Discussion, thus, S5 was rarely found in the slides. The downranking of the conventional steps into optional steps could be explained by that the time for presentation is limited during the thesis defense, thus the writers only select what they regarded as the most important points to be shown in the slides. Furthermore, since there is no convention or instruction on the preparation of thesis defense presentation slides, the writers' choices on the important points are varied. Hence, the conventional steps found with a high frequency in the original thesis become optional in the slides with a lower frequency.

Moreover, all the obligatory steps in the MTIs changed their status when being transferred into the presentation slides. On the one hand, S1 *Indicating purposes/aims/objectives* in the MTIs was obligatory, while it became a conventional step instead, although it had a high frequency of 90% in the PSIs. On the other hand, the obligatory steps of S13 *Indicating value or significance*, and S15 *Indicating thesis structure* in the MTIs became optional steps with lower frequencies in the PSIs of 40% and 15%, respectively. It was understandable that the thesis structure was not necessary to be presented in the oral defense since the writers do not need to guide the readers to read their thesis in the oral defense. Nonetheless, for the significance of the research, it was surprising that most writers chose not to explicitly present it in the slides, which indicated that they assumed the audience had already known and the demonstration of it may take some time from the limited time they had for their thesis defense.

As for the step sequence, in the original MTIs, some steps were recursively employed within one thesis. Nevertheless, the steps identified in the corresponding PSIs occurred once only. For example, step S13 *Indicating value or significance* occurred five times in MTI17, while it was found only once in the corresponding PSI17. Moreover, one particular step sequence was frequently utilized by the writers in the MTIs. To be specific, 15 out of the 20 MTIs included the step sequence of S8 *Defining terms* followed by S15 *Indicating thesis structure*. However, a different step sequence was identified in the corresponding PSIs. It was found that 12 out of the 20 presentations had the sequence of S1 *Indicating purposes/aims/objectives* followed by S7 *Stating research questions/hypotheses*.

From the above comparison between the steps in the original MTIs and the corresponding PSIs, three strategies were adopted by the writers when conducting the genre transfer. The most frequently employed strategy was the omission of steps. This strategy was found in all the realization of the three moves. Under Move 1, the most frequently omitted steps were S2 *Indicating centrality/importance*, of topic, and S4 *Reviewing previous research*, both of which were transferred from conventional steps into optional steps that were not necessary to be included in the slides. In addition, S5 *Indicating a problem/need* under Move 2 was also frequently excluded, which was not found at all in the corresponding PSIs. Moreover, the steps under Move 3 being often omitted in the corresponding PSIs were two obligatory steps, S13 *Indicating value or significance* and S15 *Indicating thesis structure*, as well as two conventional steps, S5 *Announcing research/work* carried out and S8 *Defining terms*. All these four steps became optional steps in the PSIs. The omission strategy of these steps being frequently utilized suggests that they were not expected by the audience in the slides so that they could be excluded by the writers when preparing slides.

The second strategy of the step level is the addition of the step. There was only one step found being added in the corresponding PSIs. In the original MTIs, S7 *Stating research questions/hypotheses* under Move 3 merely had a frequency of 25%, while in the PSIs, the frequency of this step increased to 75%. Therefore, it can be seen that it is more acceptable to have the audience being informed of the research questions or hypotheses in the introductory part of the slides. It should be mentioned that when merely comparing the Introduction in the genre pairs, the step was added in the slides which was not found in the original thesis Introduction. Nevertheless, from a closer examination of the whole texts of the MTs and the PSs, the content of S7 was moved from the later Methodology chapter. Therefore, this strategy is more appropriately called the relocation of the step.

Another strategy is the change of step which was found under Move 2 in one instance. The writer changed S4 *Continuing/extending a tradition in the original thesis* to S1 *Indicating gaps in previous research* in the corresponding slides. It seems that the former step is more used in the thesis, while the latter one is more accepted when presenting in the defense session because the writer revealed in the interview that he observed one senior's presentation slide set which explicitly presented the research gap in the slide. It may be caused by the writer's lack of critical thinking and genre knowledge about establishing the research niche as well, the limitation which calls for explicit instruction about this particular genre.

6.1.4　Changes and Transfer Strategies of the Textual Features

Comparing the texts between the original MTIs and the corresponding PSIs pair by pair, certain changes and modifications were identified as an impact of genre transfer through the forms of the texts and the sources of the texts in the slides in terms of how the texts were re-presented in the slides.

In the original MTIs, the texts were organized by sentences and paragraphs, except that in some instances, the research objectives and research questions were listed by numbers. When being transferred into the slides, the majority of the texts were omitted and only the important information was selected to display in the slides, as indicated by the omission of certain moves and a lot of steps shown in the above sections. However, the forms of the selected texts had to be altered and modified through the process of genre transfer as well. Alteration indicates that the form of the selected texts has been changed completely, whereas modification involves only a partial change.

In the corresponding PSIs, most of the selected texts were listed as items in the slides. All the PSIs included itemized lists in the slides. The items were listed in a variety of ways to signal their orders, such as bullets, numbers, text boxes, graphics, and letters. The most frequently utilized form of the list was bullets, which is a kind of typographical symbol.

The bullets being employed were in a variety of shapes, such as circles, squares, or arrows, and other shapes which were provided by Microsoft PowerPoint or downloaded from the Internet by the writers. All the PSIs contained bulleted lists. Moreover, the items were frequently listed by numbers, which clearly reveals how many items were presented in the slides. 13 out of the 20 PSIs (65%) contained numbered lists, in which the research objectives and research questions were often itemized in numbers. In addition, eight of the corresponding PSIs (40%) put the texts in a sequence of text boxes within a single slide serving as a list. The text boxes were either in a different color background or in a plain frame of a rectangle. Besides, two PSIs used graphics to indicate the list. As shown in Figure 6.1, the key points were listed by a graphic that the writer downloaded from the Internet. Moreover, letters were also employed to list the selected texts. For example, in PSI05, the research objectives were listed as "a. classification, b. pragmatic functions, c. reasons".

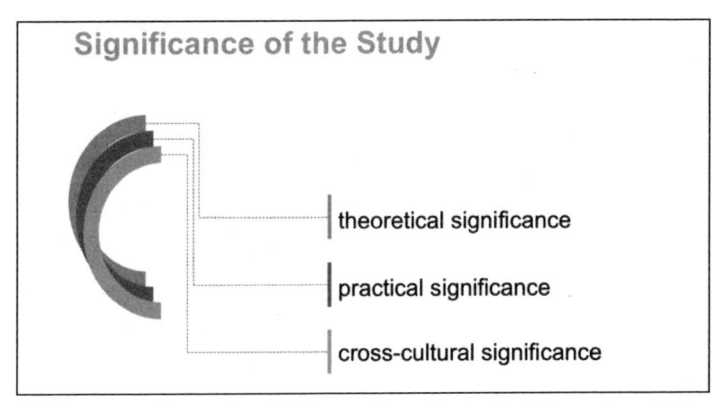

Significance of the Study

- theoretical significance
- practical significance
- cross-cultural significance

Figure 6.1   Example of Using a Graphic to List Items in a Slide

These five forms of the list were used in a combination in a single PSI which may contain a bulleted list, a numbered list, and an alphabetical list. Moreover, the listed items were in diverse length, ranging from keywords, short phrases, sentence fragments, and full sentences, to a paragraph. In addition, it was found that certain words in the lists were highlighted in different colors or underlined in three PSIs.

Apart from text being transferred and modified to become bullet points in the slides, diagrams were found in three PSIs to demonstrate the selected texts. As revealed in Figure 6.2, the information related to the research background was presented in a diagram that clearly indicates the relationship between the texts and the mind map created by the writer. In the boxes of the diagram, the texts were presented in different forms, i.e., keywords and full sentences. The creation of the diagram requires more skills and techniques of the writers compared with the itemized lists. From the diagram, it was easier for the audience to comprehend the relationship of the texts, thus the motivation and the justification of the writer's research were clearly delivered to the audience.

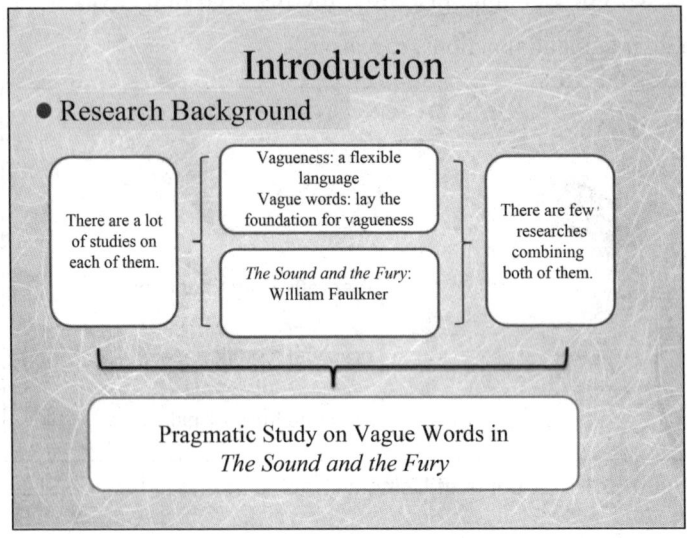

Figure 6.2 Example of Using Diagrams to Demonstrate Selected Texts (PSI5_S3)

Furthermore, certain texts in three corresponding PSIs were demonstrated as a paragraph or paragraphs which looked like a speech note of the writer's oral commentary. As shown in Figure 6.3, the texts were not listed but were displayed in two paragraphs which seems to keep the form of the texts from the original MTI. Moreover, the texts in the slide seem to be the exact oral commentary of this slide which will be read out during the presentation rather than being expanded by the writer.

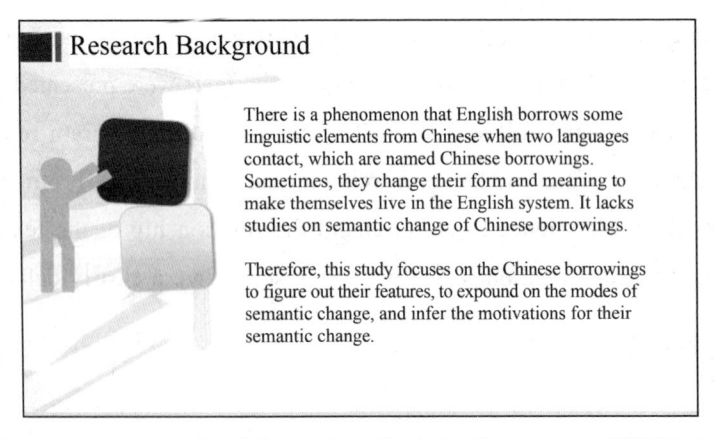

Figure 6.3 Example of Presenting Texts in Paragraphs (PSI19_S4)

A closer examination of the length of the texts revealed that the PSIs were organized in the continuum of concise texts to heavy texts. The most concise one only listed several keywords in every slide, while the most crowded one provided full sentences as an itemized list which looked like a paragraph in most slides. The majority of the PSIs fell into somewhere of the continuum, which contained keywords, phrases, sentence fragments, or a full sentence as the listed items in the slides. The finding of the slide texts was similar to the results found in the graduate seminars by Weissberg (1993) that the presentations in the seminar were varied "along a discourse continuum ranging from most planned and formal (i.e., writing-like) to most spontaneous and intimate (speech like)". The most text heavy slides correlated to the most planned and formal discourse which seems like a read-aloud paper. However, it seemed impossible for the writers to read out every slide in the defense session since only 15 minutes were given to the presentation. The interviews with these writers revealed that they only selected the key information from the itemized lists to orally deliver, though they prepared many texts in the slide. The reason why they provided many texts in a slide was that they aimed to demonstrate the complete information of every issue so that the audience could understand it without their oral commentary. This corresponded with the findings of Schoeneborn (2013) and Yates and Orlikowski (2007) that the slides or PowerPoints tend to have two functions, that is, presentation and documentation which contradict with each other. The former provides as little texts as possible, and then the writers recontextualize them into full sentences during the delivery. On the other hand, the latter offers sufficient texts so that the reader can comprehend the content contextually (Schoeneborn, 2013). Nevertheless, the thesis defense presentation slides were used for the presentation rather than for the documentation since there is a live audience instead of readers. Therefore, concise texts are recommended for the thesis defense presentation slides. The interview with the supervisor informants confirmed that they prefer concise slides in outline forms since too many texts on the slide are difficult for the audience to grasp the key information, which is in line with the findings of Weissberg (1993). In addition, as Hertz et al (2016) indicated, the heavy text on the slides is problematic since it may cause the presenters to turn to the screen and read the words rather than communicate verbally directly with the audience.

From the forms of the texts in the slides, it can be seen that the texts were transferred into the slides in various ways based on the writers' preferences. Nevertheless, certain strategies were identified. The frequent strategy used was to merely select the important texts and then modify the texts into bulleted or numbered lists in the slides. The bulleted lists were ordered nearly with the speech flow of the commentary, and the numbered lists implied a certain sequence or order, such as the research objectives and research questions which were achieved one by one. Besides, the length of the listed items can be various, ranging from simple keywords to a paragraph. Moreover, another strategy being utilized by the writers was to employ diagrams to reveal the relationship between the texts or to indicate a process.

A closer investigation of the text itself found that certain strategies were employed by the writers to re-present the selected texts in the slides. Taking a listed item in the corresponding PSIs as an analysis unit to compare with the original texts identified in the MTIs, several strategies were identified through the constant comparison. It should be mentioned that the issue indicator of the items, which is a noun or a phrase to indicate the issue that will be presented or discussed as items on a list, was not taken into account when examining the textual transfer strategies. For example, in the listed item "Theoretical Significance: At first, it is…within the paradigm of EDA" (PSI13_S6), the phrase "Theoretical Significance" was excluded when compared the text of the item with the original text identified in the thesis. Furthermore, the identified strategies were grouped into the single strategies and the combined strategies in which more than one strategy was utilized. The detailed findings in terms of the identified strategies at the level of textual features are demonstrated in Table 6.5 below, in which the definitions and typical examples are also provided. In the examples, the changed parts or the corresponding parts were bolded and underlined.

CHAPTER 6

Table 6.5 Transfer Strategies Identified in the 20 Pairs of MTIs and PSIs at the Textual Feature Level

Strategy & Definition	Example	
Single Strategies	**MT**	**PS**
SS1. Directly quoting texts: To cut a full sentence or sentences from the original thesis and to paste it/them as a listed item in the slide	"What is the cognitive mechanism of phonetic metaphor of homophonic person names in ROE?" (MTI03_p.4)	"What is the cognitive mechanism of phonetic metaphor of homophonic person names in ROE?" (PSI03_S4)
SS2. Rewording texts: To change certain word(s) of the sentence selected from the original thesis to form a listed item in the slide	"With the coherent efforts of researchers at home and abroad, the genre analysis on Introductions has been explored deeply." (MTI09_p.1)	"With the coherent efforts **made by** researchers at home and abroad, the genre analysis on Introductions has been explored deeply." (PSI09_S3)
SS3. Reordering texts: To reorganize the sequence of several sentences selected from the original thesis to form a listed item in the slide	"The present paper **offers the government** a reference from which to make language policy and language planning. **This study presents** an overall trend of language use and language attitudes of Hmong students inside and outside college. **Systematic studies** of language use and attitudes of these students can predict the trend of the whole groups, and give references in making language plan as well as ethnic minorities' education policies." (MTI16_p.13)	"**Systematic studies** of language use and attitudes of these students can predict the trend of the whole groups, and give references in making language plan as well as ethnic minorities' education policies, **offers the government** a reference from which to make language policy and language planning. **This study presents** an overall trend of language use and language attitudes of Hmong students inside and outside college" (PSI16_S6)

Cont.

Strategy & Definition	Example	
Single Strategies	MT	PS
SS4. Grafting texts: To take a part from two different sentences in the original thesis and then combine them together to form a listed item in the slide	"<u>Rap music, as a representative of hip-hop culture</u>, successfully attracts people's attention for its energetic beats and controversial lyrics. By 1979, hip-hop music had become a music genre in the mainstream music industry. In recent years, since the boom of hip-hop culture, rap music has not only gained its position in music industry, but it also has been noticed by linguistics for its special wording and rhyming. The reasons why this subject is chosen are as follows: To begin with, since the emergence of rap music, it has been very phenomenal in America, and rapidly it has become popular worldwide. For one thing, **its popularity and influence are so immense**." (MTI14_p.1)	"Rap music, as a representative of hip-hop culture, its popularity and influence are so immense." (PSI14_S3)
SS5. Extracting sentence fragments to be listed items: To extract a fragment from a full sentence in the original thesis to form a listed item in the slide	"Classifier is **widely used in people's daily life and academic works** because of its vividness." (MTI01_p.1)	" • widely used in people's daily life & academic works" (PSI01_S3)
SS6. Extracting keywords or phrases to be listed items: To extract several keywords or phrases from the sentence(s) in the original thesis to form listed items in the slide	"Presenting the **semantic prosody features** of English synonymous verbs indicating happen from three perspectives: **positive, neutral** and **negative**." (MTI02_p.2)	" • Semantic prosody features • Positive • Neutral • Negative" (PSI02_S4)

Cont.

Strategy & Definition	Example	
Single Strategies	MT	PS
SS7. Paraphrasing texts: To paraphrase the sentence selected from the thesis to form a new sentence fragment or a sentence and present it as a listed item in the slide	"However, Liu (2006) further studies decategorization and put forward the systematic theory of it." (MTI01_p.2)	" · developed as a theory by Liu (2006)" (PSI01_S3)
	"These three objectives will compose a systematically study on pragmatic vagueness in netspeak." (MTI15_p.3)	"The three objectives will bring about a systematic knowledge of pragmatic vagueness in netspeak." (PSI15_S4)
SS8. Adding texts: To add new texts in the slide as a listed item, which are not found in the original thesis	Not found	"Language exchanges" (PSI10_S3)
Combined Strategies	MT	PS
CS1. Directly quoting and omitting texts: To cut a sentence or sentences from the original thesis, to omit the clause of the sentence or some sentence(s) in the middle, and to paste it/them as a listed item in the slide	"**At first, it is a supplement to ecosophy in ecolinguistics.** According to the development in China and the valuable ecosophy in Chinese traditional culture, this thesis builds an ecosophy of strengthening national efforts to climate change combat and promoting sound development of the ecosystem – Put ecology first to seek win-win cooperation, shape green development with low-carbon emission to pursue harmonious co-existence. **Then, the study contributes to the research contents of SFG, even in the application of Fairclough's model within the paradigm of EDA.**" (MTI13_p.5)	"**At first**, it is a supplement to ecosophy in ecolinguistics. **Then, the study** contributes to the research contents of SFG, even in the application of Fairclough's model within the paradigm of EDA." (PSI13_S6)

Cont.

Strategy & Definition	Example	
Combined Strategies	**MT**	**PS**
CS2. Directly quoting and relocating texts: To cut a sentence or sentences, to move it/them from a location in the original thesis into a different location in the corresponding slides, and to paste it/them as a listed item in the slide	"What are the semantic prosody features of English synonymous verbs indicating *happen*?" (MTM02_p.26)	"What are the semantic prosody features of English synonymous verbs indicating *happen*?" (PSI02_S5)
CS3. Rewording and relocating texts: To change certain word(s) of the selected sentence(s) to form a listed item, and to move it/them from a location in the original thesis into a different location in the corresponding slides	"What are the communicative functions of pragmatic vagueness in **netspeak during internet communication process**?" (MTM15_p.21)	"What are the communicative functions of pragmatic vagueness in **online communication**?" (PSI_S5)
CS4. Grafting, and adding texts: To extract a part from different sentences in the original thesis and combined them together, and then to add extra texts to it to form a listed item in the slide	"In the theoretical aspect, it **enriches the theoretical system of language use and attitude from the sociolinguistics perspective**. Taking Guizhou Hmomg college students as the research participants, the current research explores the relationship between language use and language attitude, digging deep into the characteristics and laws of their development and change, further exploring the relationship between language use and language attitude, and differences in language attitudes between different groups, etc. Therefore, this study can also enrich and deepen the theoretical system itself, and **expand the research ideas** as well as theoretical systems **in the field of sociolinguistics**." (MTI16_p.13)	"In the theoretical aspect: **enriches the theoretical system of language use and attitude from the sociolinguistics perspective**. Taking Guizhou Hmong college students as the research participants expands the research objects and ideas in the field of sociolinguistics" (PSI16_S6)

Cont.

Strategy & Definition	Example	
Combined Strategies	MT	PS
CS5. Paraphrasing and relocating texts: To paraphrase a sentence or sentences to form a listed item, and to move it/them from a location in the original thesis into a different location in the corresponding slides	"Chinese Xiehouyu is a special language and it is full of images. Previous studies mainly focus on the semantic metaphor and phonetic metaphor in Xiehouyu and neglect the image metaphors in Xiehouyu." (MT20_**Abstract**)	"Chinese Xiehouyu contains a large number of images. However, scholars mainly study semantic metaphors and phonetic metaphors in Xiehouyu and few scholars devote to the research on image metaphors in Xiehouyu." (**PSI**20_S4)
CS6. Extracting and relocating texts: To extract keywords, phrases, or fragments from the sentence(s) to form a listed item, and to move it/them from a location in the original thesis into a different location in the corresponding slides	"First of all, most studies related to classifiers are **static description** rather than **dynamic research**." (MTLR01_p.21)	" · static description > dynamic research" (**PSI**01_S4)
CS7. Extracting and rewording texts: To extract a part from a full sentence in the original thesis and to change certain word(s) to form as a listed item in the slide	"Secondly, the author tries **to explore the communicative functions of pragmatic vagueness in netspeak under different communicative contexts.**" (MTI15_p.3)	" · to explore the communicative functions of pragmatic vagueness <u>in online communication</u>." (**PSI**15_S4)
CS8. Extracting and adding texts: To extract a part from a full sentence in the original thesis and to add extra texts to form a listed item in the slide	"However, it is a pity that there are **few contrastive studies on causative structures between the Dong language and English**, which will become the bottleneck of studies on causative structure in the Dong language." (MTI10_p.3)	"<u>Few studies on causative structure in the Dong language,</u> and **few contrastive studies on causative structures between the Dong language and English**." (**PSI**10_S3)
CS9. Extracting and restructuring texts: To extract a part or parts from a full sentence in the original thesis, and to reorganize it/them to form a listed item in the slide	"With the introduction of lexical chunks and related corpus-based studies, first of all, with the help of the self-built corpus, the present study aims to reveal the general distributions <u>of lexical chunks</u> in the corpus and **analyze the classifications** and functional roles of them used in students' argumentative writings." (MTI7_p.5)	" · · analyze the classification the classifications <u>of lexical chunks</u>" (**PSI**7_S3)

Cont.

Strategy & Definition	Example	
Combined Strategies	MT	PS
CS10. Extracting, rewording, and adding texts: To extract a part from the selected sentence in the original thesis, then to change certain words and add extra texts to form a listed item in the slide	"With the introduction of lexical chunks and related corpus-based studies, first of all, with the help of the self-built corpus, the present study aims to reveal the general distributions of lexical chunks in the corpus and analyze the classifications and **functional roles of** <u>them</u> used in students' argumentative writings." (MTI7_p.5)	" · **discuss** the functional roles <u>of lexical chunks</u>" (PSI7_S3)
CS11. Extracting, restructuring, and rewording texts: To extract a part or parts from the selected sentence in the original thesis, to reorganize it/them and to change certain words to form a listed item in the slide	"Second, for the sake of **exploring the correlation** relationship between the use of the lexical chunks and the argumentative **writing** scores and comparing the differences **on the** <u>use of lexical chunks</u> **between high and low score groups**, the study adopts Independent-sample tests and Pearson correlation analysis on the top ten lexical chunks used by students in high and low score groups." (MTI7_p.5)	" · explore the correlation between <u>HSG & LSG</u> on the use of lexical chunks & writing scores" (PSI7_S3)
CS12. Extracting, adding, and relocating texts: To extract a part from the selected sentence in the original thesis, to add certain words into it to form a listed item, and to move it from a location in the original thesis into a different location in the corresponding slides	"Phonetic metaphor is **pervasive in Chinese** because Chinese contains a large number of …" (MT03_**Abstract**)	"Phonetic metaphor: **pervasive in Chinese** <u>while long-neglected</u>" (**PSI**03_S3)

In total, there were 87 instances of strategy identified in all the 20 pairs of MTIs and PSIs, ranging from one to nine in one pair, and about four strategies on average. To better understand the most frequently used strategies, the occurrence of each strategy was counted (Table 6.6) since certain strategies were found more than once in a single pair of MTIs and PSIs. Moreover, the number of the pairs which contained the strategy was also counted to show the frequency of each adopted strategy among the total 20 pairs.

Table 6.6 Single Strategies Identified in the 20 Pairs of MTIs and PSIs

Single strategies	Occurrence	No. of pairs	%
SS6 Extracting keywords or phrases to be listed items	46	11	55
SS1 Directly quoting texts	33	7	35
SS8 Adding texts	26	9	45
SS5 Extracting sentence fragments to be listed items	22	9	45
SS7 Paraphrasing texts	11	9	45
SS2 Rewording texts	3	2	10
SS3 Reordering texts	1	1	5
SS4 Grafting texts	1	1	5

As demonstrated in Table 6.6, eight single strategies occurred 143 times among the 20 pairs of the MTIs and PSIs, around seven occurrences of the single strategies per slide set on average. The most frequently used single strategy was SS6 *Extracting keywords or phrases to be listed items*. It indicates that the writers tend to re-present the texts as keywords or phrases to make the slides more concise and relieve the reading workload of the audience, which suggests that when creating slides, the writers need to be taught how to extract keywords and phrases to better re-present significant information in the slides. The second single strategy that frequently occurred was SS1 *Directly quoting texts* with the occurrence of 33, however, it was only used by seven writers in the present subcorpus with the frequency of 35%. Therefore, it was not regarded as a frequent strategy. While the least utilized single strategies were SS3 *Reordering texts* and SS4 *Grafting texts*, each of which only occurred once in one pair of MTI and PSI. It suggests that these two single strategies are utilized by only one writer, so they reflect a kind of personal preference rather than a tendency of the data in the subcorpus.

Compared with the single strategies, the combined strategies were used less frequently. As shown in Table 6.7, the combined strategies occurred 60 times among the 20 pairs of MTIs and PSIs, with only three occurrences on average. The most popular combined strategy was CS2 *Directly quoting and relocating texts* with the occurrence of 25 and the frequency of 50%. Most of the relocated texts were from the Methodology chapter by which the research questions were moved into the Introduction part. In addition, a small part of them was from the Literature Review chapter. It reveals that when the writers prepared the slides, they already had a whole picture of their thesis projects, thus, they could relocate certain texts to suit the new communicative purposes of the genre. The other combined strategies were less frequently used by the writers with fewer occurrences and frequencies.

Table 6.7 Combined Strategies Identified in the 20 Pairs of MTIs and PSIs

Combined strategies	Occurrence	No. of pairs	%
CS2 Directly quoting and relocating texts	25	10	50
CS8 Extracting and adding texts	8	5	25
CS6 Extracting and relocating texts	7	3	15
CS5 Paraphrasing and relocating texts	5	3	15
CS7 Extracting and rewording texts	4	3	15
CS1 Directly quoting and omitting texts	3	4	20
CS3 Rewording and relocating texts	3	2	10
CS4 Grafting and adding texts	1	1	5
CS9 Extracting and restructuring texts	1	1	5
CS10 Extracting, rewording, and adding texts	1	1	5
CS11 Extracting, restructuring, and rewording texts	1	1	5
CS12 Extracting, adding, and relocating texts	1	1	5

To conclude, most of the texts in the slides were identifiable in the original thesis and the writers employed diverse strategies to re-present them from the original thesis or even add new texts based on the communicative purposes of the thesis defense presentation slides. Among the employed strategies, the single ones occurred two times more than the combined ones, which indicates that the single strategies are preferred by the writers since they are easier for the writers, though the number of the combined strategies was more than that of the single ones.

6.2 The Literature Review Pair

6.2.1 Changes and Transfer Strategies of the Overall Structure

When comparing the subcorpora of the thesis Literature Reviews (MTLrs) and the Literature Review Sections in the corresponding thesis defense presentation slides (PSLrs), it was found that, as the second-largest subcorpus of the original theses, only eight out of the 20 MTLrs were transferred to the corresponding slides. In other words, during the genre transfer process, most of the MTLrs were omitted by the writers. This result echoes that of Pramoolsook's (2007) study that the omission of the Literature Review chapter was found during the genre transfer between the theses and the corresponding research articles. It indicates that the majority of the writers considered the Literature Review not significant to be presented during the thesis defense. It could be explained that the literature review mainly aims to showcase the writer's familiarity with the field rather than their own research findings, thus, it could be omitted without affecting the quality of the presentation of the writers' own study. The interviews with the supervisors and the students obtained different perspectives about whether the Literature Review needs to be presented in the slides or not. The two supervisor informants regarded it as a significant component to be provided to make the thesis presentation complete. On the other hand, two out of the five student informants considered it less important than the other sections, such as the "Introduction" and "the Results and Discussion". Thus, they preferred to omit it considering the limited presentation time. According to this result, further studies need to be conducted to examine the perceptions of the audience, i.e., the committee members, to explicitly demonstrate their expectations of this genre to support the students for a more effective presentation. It can be drawn that at the macrostructure level, one transfer strategy was found, i.e., the omission of the LR section in the slides.

Furthermore, as revealed in *Section 4.2*, the original 20 MTLrs were mostly configured in an Introduction-Body-Conclusion structure, with 16 Introductory texts and 12 Concluding texts found. In the eight pairs of the MTLrs and PSLrs, five MTLrs had an Introduction at the beginning of the chapter, however, three of the corresponding

PSLrs omitted the introductory texts in the slides. It was interesting that when the other three MTLrs without an Introduction were transferred to the PSLrs, an Introduction was observed to be added to the slides. It is because these three writers omitted the detailed content of this section in the slides. Instead, they just provided the outline from the Literature Review chapter in the original thesis to show what had been reviewed in their theses. The conversations with these writers reveal that due to the limited time, they decided to only provide the outline of this section, by which they not only showed the themes to be reviewed but also kept the whole structure of the thesis being provided in the corresponding slides. This result indicates that manifesting the complete structure of the original thesis in the slides is considered essential to a small part of the students, which could be further confirmed by future studies that interview more writers of this genre.

In addition, as for the Conclusion part, five MTLrs contained it at the end of the LR chapter, while this Conclusion was omitted in all the corresponding PSLrs. Specifically, no concluding texts were identified in the slides of PSLrs, which might be attributed to the small size of the content of the PSLr that it is not necessary to summarize what has just been presented to the audience in a short time.

Moreover, three out of the eight PSLrs omitted the Body parts in the slides, only demonstrating the Introduction of what themes had been reviewed by the writers. In the remaining five PSLrs with a Body part, it was found that the number of thematic units in the three PSLrs was reduced, which could be due to the limited presentation time given to the writers. Additionally, it should be mentioned that it was difficult to identify and categorize the thematic units in PSLr12, since no slide heading or other signals that would help the present researcher to make a decision. Besides, the texts in the slides were not identified in the original thesis, thus, the present researcher regarded the Body part of PSLr12 as a whole.

To sum up, at the overall structure level, five transfer strategies were found. The most frequently employed one was the omission of the Conclusion part of the MTLr, which is probably ascribed to the amount of the content being delivered. The other four transfer strategies were utilized with the same frequency, i.e., the omission of the

Introduction part, the addition of the Introduction part, the omission of the Body part, and the reduction of the number of thematic units in the Body part.

The analysis of the slide headings found that the chapter title "Literature Review" was identified in seven out of the eight PSLrs, among which three of them employed this chapter title in every slide of the PSLrs as the slide heading. The remaining one, i.e., PSLr03, utilized "Review of Previous Researches" as the slide heading. Apart from the adoption of the chapter title as the slide heading, a section heading from the original thesis indicating one thematic unit was identified in PSLr16 as the slide heading as well. The results show that the writers tended to adopt the same chapter title to be the slide heading on the slides. One transfer strategy at the slide heading level was the modification of the heading, i.e., from "Literature Review" to "Review of Previous Researches". Nevertheless, this strategy was found in only one instance, suggesting that it was only a possible option for the writers in the present discourse community to use.

6.2.2 Changes and Transfer Strategies of the Moves

For the moves and steps, merely five out of the eight PSLrs maintained the Body parts from the original MTLrs. Hence, only these five pairs were compared at the move and step level. Table 6.8 sets out the frequency of the moves found in these five pairs. According to the table, both the five MTLrs and the corresponding five PSLrs utilized Move 1 *Establishing a territory*, which indicates that showing familiarity with the field is of great importance in both genres in the present discourse community.

Table 6.8 Move Frequency in the 5 Pairs of MTLrs and PSLrs

Move	%(MTLrs)	%(PSLrs)
Move 1 Establishing a territory	100	100
Move 2 Establishing a niche	100	60
Move 3 Occupying the niche	80	80

As for Move 2, it was found to be obligatory in the five MTLrs, whereas it was conventional when transferred to the PSLrs. It demonstrates that Move 2 could be omitted in the slides. It is probably because the writers considered establishing a niche not one of the main communicative purposes of the PSLrs.

Regarding Move 3 *Occupying the niche*, it was found conventional in both the MTLrs and the PSLrs. Nonetheless, the detailed analysis of these five pairs revealed that Move 3 was observed in PSLr12 but not in the original MTLr12. In other words, Move 3 was added by the writer in the PSLr12. Moreover, this move was found to be omitted in the corresponding PSLr16, while it was included in the original MTLr16. To put it simply, one PSLr added Move 3, and one omitted it in the slides. The results revealed that the writers had different comprehension of the communicative purposes of the Literature Review chapter or section, which resulted in the contents related to the writer's research being added or omitted in the corresponding slides.

In terms of the move pattern, all the MTLrs and PSLrs were structured variously, thus, no move pattern was identified in both genres. In a nutshell, apart from maintaining the moves, two transfer strategies were identified at the move level. One was the omission of the move, i.e., the omission of Move 2 *Creating a niche* and, the omission of Move 3 *Occupying the niche*. The other one was the addition of move, i.e., the addition of Move 3. The reason for the addition of Move 3 may be because the writer considered it more appropriate to link her own research with the reviewed literature during the thesis presentation in order to directly showcase her research and where it was situated in the field.

6.2.3 Changes and Transfer Strategies of the Steps

Table 6.9 below displays the frequency of the steps of Move 1 *Establishing a territory*. It can be seen that S1 was retained in the corresponding slides, which suggests that the theory or knowledge claims were significant to be presented in the slides for the writers in the present discourse community. Nevertheless, S2 was absent in the PSLrs, which reveals that the writers regarded centrality claiming not essential to be displayed to the audience since it may be orally delivered by the writers during the presentation.

Table 6.9 Step Frequency under Move 1 in the 5 Pairs of MTLrs and PSLrs

Step	%(MTLrs)	%(PSLrs)
S1 Surveying the non-research-related phenomena or knowledge claim	100	100
S2 Claiming centrality	60	0
S3 Surveying the research-related phenomena	100	60

Moreover, S3, which was obligatory in the original MTLrs, was found to be reduced as conventional in the PSLrs. The result demonstrates that the research practices of the previous studies were not necessarily provided in the slides during the defense session because of the limited presentation time.

As for the six steps of Move 2 *Creating a niche*, all but one was identified in the five MTLrs (Table 6.10). However, when they were transferred to the corresponding PSLrs, only S2 was observed in the slides. To be specific, among all the five step options found in the original MTLrs, the writers merely selected the research gaps to be presented in the slides to indicate the niche from the literature. The conversation with one of these writers reveals that she considered the research gap the most important element to be provided in the Literature Review section and to attract the audience's attention. It should be mentioned that in MTLr16, S2 was found in the Conclusion part rather than in the Body part but it was transferred to the Body part of the corresponding PSLr16. It indicates that the whole MTLr, including the concluding texts, is the content source of the PSLr.

Table 6.10 Step Frequency under Move 2 in the 5 Pairs of MTLrs and PSLrs

Step	%(MTLrs)	%(PSLrs)
S1 Counter-claiming	0	0
S2 Gap-indicating	80	60
S3 Asserting confirmative claims	60	0
S4 Asserting the relevancy of the surveyed claims	40	0
S5 Abstracting or synthesizing knowledge claims	80	0
S6 Concluding a part of the review	60	0

Furthermore, changes were also identified in the steps of Move 3 (Table 6.11). It was found that the frequencies of S1, S3, and S4 were reduced in the PSLrs, indicating that these three steps could be omitted when composing a PSLr. This could be explained that these three steps might be presented in other sections already, such as in Introduction, Theoretical Framework, and Methodology. Thus, the writers tended not to repeat them to waste the limited presentation time.

Table 6.11 Step Frequency under Move 3 in the 5 Pairs of MTLrs and PSLrs

Step	%(MTLrs)	%(PSLrs)
S1 Indicating research aims, focuses, research questions or hypotheses	20	0
S2 Indicating theoretical positions/theoretical framework	20	40
S3 Indicating research design/processes	40	20
S4 Interpreting terminology used in the thesis	60	20

It was interesting to find that S2 was added by one writer in PSLr12 to indicate the theoretical position. A closer investigation of this instance reveals that in the original MT12, the Literature Review and the Theoretical Framework were separated into two individual chapters. Nevertheless, this writer omitted the Theoretical Framework section in the corresponding slides where the theoretical position was provided. The conversation with this writer demonstrates that her adoption of the theoretical framework followed one previous study reviewed in the Literature Review chapter, thus, she tended to embed it in the Literature Review section to make the slides succinct.

According to the changes above, two transfer strategies were identified. The most frequently employed one was the omission of steps, which was observed in all the three moves. Understandably, it is because the presentation time was limited to 15 minutes, hence, only the salient elements were maintained in the slides. The other strategy was the addition of step, i.e., the addition of *Indicating theoretical position/framework* of Move 3 *Occupying the niche*, which was found in merely one instance, suggesting that it was not favored by the writers in the present discourse community.

6.2.4 Changes and Transfer Strategies of the Textual Features

From the perspective of the forms of the texts in the original MTLrs and the corresponding PSLrs, it was found that most of the texts were transferred to be items listed in the slides. Those items were organized in different ways, such as bullets, text boxes, numbers, or graphics. The most frequently used form of the items was the bullets, which were identified in five out of the eight PSLrs. The second most frequently used ones were text boxes and numbers observed in three PSLrs, respectively. Moreover, one PSLr, i.e., PSLr07, was found to employ the shape of a ball to list the items. Apart from the item form, PSLr12 was observed to display the texts as a small paragraph in one slide. These results manifest that the writers tend to utilize different forms to demonstrate the texts in the slides and those forms are all accepted by the present discourse community.

Furthermore, as mentioned in *Section 3.5*, the preliminary framework about the transfer strategies found in the pilot study of the MTIs and the PSIs, which was relocated to *Section 6.1.4*, will be adopted as the departure point for the remaining data analysis. Therefore, the framework shown in Table 6.5 in *Section 6.1.4* was employed to analyze the changes and the transfer strategies from MTLrs to PSLrs. Based on this framework, a constant comparison of the texts or the items in the PSLrs and their original texts in the MTLrs was conducted. The identified single strategies are listed in Table 6.12 below.

Table 6.12 Single Strategies Identified in the 8 Pairs of MTLrs and PSLrs

Single strategies	Occurrence	No. of pairs	%
SS1 Directly quoting texts	14	5	62.5
SS6 Extracting keywords or phrases to be listed items	13	4	50.0
SS5 Extracting sentence fragments to be listed items	7	3	37.5
SS2 Rewording texts	2	2	25.0
SS9 Directly copying graphic items	**2**	**2**	**25.0**
SS8 Adding texts	4	1	12.5

(* *The newly identified strategy is in bold.*)

From the table above, it can be seen that six single strategies were identified in the eight pairs of MTLrs and PSLrs, among which SS1 was the most frequently used one with a frequency of 62.5%. It should be mentioned that aside from directly quoting the full sentence or sentences, the headings could be directly quoted into the slides to be listed items, as found in PSLr03, PSLr09, and PSLr10. To illustrate, the four listed items in the slide shown in Figure 6.4 were the exact section headings from 2.1 to 2.4 in the original MTLrs. The writer directly cut and pasted these section headings to the corresponding slide to manifest the themes she reviewed rather than going into detail, which could be ascribed to the limited time for presentation and the insignificance of the PSLr in the writer's view. To conclude, the quotation of the sentence(s) and section headings were all categorized as SS1 *Directly quoting texts*. This result reveals that when the writers composed the PSLrs, they tended to utilize the texts from the original MTLrs and re-presented them in the slides without change.

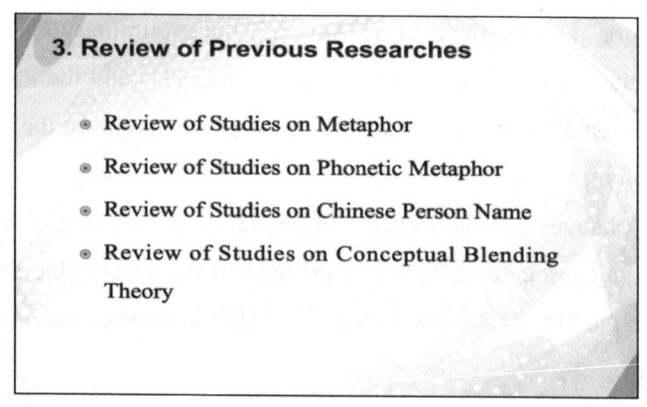

3. Review of Previous Researches

- Review of Studies on Metaphor
- Review of Studies on Phonetic Metaphor
- Review of Studies on Chinese Person Name
- Review of Studies on Conceptual Blending Theory

Figure 6.4　Example of Directly Quoting Section Headings (PSLr03_S1)

Moreover, the second frequently used single strategy was SS6 *Extracting keywords or phrases* to be listed items, which was found in half of the eight pairs. In addition, SS5 *Extracting sentence fragments to be listed items* and SS2 *Rewording texts* were found less in these pairs, with a frequency of 37.5% and 25%, respectively. It should be noticed that in the instances of SS6 and SS5, certain words from the thesis were replaced by shorthand symbols. To illustrate, the word "and" was transferred as "&" and "for example" was replaced by "e.g." in PSLr07. These shorthand symbols were regarded as the same word in the original thesis when categorizing the transfer strategies. The reason for the employment of these shorthand symbols could be that the writers want to make the content in the slide concise and easier for the audience to comprehend. The interviews with the supervisors indicate that it is acceptable to utilize these shorthand symbols, but the students need to make sure that these symbols are widely used so the audience can understand them without extra explanations.

In addition, one new single strategy was identified in these pairs, i.e., SS9 *Directly copying graphic items*. As the example in Table 6.13, the writer directly cut the table from the original MTLr and then pasted it in the corresponding slide. This strategy was found in two pairs (25%) of the MTLrs and the PSLrs.

Table 6.13 Definition and Example of SS9 *Directly Copying Graphic Items*

Definition		SS9 Directly copying graphic items To cut a graphic (e.g., table, figure) from the original thesis and paste it in the slide
Example	MT	Table 2.2 Nattinger & DeCarrico's Classification of Lexical Chunks | Items	Grammatical level	Canonical/ Non-canonical	Variable/ Fixed	Continuous/ Discontinuous
---	---	---	---	---
Poly-words	Word	Both	Fixed	Continuous
Institutionalized expressions	Sentence	Canonical	Fixed	Continuous
Phrasal constraints	Word	Both	Somewhat variable	Mostly Continuous
Sentence builders	Sentence	Canonical	Highly variable	Often Discontinuous	 (MTLr07_p.14)
	PS	**2. Literature Review** Classification ▷ Nattinger & DeCarrico(1992): |	Grammatical level	Canonical/ Non-canonical	Variable/ Fixed	Continuous/ Discontinuous
---	---	---	---	---
Poly-words	Word	Both	Fixed	Continuous
Institutionalized expressions	Sentence	Canonical	Fixed	Continuous
Phrasal constraints	Word	Both	Somewhat variable	Mostly Continuous
Sentence builders	Sentence	Canonical	Highly variable	Often Discontinuous	 (PSLr07_S2)

The least employed single strategy was SS8 *Adding texts* that only occurred in one PSLr, in which the writer created new texts that were not identified in the original thesis. The results of the single strategies demonstrate that the writers employed various ways to compose the items in the slides and both the texts and graphics could be transferred to the slides. Nevertheless, most of the single strategies were personal preferences rather than a trend in the present discourse community.

Aside from the single strategies, combined strategies were also identified in these eight pairs of MTLrs and PSLrs. Four combined strategies were newly observed in the pairs of Literature Review, as shown in Table 6.14 where their definitions and typical examples are provided.

Table 6.14 Newly Identified Combined Strategies in the Eight Pairs of MTLrs and PSLrs

Strategy & Definition	Example	
	MT	PS
CS13 Directly quoting and adding texts: To cut a full sentence or sentences from the original thesis and add extra texts to form a listed item in the slide	"Mao (2019) also conducts a research in Hainan from the perspective of sociolinguistics." (MTLr16_p.6)	"**For example**: Mao (2019) also conducts a research in Hainan from the perspective of sociolinguistics." (PSLr16_S3)
CS14 Directly quoting and omitting the texts but keeping the citation(s): To cut one sentence from one paragraph(s) and omit the remaining sentences but keep the citations as non-integral citations to be added to the end of that sentence or the relevant place to form a listed item in the slide	"**The term discourse has been used in many ways across the social sciences, especially in the field of discourse analysis, even in EDA.** Foucault (1972) defines ... It is also generally... (**Brown & Yule, 1983**)." (MTLr13_p. 22)	"The term discourse has been used in many ways across the social sciences, especially in the field of discourse analysis, even in EDA (Foucault, 1972; Brown & Yule, 1983)." (PSLr13_S1)

Cont.

Strategy & Definition	Example	
	MT	PS
CS14 Directly quoting and omitting the texts but keeping the citation(s): To cut one sentence from one paragraph(s) and omit the remaining sentences but keep the citations as non-integral citations to be added to the end of that sentence or the relevant place to form a listed item in the slide	"Compared with … **It can be seen as the related literature focuses on theoretical and description introductions, and application studies, which is similar with abroad.** The first part is … **Xiang (2004)** introduces … **Liu & Zhu (2011)** analyze … Besides brochures… Dai & Qiu (2012) define … **Xin & Huang (2013)** point … **Huang (2016)** focuses on … **He & Wei (2017b)** put forward … At the same time, researchers … (Huang, 2016 & 2017). Huang (2016) shows … Huang (2016) comes up … **(Huang & Chen, 2018).** He & Wei (2018) make … The second part is … Wang (2002) studies … **Xin (2006)** compares … **He & Wei (2017a)** establish … **He & Zhang (2017)** establish … **Miao & Lei (2019)** analyze …" (MTLr13_p.8-9)	"It can be seen as the related literature focuses on theoretical and description introductions **(Xiang, 2014; Liu & Zhu, 2011; Xin & Huang, 2013; Huang, 2016; Huang & Chen, 2018; He & Wei, 2018),** and application studies **(Xin, 2006; He &. Wei, 2017; He & Zhang, 2017; Miao & Lei, 2019),** which is similar with abroad." (PSLr13_S4)
CS15 Directly quoting, omitting, and adding texts but keeping citation(s): To cut one sentence(s) from one paragraph(s), omit the remaining sentences but keep the citation(s) as non-integral citations to be added to the end of that sentence or to the relevant place, and add extra texts to form a listed item in the slide	"The study of news discourse… **It can be divided into two parts: news discourse on politics, news discourse on society and environment.** The details are in the following. **The review focuses on the news discourse on politics, … He & Wang (2018)** study … **The second part is about the news discourse on society and environment. Xu (2014)** studies … **Yang (2018)** indicates … **Yuan (2018)** studies …" (MTLr13_p. 12-13)	"It can be divided into two parts: news discourse on politics, news discourse on society and environment. The **first** review focus on the news discourse on politics (He & Wang, 2018). The second part is about the news discourse on society and environment. (Xu, 2014; Yang, 2018; Yuan, 2018)" (PSLr13_S5)

237

Cont.

Strategy & Definition	Example	
	MT	PS
CS16 Rewording and omitting texts: To change certain word(s) and omit certain word(s) of the selected sentence(s) to form a listed item	"Therefore, **the writer adopts** the term of climate change as the target problem to use and study in this thesis. At the same time, the term is defined as global warming affected by human beings for avoiding the confusion to readers." (MTLr13_p. 2)	"The term of climate change **is adopted** as the target problem to use and study in this thesis. At the same time, the term is defined as global warming affected by human beings for avoiding the confusion to readers." (PSLr13_S2)

In total, eight combined strategies were found in these pairs of MTLrs and PSLrs, as displayed in Table 6.15. The most frequently used combined strategy was CS7 *Extracting and rewording texts*, which had a low frequency of 37.5%. In the instances of CS7, the verbs were usually reworded to initiate a listed item, such as "occupying" being transferred as "occupy" in the slide of PSLr07 and "emphasizes" being "emphasize" in the slide of PSLr09. Moreover, synonyms were utilized to replace some of the texts from the original MTLrs. For example, in PSLr16, the text "some of the previous studies do not focus on ..." became "few studies focus on ...", which makes the text more concise.

Table 6.15 Combined Strategies Identified in the 8 Pairs of MTLrs and PSLrs

Combined strategies	Occurrence	No. of pairs	%
CS7 Extracting and rewording texts	8	3	37.5
CS8 Extracting and adding texts	5	2	25.0
CS13 Directly quoting and adding texts	4	2	**25.0**
CS2 Directly quoting and relocating texts	1	1	12.5
CS6 Extracting and relocating texts	1	1	12.5
CS14 Directly quoting and omitting the texts but keeping the citation(s)	8	1	12.5
CS15 Directly quoting, omitting, and adding texts but keeping citation(s)	1	1	12.5
CS16 Rewording and omitting texts	1	1	12.5

(*Note: The newly identified strategies are in bold.*)

The remaining seven combined strategies had far fewer frequencies and most of them were employed by only one writer. The last three strategies were all found in the pair of MTLr13 and PSLr13. These results manifest that the writers made a great effort to compose the contents on the slides by themselves, which reveals that they may have scarce knowledge of how to transfer the texts to the corresponding slides. Thus, more attention is called to be paid to the activities of the genre transfer between these two genres.

6.3 The Theoretical Framework Pair

6.3.1 Changes and Transfer Strategies of the Overall Structure

In the corpus of original theses, 12 of them contained a Theoretical Framework chapter whereas only eight thesis defense presentation slide sets were observed to include the content from this chapter. Thus, there were 12 MTTfs and eight PSTfs found in the present study. A closer investigation found that PSTf02 was added to the slides by the writer as MTTf02 was absent in the subcorpus. In other words, among the 12 MTTfs, merely seven of them were transferred to the corresponding slides. The conversation with the writer of PSTf02 reveals that the reason why he added this section to the slides was that the model of the senior he observed included this section, hence, he decided to add it as well. The content of this section that he added to the slides was from one thematical unit of the original Literature Review chapter, which again confirms that the Theoretical Framework chapter is a part of the Literature Review chapter.

It can be concluded that two strategies were identified from the perspective of the overall structure when the writers transferred the Theoretical Framework chapter to the corresponding slides. The first strategy was the omission of the Theoretical Framework chapter as 5 out of the 12 writers who had this chapter in the original theses omitted related content of this chapter in the slides, which makes this chapter optional to be provided in the slides. This echoes the finding of Hu and Liu (2018) that *Framework* was found to be an optional move in the three-minute thesis presentation, which indicates that the theoretical framework the writers adopted for their thesis was not necessary to be delivered to the audience during the presentation. The second strategy was the addition of the Theoretical Framework section in the slides. Nevertheless, it was observed in only one instance, thus, it was not preferred by the writers in the present discourse community.

Moreover, a comparison of the chapter titles in the original theses and those in the corresponding slides found that the same titles were transferred to the slides by the writers to indicate the content from this chapter. Specifically, apart from one PSTf which was added in the thesis defense presentation slides, the chapter titles "Theoretical Framework" and "Theoretical Foundation" were used by six MTTfs and one MTTf, respectively. The results demonstrate that in order to transfer the Theoretical Framework chapter, the writers tended to maintain the same chapter title on the slides.

6.3.2 Changes and Transfer Strategies of the Moves

As revealed in the preceding section, PSTf02 was newly found in the corresponding slides. Therefore, the moves and steps in PSTf02 were all added by that writer rather than being transferred from the original MTTf02. Thus, this section mainly depicts the changes and transfer strategies found in the remaining seven pairs of MTTfs and PSTfs.

Table 6.16 displays the moves frequency identified in both the MTTfs and PSTfs. The obligatory *Introduction* in MTTfs became optional with a far lower frequency of 14.3% in the PSTfs. This indicates that the *Introduction*, aiming to provide the structure of this chapter or section, was not significant when presenting the Theoretical Framework during the thesis defense.

Table 6.16 Move Frequency in the 7 Pairs of MTTfs and PSTfs

Move	% (MTTfs)	%(PSTfs)
Introduction	100	14.3
Move 1 Establishing one part of the territory	100	42.9
Move 2 Creating a research niche	71.4	14.3
Move 3 Occupying the niche	100	100
Conclusion	28.6	0

Moreover, Move 1 was obligatory in the original MTTfs, whereas it was optional when being transferred to the PSTfs. Similarly, Move 2, conventional in the MTTfs, became optional in the PSTfs as well. The results reveal that the territory and the research niche were not the vital information to be provided when presenting the content related to the Theoretical Framework to the audience. It is probably because the audience, i.e., the committee members, is experts who already know the background of the field. Additionally, the optional status of the research niche might be explained that the writers at the M.A. level are less confident to criticize the existing theories or knowledge claims.

Furthermore, when the writers transferred the MTTfs to the PSTfs, all of them maintained Move 3 *Occupying the niche* to be displayed in the slides. This suggests that this move is essential and needs to be transferred to the slides if the writer decides to provide the Theoretical Framework section during the thesis defense.

In addition, the *Conclusion* found in the MTTfs was absent in the PSTfs, which could be ascribed to the different lengths of these two genres since the PSTfs merely consisted of around two slides in which the content is clear to the audience. Thus, it is not necessary to summarize it given the limited presentation time.

In terms of the move pattern, the seven MTTfs were organized in varied ways, thus, no move pattern was identified. However, the move sequence of M1-M3 was identified in the majority of the MTTfs (85.7%), while it was observed in two PSTfs (28.6%), which is understandable as Move 1 was optionally transferred to the slides.

According to the above results, one transfer strategy was identified at the move level, that is the omission of the move. The frequently omitted moves were *Introduction*, Move 1 *Establishing one part of the territory*, Move 2 *Creating a research niche*, and *Conclusion*. Therefore, it can be inferred that these moves were not essential to be displayed in the slides, thus, they are suggested to be omitted when producing a PSTf.

6.3.3 Changes and Transfer Strategies of the Steps

Table 6.17 provides the frequency of the steps of Move 1 identified in the seven pairs of MTTfs and PSTfs. According to the table, S1 was obligatory in the original

MTTfs, whereas it was optional after being transferred to the slides. Moreover, S2 which was optional in the MTTfs was not found in the corresponding PSTfs. The results imply that these two steps were not necessary to be provided in the slides. The reason could be that the primary communicative purpose of this Theoretical Framework section is to demonstrate the theoretical framework adopted for the writer's research, thus, the writers tended to provide less information that is not directly related to the primary communicative purpose of this section.

Table 6.17 Step Frequency under Move 1 in the 7 Pairs of MTTfs and PSTfs

Step	% (MTTfs)	%(PSTfs)
S1 Surveying the non-research phenomena or knowledge claims	100	42.9
S2 Claiming centrality	33.3	0
S3 Surveying the research-related phenomena	0	0

As for the steps of Move 2 *Creating a niche*, three steps, i.e., S1, S3, and S5, were found in the seven MTTfs (Table 6.18). However, only S1 was maintained in the corresponding slide. The small number of the steps of Move 2 identified in the MTTfs was a result of the omission of Move 2 found in the genre transfer process as indicated in the above section.

Table 6.18 Step Frequency under Move 2 in the 7 Pairs of MTTfs and PSTfs

Steps	%(MTIs)	%(PSIs)
S1 Counter-claiming	14.3	14.3
S2 Gap-indicating	0	0
S3 Asserting confirmative claims	14.3	0
S4 Asserting relevancy of the surveyed claims	0	0
S5 Abstracting or synthesizing knowledge claims to establish a theoretical position or framework	42.9	0.
S6 Concluding a part of the literature review	0	0

Regarding the steps of Move 3 *Occupying the niche*, Table 6.19 displays the frequencies of these steps found in both the MTTfs and PSTfs. It can be seen that only S2 was reserved in the corresponding PSTfs when the writers transferred the

Theoretical Framework chapter to the slides. The other three steps were all absent in the PSTfs, indicating that they were of less importance during the presentation of the Theoretical Framework since they were presented in other sections, such as the Introduction and the Methodology.

Table 6.19 Step Frequency under Move 3 in the 7 Pairs of MTTfs and PSTfs

Step	%(MTIs)	%(PSIs)
S1 Indicating research aims, focuses, research questions or hypotheses	28.6	0
S2 Indicating theoretical positions/ theoretical framework	100	100
S3 Indicating research design/process	28.6	0
S4 Interpreting terminology used in the thesis	28.6	0

To conclude, one transfer strategy was identified at the step level, that is the omission of the steps. This strategy was found in all the seven pairs of the MTTfs and PSTfs and in all the three moves, which could be attributed to the limited time for presentation so the details of the theoretical framework of the writer's thesis are not provided in the slides.

6.3.4 Changes and Transfer Strategies of Textual Features

After the identification of the texts between the MTTfs and the PSTfs, it was found that almost all the texts in the PSTfs were observed in the original MTTfs. Nevertheless, the forms of the texts were transferred to the corresponding slides in various ways. On the one hand, the texts were found to become listed items in five of the seven PSTfs. These items were listed as bullets in four PSTfs. Moreover, numbers and graphics were identified to be employed to list the items in one PSTf, respectively. On the other hand, it was found that the texts from the original thesis were re-presented by diagrams in three PSTfs, as shown in Figure 6.5 below. The writers utilized the diagrams to replace the detailed description in the original MTTfs to clearly show the relationship between the items. These diagrams were used to demonstrate the categorizations of the concepts. It should be mentioned that all the seven PSTfs were observed to contain diagrams, however, the diagrams, including tables and figures, in four PSTfs were directly copied from the original MTTfs rather than being re-created by the writers during the process of genre transfer. It can be concluded that in terms of the forms of the texts in the PSTfs, bullets, numbers, and graphics were all accepted in the present discourse community. In addition, it is suggested that categorizations of the concepts in theories could be re-presented by diagrams in the slides which would make the theories easier and faster to understand.

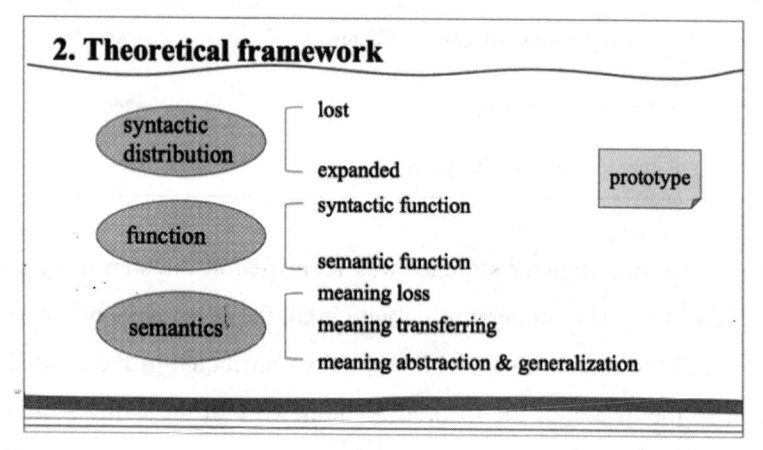

Figure 6.5 Example of Re-presenting Texts in Diagram (PSTf01_S2)

As for the items in the slides, both single strategies and combined strategies were found through the constant comparison of the MTTfs and the corresponding PSTfs. There were 24 instances of strategy in total identified in these eight pairs, ranging from two to five strategies in each pair. On average, each pair used three strategies to produce the PSTfs.

Regarding the single strategies, Table 6.20 provides the occurrence and frequency of every single strategy found in the Theoretical Framework pair. Totally, six single strategies were observed. The most frequently employed one was SS9 which was found in six out of the eight pairs (75%). This indicates that the writers tended to utilize graphics, i.e., tables or figures, to demonstrate the theoretical framework they adopted, and as for these graphics they preferred to directly copy them from the original MTTfs.

It is probably because the theories or concepts are too complicated to be comprehended by the audience merely by the words, thus, the writers selected the graphics to manifest these complicated concepts.

Table 6.20 Single Strategies Identified in the 8 Pairs of MTTfs and PSTfs

Single strategies	Occurrence	No. of pairs	%
SS9 Directly copying graphic items	9	6	75.0
SS6 Extracting keywords or phrases to be listed items	34	5	62.5
SS5 Extracting sentence fragments to be listed items	3	3	37.5
SS1 Directly quoting texts	3	1	12.5
SS7 Paraphrasing texts	1	1	12.5
SS10 Grafting graphic items	1	1	12.5

(*Note: The newly identified strategy is in bold.*)

The second most frequent single strategy was SS6, which was found in 62.5% of these eight pairs with the most occurrence of 34 instances. It reveals that the items in the slides were primarily presented by keywords or phrases that were extracted from the original thesis. It suggests that the extraction of keywords or phrases to the slides might be effective when producing a PSTf.

Moreover, SS5 *Extracting sentence fragments to be listed items* was identified in three pairs (37.5%) of the MTTfs and the PSTfs. Additionally, the remaining three single strategies, i.e., SS1 *Directly quoting texts*, SS7 *Paraphrasing texts*, and SS10 *Grafting graphic items*, were the least used ones that were only observed in one pair. It should be pointed out that SS10 was newly found in this Theoretical Framework pair. SS10 *Grafting graphic items* means that the writer extracts several graphic items in different locations in the original thesis and then combines them as a new graphic item in the slide. As revealed in Figure 6.6 below, the five elements of this graphic item in the slide were extracted from different places of the MTTf03, and then combined by the writer to form a new graphic in the slide.

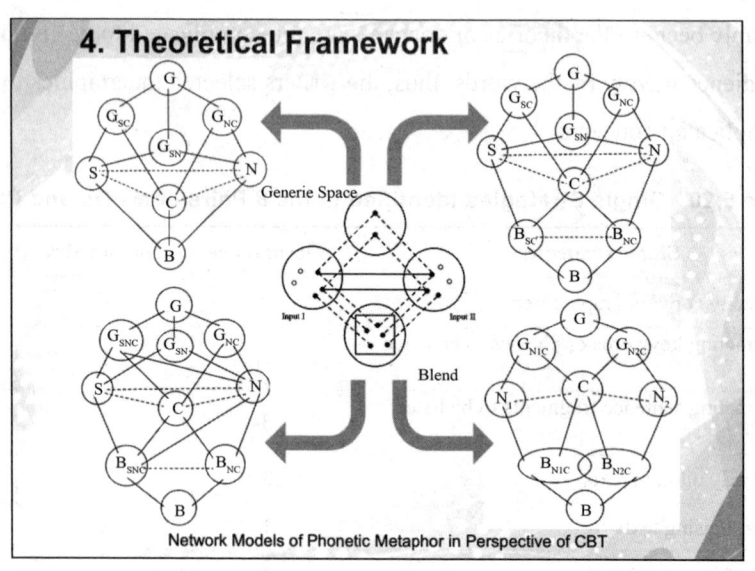

Figure 6.6　Example of SS10 *Grafting Graphic Items* (PSTf03_S2)

　　Apart from these single strategies, four combined strategies were identified, as shown in Table 6.21 below. All these four strategies had quite low frequencies. Among them, CS6 was found in two pairs of the MTTfs and the PSTfs. To be specific, PSTf01 extracted certain phrases from the integrated Results and Discussion chapter of the original thesis and then relocated them in a paraphrased version to the Theoretical Framework section in the slides. According to the conversation of this writer, it could be explained that the exploration of the results was guided by certain theories and the writer restated her theoretical framework briefly to remind the readers when reporting the results. Then, when she produced the PSTf, she preferred this brief version of the theoretical framework due to the limited time for the presentation. Therefore, the key phrases from this brief version were extracted and relocated to the PSTf. In addition, PSTf02 was added by the writer since no original MTTf02 was found, as mentioned in *Section 6.3.1* above. A closer investigation of the texts revealed that the texts in PSTf02 were extracted from MTLr02. These results manifest that the theories could be provided in the Literature Review chapter and the integrated Results and Discussion chapter, thus, these two chapters could be the sources of the texts in the PSTfs.

Table 6.21 Combined Strategies Identified in the 8 Pair of MTTfs and PSTfs

Combined strategies	Occurrence	No. of pairs	%
CS6 Extracting and relocating texts	5	2	25.0
CS1 Directly quoting and omitting texts	1	1	12.5
CS5 Paraphrasing and relocating texts	1	1	12.5
CS17 Extracting and paraphrasing texts	1	1	12.5

(*Note: The newly identified strategy is in bold.*)

Furthermore, as indicated in Table 6.21, the other three combined strategies, i.e., CS1, CS5, and CS17, were only used by one writer, respectively. It could demonstrate that these three strategies were personal preferences, but they were all accepted by the present discourse community. It seems that the writers were encouraged to produce the PSTf in innovative ways. It should be mentioned that CS17 *Extracting and paraphrasing texts* was newly identified in the constant comparison of the Theoretical Framework pair. The definition and the example of this strategy are demonstrated in Table 6.22 below.

Table 6.22 Definition and Example of CS17 *Extracting and Paraphrasing Texts*

Definition	Example MT	Example PS
To extract a part from one sentence in the original thesis and paraphrase it as a listed item in the slide	"On the one hand, by applying **the textual metaphor theories put forward by Martin J.R.** into studying English rap songs." (MTTf14_p.3)	"·Martin's textual metaphor theory" (PSTf14_S1)

In short, six single strategies and four combined strategies were identified in the pairs of the MTTfs and the PSTfs. One single strategy and one combined strategy were newly found in these pairs. Nevertheless, most of the strategies were employed merely by a small number of the writers. The frequently used strategies were the copying of the graphic items and the extraction of the keywords and phrases from the original MTTfs.

6.4 The Methodology Pair

6.4.1 Changes and Transfer Strategies of the Overall Structure

Comparing the subcorpora of the MTMs and the PSMs, 16 pairs were identified, whereas four MTMs were omitted in the slides by the writers. In other words, the majority of the writers transferred the Methodology chapters to the corresponding Methodology sections in the slides, which coincides with what was observed by Hu and Liu's (2018) study that *Methods* was found to be conventional to be presented in the three-minute thesis presentations. The result suggests that the content pertinent to the Methodology is better to be provided when producing the thesis defense presentation slides.

According to the changes at the macrostructure level, one strategy was identified, i.e., the omission of the MTM. Nevertheless, this strategy was utilized merely by a small number of writers (20%), suggesting that the writers in the present discourse community have less tendency to omit the content related to Methodology in the slides. It is understandable that the following reported results were obtained based on the methodology the writers adopted, thus, the information related to the methodology is significant to be presented.

Furthermore, when comparing the chapter title of the original MTMs and the corresponding section heading of the PSMs, it was found that six PSMs did not transfer the chapter title of the MTM to the slide. In addition, the chapter title "Research Design and Methodology" in MTM02 was changed to "Methodology" in the corresponding PSM02, whereas the "Methodology" in MTM09 became "Research Methodology" in the PSM09. The results show two transfer strategies between the MTMs and the PSMs, i.e., the omission of the title and the variation of the title. It suggests that the section title of the PSM which indicates the boundary of the section from other sections could be omitted during the genre transfer process. Additionally, it demonstrates that the synonyms of the section title could be utilized alternatively.

6.4.2 Changes and Transfer Strategies of the Moves

As indicated in the preceding chapter, PS11 had a cyclical structure of PSM-PSRD, thus, it will be reported separately in *Section 6.5.4* later. This section thus primarily provides the results found in the genre transfer of the remaining 15 pairs of MTMs and PSMs. Table 6.23 below demonstrates the move frequencies in these MTMs and PSMs. It was found that Move 1 which was conventional in the original MTMs tended to be optional in the corresponding PSMs, which reveals that the introduction of the section in the slides was not a convention in the present discourse community.

Table 6.23 Move Frequency Identified in the 15 Pairs of MTMs and PSMs

Move	% (MTMs)	%(PSMs)
Move 1 Introducing the Method chapter	93.3	33.3
Move 2 Describing data collection method and procedure(s)	100	93.3
Move 3 Delineating methods of data analysis	80	33.3
Move 4 Elucidating data analysis procedure(s)	100	60

Furthermore, Move 2 was obligatory in the MTMs, while it became conventional in the corresponding slides. Nonetheless, after being transferred, Move 2 had a high frequency of 93.3%, which could be regarded as a quasi-obligatory move (Chen & Kuo, 2012). Therefore, the results manifest that the pertinent information about the data collection is essential to be selected and provided in the slides.

In addition, Move 3, which was conventional in the original MTMs, tended to be optional when being transferred to the PSMs. The majority of the writers preferred not to explicitly exhibit the data analysis methods. The interviews with the students demonstrate that they thought the data analysis methods were indicated by the data analysis procedures already, thus, they tended not to repeat this information in order to save more time. Moreover, they said that merely showing the data analysis methods is not helpful for the audience to understand how the data were analyzed. The result suggests that data analysis methods are less significant to be presented in the slides.

Moreover, the status of Move 4 *Elucidating data analysis procedures* changed from obligatory to conventional after being transferred from MTMs to PSMs. It could be possibly explained that the writers may consider that their data analysis procedures are easy for the audience to comprehend, so they tended not to demonstrate them in the slides because of the limited time for presentation.

It should be pointed out that a new move *Providing chapter summary* was found in three out of the original 15 MTMs, whereas it was not observed in the corresponding PSMs. This could be attributed to the size of these two different genres that MTMs are far lengthier than the PSMs so the writers could utilize a summary to recapitulate the key issues provided in the preceding texts. This result shows that the size of the texts in one genre plays a role in the selection of the contents to be displayed.

In terms of the move patterns, most of the MTMs and PSMs were structured in various ways. In other words, the repeated move sequences were identified in merely a small number of the texts. The most frequently used move pattern in the 15 original MTMs was M1-M2-M3-M4 with a frequency of 20%. Nevertheless, the most frequently employed one in the PSMs was M2-M4 (20%), which results from the omission of Move 1 in the PSMs.

In sum, the omission of the move was found to be the transfer strategy at the move level. The most frequently omitted move was Move 1 *Introducing the Method chapter*, followed by Move 3 *Delineating the methods of data analysis*, and Move 4 *Elucidating data analysis procedures*. However, after the omission, Move 4 was conventional in the PSMs, suggesting that it is better to demonstrate the data analysis procedures in the slides to be more acceptable in the current discourse community.

6.4.3　Changes and Transfer Strategies of the Steps

Apart from the moves, the comparison of the steps in each move was conducted as well. Table 6.24 below shows the steps of Move 1 *Introducing the Method chapter* in the 15 pairs of MTMs and PSMs. It was observed that S1 was sharply reduced from 73.3% to 6.7% in the corresponding PSMs, which could be due to the concise nature of the slides that the section structure is not necessary to be displayed in the slide.

Table 6.24 Step Frequency of Move 1 in the 15 Pairs of MTMs and PSMs

Step	%(MTMs)	%(PSMs)
S1 Indicating chapter/section structure	73.3	6.7
S2 Providing an overview of the study	73.3	26.7
S3 Indicating theory/approach	13.3	6.7

Furthermore, S2 was conventional in the MTMs, while it became optional when being transferred to the PSMs. It could be explained that the Methodology chapter was the third or the fourth chapter in the original theses, which is distant from the Introduction chapter where the overview of the study was delineated, thus, the writers may want to remind the readers of the related information so the readers could clearly comprehend the research methodology. Therefore, S2 was found to be conventional in the original MTMs. On the other hand, during the thesis defense presentation, the information was condensed and delivered in a short period of time, hence, it was not necessary for the writers to repeat certain information to remind the audience, which leads to the optional status of S2 in the PSMs. Additionally, S2 was identified to be mainly about the research questions of the writers' studies which could be provided in the Introduction chapter or the Methodology chapter, thus, the texts pertinent to the research questions were either in the Introduction section or the Methodology section in the slides rather than being repeated in both of these two sections. The results reveal that the repetition of information is rare in the slides.

Moreover, S3 *Indicating theory or approach* stayed optional after being transferred to the corresponding PSMs, which suggests that it was not significant and was not one of the communicative functions of Move 1 *Introducing the Method chapter.*

Table 6.25 Step Frequency of Move 2 in the 15 Pairs of MTMs and PSMs

Step	%(MTMs)	%(PSMs)
S1 Describing the sample	100	73.3
S2 Describing methods and steps in data collection	100	60
S3 Justifying data collection procedure(s)	80	0

For the steps of Move 2 *Describing data collection method and procedures*, it can be seen from Table 6.25 that the two obligatory steps found in the original MTMs were all conventional in the PSMs. A small number of writers tended not to utilize these two steps in the slides. Moreover, S3 was omitted after the genre transfer between the MTMs and the PSMs. The result shows that the justification for the data collection procedures, which may be delivered in the oral commentary accompanying the presentation of S2, was not significant enough to be displayed in the slides.

Table 6.26   Step Frequency of Move 3 in the 15 Pairs of MTMs and PSMs

Step	%(MTMs)	%(PSMs)
S1 Presenting an overview of the design	73.3	13.3
S2 Explaining specific method(s) of data analysis	20	13.3
S3 Explaining variables and variable measurement	6.7	6.7
S4 Justifying the methods of measuring variables or data analysis	0	0

In terms of the steps of Move 3 *Delineating methods of data analysis* (Table 6.26), one change was identified between the MTMs and PSMs pair, that is S1 became optional from being conventional in the original MTMs. It could be caused by the frequent omission of Move 3 in the slides during the genre transfer, as mentioned in the preceding section.

It should be mentioned that although S3 had the same frequency in these two genres, a closer examination of it found that S3 was observed in MTM16 and PSM07. It means that this step was omitted by the writer of the PSM16, while it was added by the writer of the PSM07. Therefore, two changes were identified in terms of the adoption of S3 in the corresponding slides, i.e., S3 being omitted and S3 being added.

Table 6.27   Step Frequency of Move 4 in the 15 Pairs of MTMs and PSMs

Step	%(MTMs)	%(PSMs)
S1 Relating (or recounting) data analysis procedure(s)	100	60
S2 Justifying the data analysis procedure(s)	6.7	0
S3 Previewing results	13.3	0

As for the steps of Move 4 *Elucidating data analysis procedures*, it can be seen from Table 6.27 that S1 was obligatory in the original MTMs but not every corresponding PSM maintained this step after the genre transfer, thus, it became conventional in the slides. Additionally, S2 and S3 were all omitted in the slides, which reveals that these two steps were of less importance in both the MTMs and the PSMs.

Accordingly, the transfer strategies found at the step level were the omission of step and the addition of step. The most frequently employed strategy was the omission of step, which was observed in the steps of all four moves. The considerably omitted steps were S1 *Indicating chapter/section structure* of Move 1, S3 *Justifying data collection procedures* of Move 2, and S1 *Presenting an overview* of the design of Move 3. The addition of step was identified in only one instance, suggesting that it was not popular among the writers in the present discourse community.

6.4.4 Changes and Transfer Strategies of Textual Features

When examining the contents between the 15 pairs of the MTMs and the PSMs, it was found that both the texts and the graphics (e.g., tables and figures) were selected to be presented in the corresponding slides. As for the texts, most of them were transferred as listed items in the slides. For these listed items, the most frequently used form was the bullets, which were found in 12 out of the 15 PSMs. The second frequent form to list the items was the numbers, utilized by eight PSMs. Graphics and text boxes were also identified to be employed to list the items in four PSMs and two PSMs, respectively. Aside from being transferred to be listed items, the selected texts were manifested by diagrams in the slides as well, which were identified in five PSMs. As shown in Figure 6.7 below, the texts were re-presented in a diagram by which the relationship among the items was demonstrated in a clear and succinct way.

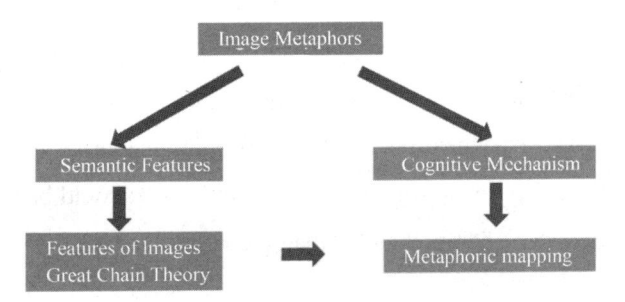

Figure 6.7 Example of Using Diagram to Re-present Texts (PSM20_S1)

As for the graphics, they were directly copied from the original MTMs to the corresponding PSMs without any change, which was observed in four PSMs. Moreover, it was interesting to find that in PSM02, pictures that were not identified in the original MTM02 were demonstrated. As displayed in Figure 6.8 below, the screenshots of the tool the writer employed to collect the data were added and presented in the slide. According to the consultation with the writer, the reason why he chose to show the picture of how the tool was used is that it could manifest the reliability of the action he conducted, which indicates the expository or evidence-providing characteristic of the images in the slides (Morell, 2015).

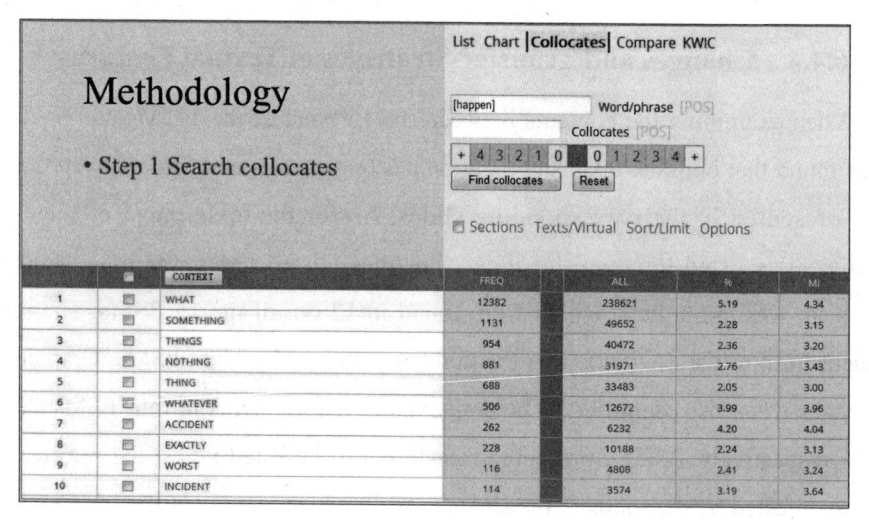

Figure 6.8   Example of Using Pictures in the Slide (PSM02_S1)

Moreover, it was found that in PSM15, certain texts from the original MTM15 were replaced by visuals. To be specific, for the second listed item in the slide as shown in Figure 6.9, its original texts were "The conversations are extracted from famous social websites, they are: Sina Weibo, Tencent QQ, Douban forum and Taobao." (MTM15, p. 2). However, when transferred to the slide, the writer utilized the icons of these four social websites to substitute the words instead. It could be probably because the visuals are easier to be comprehended than the words, especially among the Chinese people.

CHAPTER 6

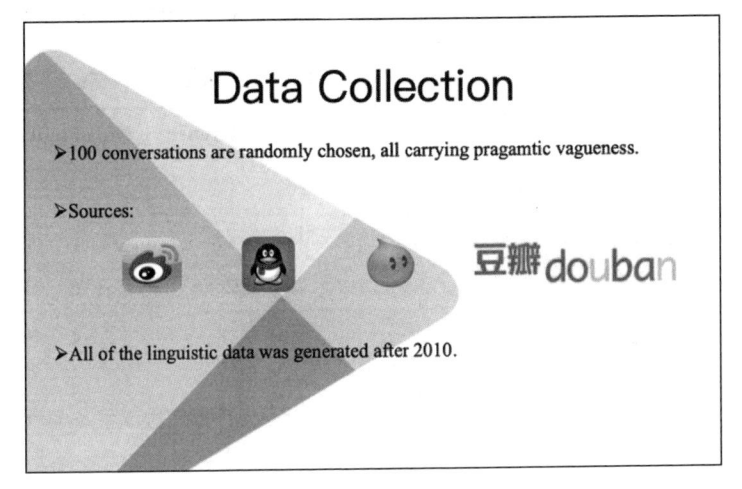

> Data Collection
>
> ➤100 conversations are randomly chosen, all carrying pragamtic vagueness.
>
> ➤Sources:
>
> 豆瓣douban
>
> ➤All of the linguistic data was generated after 2010.

Figure 6.9 Example of Using Visuals to Replace Words (PSM15_S1)

In summary, both the texts and the graphics from the original MTMs could be selected to be presented in the corresponding PSMs. For the texts, their forms were changed from paragraphs to listed items. The most frequent form used to list the items was the bullets, followed by numbers, graphics, and text boxes. For the selected graphics, their form was not changed during the process of genre transfer. In addition, the results indicate that pictures and visuals could be employed to make the content easier to understand.

Apart from the forms, both single strategies and combined strategies were found to be used through the genre transfer to create the items in the slides. Totally, 66 instances of the strategies were identified in the 15 pairs of the MTMs and the PSMs, ranging from one to eight strategies, with an average of four strategies per pair.

In terms of the single strategies, their occurrence and the number of the pairs employed are displayed in Table 6.28 below. It can be seen that the most frequent single strategy utilized by the writers to produce the PSMs was SS6 by which the keywords and phrases from the sentences in the original MTMs were extracted to list in the slides. This strategy was found in 11 out of the 15 pairs of the MTMs and the PSMs, with a frequency of 73.3%, which indicates that the writers tended to select the keywords or phrases to be demonstrated in the slides to make the slides concise for the audience.

Hence, the extraction of keywords or phrases is suggested when composing a PSM.

Table 6.28 Single Strategies Identified in the 15 Pairs of MTMs and PSMs

Single strategies	Occurrence	No. of pairs	%
SS6 Extracting keywords or phrases to be listed items	62	11	73.3
SS1 Directly quoting texts	21	6	40.0
SS8 Adding texts	20	6	40.0
SS11 Adding graphic items	7	4	**26.7**
SS7 Paraphrasing texts	7	4	26.7
SS4 Grafting texts	6	4	26.7
SS9 Directly copying graphic items	5	4	26.7
SS2 Rewording texts	1	1	6.7
SS12 Summarizing texts	1	1	**6.7**

(*Note: The newly identified strategies are in bold.*)

The second frequently used single strategies were SS1 and SS8, both of which were found in six PSMs with a frequency of 40%. Regarding SS1, a closer examination found that four out of the six PSMs employing this strategy involved the direct quotation of the research questions from the original MTMs, which reveals that the research questions are significant content so that the writers prefer to display them in full sentences. Moreover, SS8 was utilized when the writers tried to make the texts in the slides more comprehensible as a result that the context in the slides was not as elaborate and clear as that in the original MTMs. Thus, the writers added necessary texts to the slides to help the audience to understand their research procedures. This result shows that the PSM is an independent genre that needs to be comprehensible although it is closely related to the MTM.

Furthermore, a new single strategy, i.e., SS11 *Adding graphic items*, was identified in four PSMs. SS11 refers to the situation when the writers create or add a new graphic item (e.g., tables, figures, diagrams, or images) that is not found in the original thesis. As shown in Figure 6.10 below, the diagram in the slide, which was not identified in the original MTM13, was created by the writer with the aim of succinctly presenting the data analysis procedures which were demonstrated in paragraphs in the original thesis.

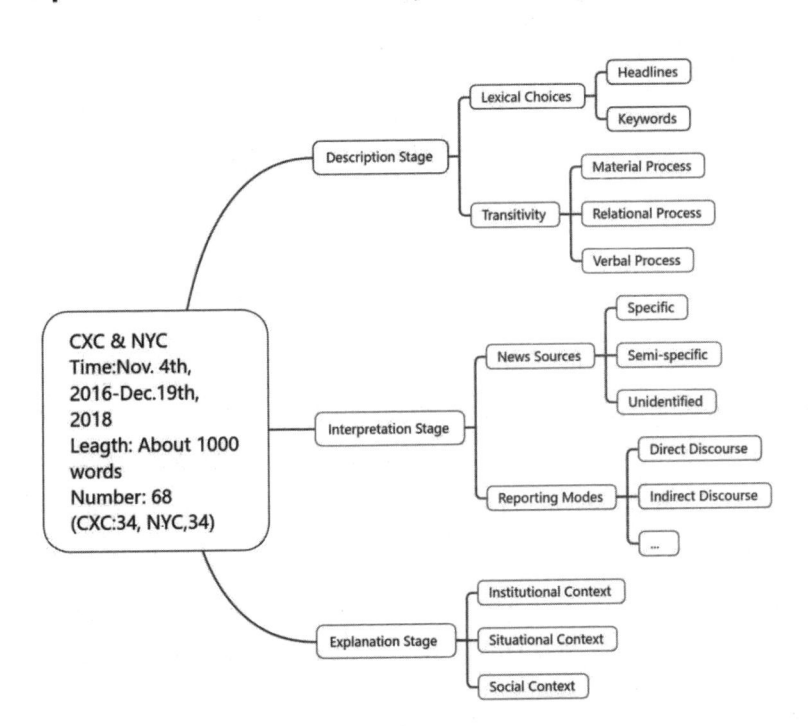

Chapter 4 Research Methodology --Data Analysis

Figure 6.10   Example of SS11 Adding Graphic Items (PSM13_S3)

In addition, SS7 *Paraphrasing texts*, SS4 *Grafting texts*, and SS9 *Directly copying graphic items* were also identified in four PSMs with a frequency of 26.7%. Besides, SS2 *Rewording texts* and SS12 *Summarizing texts* were found merely in one PSM, which was the least used single strategy in these 15 pairs of the MTMs and the PSMs. It should be pointed out that SS12 was newly found in the Methodology pair. Its definition and example are provided in Table 6.29 below. These strategies obtained a quite low frequency, suggesting that they were personal preferences rather than a trend in the present discourse community.

Table 6.29 Definition and Example of SS12 Summarizing Texts

Definition	Example	
	MT	PS
SS12 Summarizing texts: To summarize the sentences from the original thesis to form a listed item in the slide	"About the first research question, the author analyzed pragmatic vagueness's linguistic characteristics in netspeak from three levels. According to the observation on the linguistic data, the author found that there are three levels which can showed pragmatic vagueness, namely the lexical level, the sentential level and the non-verbal symbols. Then the author annotated and underlined different words, sentence patterns and non-verbal signs which give rise to pragmatic vagueness in netspeak." (MTM15_p. 5-6)	"The writer annotated the linguistic data from lexical level, sentential level. and non-verbal signs to find out linguistic characteristics of pragmatic vagueness in netspeak" (PSM15_S3)

In terms of the combined strategies, the most frequently used ones were CS7 and CS8, as displayed in Table 6.30 below, with a frequency of 40%. A closer investigation of the instances of CS7 found that certain word(s) of the extracted part was replaced by a synonym. In another way, the present participle form of the verb of the extracted part was changed to the original form, such as "extracting" being "extract" and "searching" being "search". As for the instances of CS8, certain words were added to the extracted parts from the original MTMs to make them more comprehensible in the slides.

Table 6.30 Combined Strategies Identified in the 15 Pairs of MTMs and PSMs

Combined strategies	Occurrence	No. of pairs	%
CS7 Extracting and rewording texts	15	6	40.0
CS8 Extracting and adding texts	10	6	40.0
CS17 Extracting and paraphrasing texts	7	5	33.3
CS6 Extracting and relocating texts	8	3	20.0
CS18 Directly copying and relocating graphic items	6	1	6.7
CS1 Directly quoting and omitting texts	3	1	6.7
CS10 Extracting, rewording, and adding texts	2	1	6.7
CS19 Grafting and rewording texts	2	1	6.7
CS20 Extracting and simplifying texts	2	1	6.7
CS21 Grafting and paraphrasing texts	1	1	6.7

(Note: The newly identified strategies are in bold.)

Moreover, the following frequently used combined strategies were CS17 and CS6 which were found in five PSMs (33.3%) and three PSMs (20%), respectively. In the instances of CS6, it was found that the texts from the Results and Discussion were extracted and relocated to the PSMs. The reason for this relocation of texts was that the writers tried to illustrate the procedures of the data analysis through some examples.

Additionally, the remaining seven combined strategies were employed at a far low frequency of 6.7%. Among them, five combined strategies were newly found in the 15 pairs of the MTMs and the PSMs. The definition and typical example of these five new combined strategies are demonstrated in Table 6.31 below. The low frequency of these seven combined strategies manifests that they were created by different individuals. However, these strategies were acceptable in the present discourse community, So, the effort made by these individuals would provide more options for the future writers.

Table 6.31   Definitions and Examples of the Five New Combined Strategies in the 15 Pairs of MTMs and PSMs

Definition	Example
CS18 Directly copying and relocating graphic items: To copy a graphic from other chapters in the original thesis and then relocated it as a graphic item in the slide of the PSM	Table 4.20 Semantic prosody functions of *happen* with noun collocates | Noun collocates	Assertives	Directives	Commisives	Expressives	Declarations
---	---	---	---	---	---
thing(s)	12	9	17	1,586	18
accident(s)	7	4	2	339	4
incident	4	6	3	99	2
crash	1	1	2	48	1
miracle(s)	1	1	1	44	1
disasters	0	0	1	10	0
Total	25	21	26	2,126	26
Percentage	1.12%	0.94%	1.17%	95.59%	1.17%	 (MTRD02_p. 12)

259

Cont.

Definition	Example	
CS18 Directly copying and relocating graphic items: To copy a graphic from other chapters in the original thesis and then relocated it as a graphic item in the slide of the PSM	Step 6 Calculate freq. of semantic prosody functions Table 4.20 Semantic prosody functions of *happen* with noun collocates | Noun collocates	Freq. of semantic prosody functions |||||
---	---	---	---	---	---
	Assertives	Directives	Commisives	Expressives	Declarations
thing(s)	12	9	17	1,586	18
accident(s)	7	4	2	339	4
incident	4	6	3	99	2
crash	1	1	2	48	1
miracle(s)	1	1	1	44	1
disasters	0	0	1	10	0
Total	25	21	26	2,126	26
Percentage	1.12%	0.94%	1.17%	95.59%	1.17% | (PSM02_S8)	
CS19 Grafting and rewording texts: To extract a part from different sentences and combine them together, then to change certain word(s) to form a listed item in the slide	"The data for the present research consists of two parts with each containing **50 M.A. thesis introductions in Linguistics**. The M.A. theses in Linguistics of native English speakers are randomly **selected from ProQuest** Dissertations & Theses (PQDT) published **between 2012 and 2017** and data collected from PQDT are called Pro-Quest Introductions (PQI)." (MTM09_p. 1)	"· M.A. thesis introductions in Linguistics collected from Pro-Quest (50 papers) 2012-2017" (PSM09_S2)
CS20 Extracting and simplifying texts: To extract a part from a sentence of the original sentence and simplify it to form a listed item in the slide	"On condition that the MI score of the collocate of the node word is 3 or more than 3 and ... the collocate of the node word is the typical collocate of the node word." (MTM02_p. 4)	"· MI≥3" (PSM02-S2)

CHAPTER 6

Cont.

Definition	Example	
CS21 Grafting and paraphrasing texts: To extract a part from different sentences and combine them together and then paraphrase it to form a listed item in the slide	"**The first part**, April 7th, 1928, is **narrated by** Benjamin, who is also called **Benjy** by other people in the novel. He is 33 years old, however, he is **not normal** as common people because of his **serious** mental **handicaps**... There are a great number of vague words in the whole story, nevertheless, the author only selects the first part to collect the relative data, because **the section is more different from other three parts** and..." (MTM05_p. 2-4)	"The first part in the novel is narrated by Benjy, who has serious handicaps, so that his thinking is confused. Therefore, the section is different from others." (PSM05_S1)

To sum up, nine single strategies and ten combined strategies were identified in these 15 pairs of the MTMs and the PSMs. Among them, one single strategy and five combined strategies were particularly found in the Methodology pair. The most frequently employed strategy was SS6 *Extracting keywords or phrases to be listed items*, which could be explained by the limited space of a single slide and the intention of making a concise slide for the audience.

6.5 The Integrated Results and Discussion Pair

6.5.1 Changes and Transfer Strategies of the Overall Structure

The comparison of the MTRDs and the PSRDs found that all the MTRDs were transferred to the corresponding PSRDs, which suggests that the contents related to the Results and Discussion chapter were vital to be provided in the slides. However, as mentioned in *Section 5.4*, PS11 had a recurrent structure of PSM-PSRD, thus, it will be singled out to report in *Section 6.5.5* later. The results of the other 19 pairs of the MTRDs and PSRDs were demonstrated first.

When comparing the chapter titles of the original MTRDs and the corresponding section headings of the PSRDs, two changes were identified except for the maintenance of the original chapter title in seven PSRDs. On the one hand, eight PSRDs were found to change the chapter title in the corresponding slides through the genre transfer. To be specific, five out of these eight PSRDs had the chapter title "Results and Discussion" in the original MTRDs, however, two were changed to "Results and Major Findings" in the slides and the other three were changed to "Major Findings" "Findings" and "Results", respectively. In addition, the topic-specific chapter titles in three MTRDs were transferred as "Major Findings" "Results and Discussion" and "Analyses" in the paired PSRDs, respectively. These results demonstrate that the section headings of the PSRDs could be various rather than being kept the same as the one from the original thesis. On the other hand, four PSRDs omitted the original chapter title when transferred to the slides. This shows that a PSRD without a clear section heading to show its boundary from other sections could be acceptable in the present discourse community. Accordingly, two transfer strategies at the heading level were identified, i.e., the variation of the heading and the omission of the heading.

6.5.2 Changes and Transfer Strategies of the Moves

Table 6.32 displays the move frequency between these 19 pairs of MTRDs and PSRDs. Move 1 and Move 2, being obligatory in the original MTRDs, were both changed to be conventional in the corresponding PSRDs. The result reveals that the contents related to these two moves were still essential to be demonstrated in the slides even though several writers in the subcorpora decided to omit them when they transferred the MTRDs to the PSRDs.

Table 6.32 Move Frequency in the 19 Pairs of the MTRDs and the PSRDs

Move	%(MTRDs)	%(PSRDs)
Move 1 Introducing the Results-Discussion chapter	100	63.2
Move 2 Reporting results	100	89.5
Move 3 Commenting on results	100	10.5
Move 4 Summarizing results	94.7	21.1
Move 5 Summarizing the study	0	0
Move 6 Evaluating the study	0	0
Move 7 Deductions from the study	31.6	0

Moreover, it was striking to find that the compulsory Move 3 *Commenting on results*, which is the main communicative purpose of the Discussion section (Yang & Allison, 2003), was optional when being transferred from the MTRDs to the PSRDs. It makes the integrated Results and Discussion chapter be a Results section rather than an Integrated Results and Discussion section in the corresponding slides. The interviews with the supervisors suggest that the discussion of the results is crucial to be presented in the slides. This result indicates that the writers may not be aware that commenting on the results is one of the expectations of the audience. Therefore, this needs to be emphasized in the future supervision on the students' composition of the PSRD.

Furthermore, Move 4 *Summarizing the results*, which was conventional in the MTRDs, became optional in the PSRDs. It may be accounted for that more space in the original theses was available for the writers to report the results in detail and thus, after the lengthy texts about the results, the writers might summarize the results for the readers to enhance their understanding in a concise way. On the other hand, the space of the slide and the time for the presentation were limited, which resulted in only the major results being demonstrated, hence, the summary of the results presented in the slides was not necessary.

In addition, Move 5 *Summarizing the study* and Move 6 *Evaluating the study* were not found in both two genres, which reveals that summarizing and evaluating the study was not the communicative purpose of the Integrated Results and Discussion chapter or section in the present discourse community. Moreover, Move 7 *Deductions from the study* with a frequency of 31.6% in the MTRDs was omitted in the corresponding PSRDs, which could be ascribed to the preference of the writers to provide the deductions in the Conclusion section.

Aside from the above move changes, it should be mentioned that a new move *Providing chapter summary and/or next chapter introduction* found in the original theses was not identified in the slides after the genre transfer between these two genres. This could be explained by the characteristics of the slides which need to be concise for easier comprehension of the audience, and this genre encounters the time limitation for the information delivery so the chapter summary that was less significant was not necessary to be manifested in the slides.

Accordingly, it can be concluded that one transfer strategy was found to be extensively employed by the writers at the move level, which is the omission of move. The most frequently omitted moves were Move 3 *Commenting on results* and Move 4 *Summarizing the results*.

6.5.3 Changes and Transfer Strategies of the Steps

Apart from the changes at the move level, changes were also found at the step level. Table 6.33 lists the frequency of the steps of Move 1 *Introducing the Results-Discussion chapter* in the MTRDs and the PSRDs. It can be seen that the frequencies of the three steps which were obligatory in the original MTRDS were all largely reduced and they became optional in the corresponding PSRDs. Notwithstanding Move 1 being conventional through the genre transfer between these two genres, none of its steps was conventional in the slides. The results indicate that during the genre transfer process, the writers in the present discourse community had different considerations on the significant elements to introduce the Results and Discussion section to facilitate the audience's comprehension of the report of the results, hence, they had varied preferences to realize Move 1 after transferring from the MTRDs to the PSRDs. Therefore, it can be claimed that there are no fixed norms for the realization of Move 1 found in the PSRDs.

Table 6.33 Step Frequency of Move 1 in the 19 Pairs of MTRDs and PSRDs

Step	%(MTRDs)	%(PSRDs)
S1 Providing background information	100	31.6
S2 Indicating chapter purposes and/or structure	100	10.5
S3 Indicating methods used or statistical procedure applied	100	36.8

As for the steps of Move 2 *Reporting results* in the MTRDs and the PSRDs, the most obvious change was the absence of S2 *Locating graphics*, as seen in Table 6.34 below. It could be accounted for the nature and the layout of the slide that allow only one slide to be displayed at one time during the delivery of the presentation, thus, the oral commentary usually refers to the content in that particular slide being shown. Therefore, the pointing of the location of the graphic in one particular slide, which could be addressed orally, was not necessary to be written in the slide. In addition, the frequency of S3 *Reporting major findings* was slightly decreased after the genre transfer from the MTRDS to the PSRDs, which suggests that the demonstration of the major results was still essential in the PSRDs.

Table 6.34 Step Frequency of Move 2 in the 19 Pairs of MTRDs and PSRDs

Step	%(MTRDs)	%(PSRDs)
S1 Indicating section purpose/structure	90	0
S2 Locating graphics	90	0
S3 Reporting major findings	100	89.5

It should be mentioned that a new step of Move 2, i.e., *Indicating section purposes/structure*, was identified in the majority of the original MTRDs (90%), whereas it was not found at all in the corresponding PSRDs. The result reveals that this step is a particular step exclusively used only for the MTRDs. It could be explained that the MTRD was composed of several sections so the writers may need to prepare the readers for the following lengthy texts at the beginning of one section. On the contrary, the PSRD was organized by a sequence of slides where an advance introduction for the following slide was not necessary, given the limited presentation time.

In terms of the steps of Move 3 *Commenting on results*, since Move 3 was the most frequently omitted move during the genre transfer process, as mentioned in *Section 6.5.2*, its steps were found to be the most frequently omitted ones accordingly. As shown in Table 6.35, only S1 was maintained with a quite low frequency of 10.5% in the corresponding PSRDs.

Table 6.35 Step Frequency of Move 3 in the 19 Pairs of MTRDs and PSRDs

Step	%(MTRDs)	%(PSRDs)
S1 Interpreting results	78.9	10.5
S2 Comparing results with literature	36.8	0
S3 Evaluating results	0	0
S4 Accounting for results	78.9	0

Furthermore, given the fact that there were no step options for Move 4 *Summarizing the results*, no comparison of the steps of Move 4 was conducted. Additionally, Move 5 *Summarizing the study*, Move 6 *Evaluating the study*, and Move 7 *Deductions from the study* were all omitted after the transfer from the MTRDs to the PSRDs, thus, there was no possibilities for the steps of these three moves to be compared between these two genres either.

From the above comparison of the steps, the omission of step was found to be the only transfer strategy at the step level. The most frequently omitted steps were *Indicating chapter purpose and/or structure* of Move 1 and *Locating graphics* of Move 2. Therefore, it could be safe to suggest the writers to exclude these two steps when they transfer the MTRDs to the PSRDs.

6.5.4 Changes and Transfer Strategies of the Textual Features

The examination of the contents between the MTRDs and the PSRDs found that both the texts and the graphics were transferred to the slides. It is interesting to find that PSRD03 merely contained the graphics from the original MTRD03, thus, no texts were observed. The conversation with this writer reveals that she preferred the slides to be concise since the findings could be presented orally based on the graphics which were more informative and succinct than the words.

As for the texts, most of them were transferred as items in the slides listed by bullets, numbers, text boxes, letters, or graphics. Specifically, the most frequently used form to list the items was the bullets, which were found in 17 out of the 19 PSRDs. Besides, numbers were also utilized in eight PSRDs. The next frequently employed form was the text boxes which were found in five PSRDs, followed by the letters and the graphics observed in two PSRDs. It should be mentioned that for certain items, both the letters and the graphics were found to list them. As displayed in Figure 6.11 below, the three items in the slide were listed by both the letters and the graphic of the circle. The same was found in the combination of the numbers and the text boxes to list one item.

CHAPTER 6

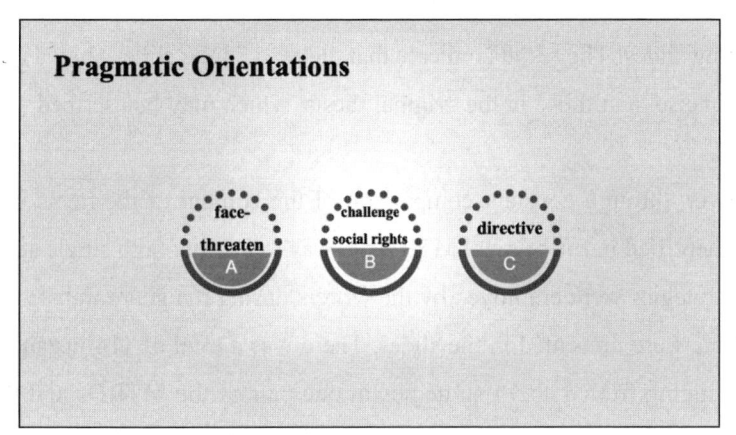

Pragmatic Orientations

face-threaten A　　challenge social rights B　　directive C

Figure 6.11　Example of Using Both Letters and Graphs to List Items (PSRD04_S15)

Furthermore, it was found that the texts selected from the original MTRDs were demonstrated by diagrams rather than sentences in the corresponding slides of six PSRDs. As shown in Figure 6.12, the texts were presented in a diagram through which the relationship among the items was manifested.

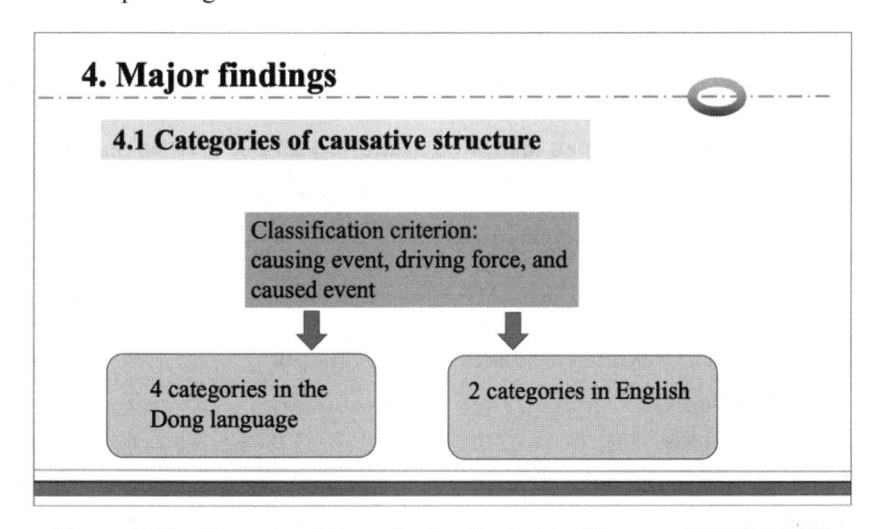

4. Major findings

4.1 Categories of causative structure

Classification criterion: causing event, driving force, and caused event

↓　　↓

4 categories in the Dong language　　2 categories in English

Figure 6.12　Example of Transferring Texts to a Diagram (PSRD10_S1)

According to the above changes about the forms of the texts, it can be concluded that the most frequently used strategy for the transfer of the forms of the texts in the slides was to change them into listed items, and the bullets were found to be employed

267

the most. In addition, the texts could be transferred to be presented by a diagram in the corresponding slides. The results indicate that the texts in the slides tended to be shorter and more concise than those in the original thesis, which may be ascribed to the nature of the slides.

Moreover, through constant comparison of the content of the items in the slides with those identified in the original MTRDs, it was found that both single strategies and combined strategies were employed by the writers during the genre transfer in terms of how the items were presented in the slides. There was a total of 114 instances of those strategies, ranging from 1 to 14 strategies in one pair of the MTRDs and the PSRDs, which makes an average of six strategies per pair.

Regarding the single strategies, Table 6.36 provides their occurrences and frequencies. SS6 and SS9 were found to be the most frequently used single strategies which were observed in 14 out of the 19 PSRDs, which indicates that the extraction of the keywords or phrases and the copying of the graphics from the original MTRDs could make the corresponding PSRDs more acceptable and effective when conducting the genre transfer. It is probably because the graphics could provide evidence for the writer's commentary and the keywords or phrases are easy for the audience to digest.

Table 6.36 Single Strategies Identified in the 19 Pairs of MTRDs and PSRDs

Single strategies	Occurrence	No. of pairs	%
SS6 Extracting keywords or phrases to be listed items	166	14	73.7
SS9 Directly copying graphic items	78	14	73.7
SS1 Directly quoting texts	92	12	63.2
SS5 Extracting sentence fragments to be listed items	30	8	42.1
SS7 Paraphrasing texts	31	7	36.8
SS12 Summarizing texts	17	6	31.6
SS2 Rewording texts	8	5	26.3
SS8 Adding texts	14	4	21.1
SS4 Grafting texts	6	4	21.1
SS11 Adding graphic items	5	4	21.1
SS13 Simplifying graphic items	1	1	5.3

(*Note: The newly identified strategy is in bold.*)

The second frequently used single strategy was SS1 *Directly quoting texts*, which obtained a frequency of 63.2%. It should be pointed out that in most of the instances of SS1, the writers tended to select typical examples from the original MTRDs to present in the slides to indicate their findings since most of the MTs were qualitative research based on textual analysis. For those examples, they were directly quoted in the slides without any change. This result reveals that the examples of the textual analysis are suggested to be directly presented in the slides when composing a PSRD.

The remaining seven single strategies in Table 6.36 were utilized in less than half of PSRDs, demonstrating that they were not popular among the writers in the present discourse community. The instances of SS12 were mainly about the interpretation of the selected example in the slide. In other words, the interpretation of the example in the original MTRD was elaborate, however, it was summarized by the writers through the process of genre transfer. This could be attributed to the limited presentation time so the writers were restricted to deliver lengthy texts. Moreover, it should be mentioned that SS13 *Simplifying graphic items* was newly found in the integrated Results and Discussion pair. It refers to the writers selecting a graphic from the original thesis and simplifying it to be a graphic item in the slide, as shown in Figure 6.13 below.

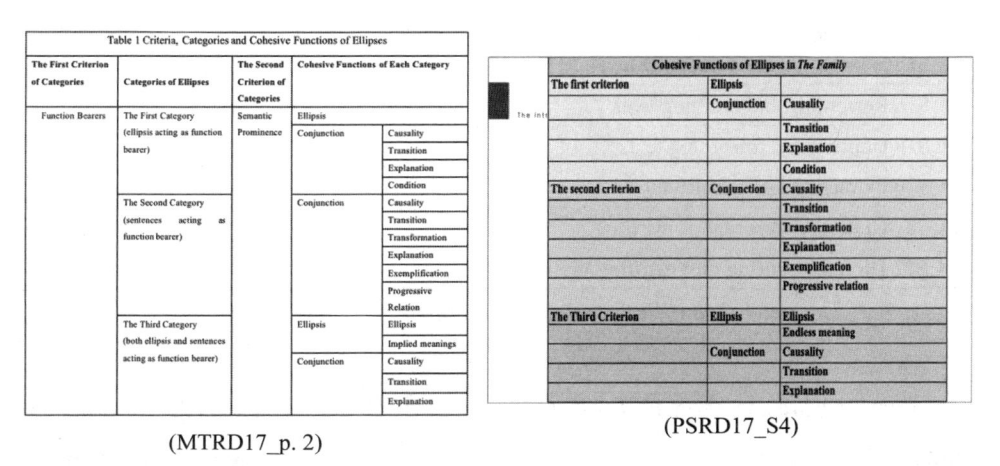

Figure 6.13 Example of SS13 Simplifying Graphic Items

In terms of the combined strategies, 15 of them were identified in the 19 pairs of the MTRDs and the PSRDs. As displayed in Table 6.37 below, the most frequently employed combined strategies were CS7 and CS17. In the instances of CS7, certain words were replaced by synonyms. In addition, the verb initiating the item which was extracted from the original thesis was changed to its original form, such as "shows" being "show" and "indicates" being "indicate" in the slide. This result implies that when the writers extract the texts from the original thesis to the corresponding slides, they need to consider the appropriateness of the texts being listed as items in the slides. It is suggested employing the original form of the verb when it is utilized to initiate an item.

Table 6.37 Combined Strategies Identified in the 19 Pairs of MTRDs and PSRDs

Combined strategies	Occurrence	No. of pairs	%
CS7 Extracting and rewording texts	16	6	31.6
CS17 Extracting and paraphrasing texts	8	6	31.6
CS18 Directly copying and relocating graphic items	14	3	15.8
CS1 Directly quoting and omitting texts	5	3	15.8
CS8 Extracting and adding texts	5	3	15.8
CS6 Extracting and relocating texts	9	2	10.5
CS2 Directly quoting and relocating texts	6	2	10.5
CS13 Directly quoting and adding texts	2	2	10.5
CS4 Grafting and adding texts	1	1	5.3
CS5 Paraphrasing and relocating texts	1	1	5.3
CS16 Rewording and omitting texts	1	1	5.3
CS19 Grafting and rewording texts	1	1	5.3
CS20 Extracting and simplifying texts	1	1	5.3
CS21 Grafting and paraphrasing texts	1	1	5.3
CS22 Directly quoting and grafting texts	**1**	**1**	**5.3**

(*Note: The newly identified strategy is in bold.*)

Furthermore, as seen in Table 6.37, apart from CS7 and CS17, the other 13 combined strategies were used at a far lower frequency. Among them, CS22 *Directly quoting and grafting texts* was a new strategy found in the present pair. Its definition and an example of it are provided in Table 6.38 below. The low frequency of these combined strategies indicates that they are just the attempt of the individuals, and their employment needs to be further explored.

Table 6.38 Definition and Example of CS22 *Directly Quoting and Grafting Texts*

Definition	Example	
	MT	PS
CS22 Directly quoting and grafting texts: To cut a sentence or sentences and then to extract a part (parts) from other sentence(s) to combine with the directly quoted sentence(s) to form a listed item in the slide	"**There are plenty of translating borrowings for Chinese borrowings, much more than the meaning borrowings of Chinese borrowings, including 135 items, accounting for 28% in 474 Chinese borrowings.**" (MTRD19_p. 9) "To examine translating borrowings of Chinese borrowings, **it finds that there are 120 items with mono-POS.**" (MTRD19_p. 10) "Accounting for 11% of all the translating borrowings, **there are 15 items with multi-POS for translating borrowings**." (MTRD19_ p. 14)	"There are plenty of translating borrowings for Chinese borrowings, much more than the meaning borrowings of Chinese borrowings, including 135 items, accounting for 28% in 474 Chinese borrowings. It finds that there are 120 items with mono-POS, while there are 15 items with multi-POS." (PSRD19_S3)

In a nutshell, 11 single strategies and 15 combined strategies were identified in the integrated Results and Discussion pair. Among them, one single strategy and one combined strategy were specifically found in this pair. The most frequently utilized strategies were the extraction of texts and the copying of the graphics from the original MTRDs to the corresponding PSRDs. The results reveal that a PSRD tends to be produced by graphics accompanying the extraction of texts from the paired MTRD.

6.5.5 A Special Case of PSMRD11

As mentioned at the beginning of *Section 6.5.1* that PS11 had a parallel structure of PSM and PSRD, this parallel structure is thus reported separately in this section. The transfer strategies of this case are demonstrated in the following paragraphs at the levels of moves, steps, and textual features the same as in the preceding sections.

As for the Methodology part, it was found that the three moves used in the original MTM11 were maintained in the slides of the Methodology section. Nevertheless, at the step level, one change was observed, that is S1 *Indicating chapter/section structure* of Move 1 *Introducing the Method chapter* was omitted in the corresponding slides. This could be understandable since the content presented in the slides is limited, and each slide usually contains a heading to indicate the theme of that slide, thus the section structure is not necessary to be provided. Accordingly, the transfer strategy this writer employed to conduct the PSM at the rhetorical structure level was the omission of step.

On the other hand, as for the integrated Results and Discussion part, the original MTRD11 employed four moves, i.e., Move 1 *Introducing the Results-Discussion chapter*, Move 2 *Reporting results*, Move 3 *Commenting on results*, and Move 4 *Summarizing results*, while only Move 2 was identified in the corresponding slides. In other words, Move 1, Move 3, and Move 4 were omitted during the process of the genre transfer. The omission of Move 1 is because the content in the slides is short and direct, so, the introduction of the section structure is not needed. The interview with this writer indicates that the omission of Move 3 is for the consideration that it could be delivered orally based on the results in the slides. Moreover, the omission of Move 4 could be explained that the results selected to be presented in the slides were shown concisely rather than lengthily as those in the thesis. Thus, it points out that the summary of the results being reported in the slides was not necessary due to the limited time for the thesis presentation. In addition, a closer examination of the steps of Move 2 found that S1 *Locating graphics* was also omitted in the corresponding slides. This may be influenced by the nature of the PowerPoint presentation during which the slide is displayed one by one, so the graphic(s) shown in one slide could be clearly referred to without confusion. It can be drawn that the transfer strategies this writer utilized to compose the PSRD in terms of the rhetorical structure were the omission of move, i.e., Move 1, Move 3, and Move 4, and the omission of step, i.e., S1 *Locating graphics*.

Furthermore, at the textual level, it was found that the texts from the original MT11 were transferred as listed items in the slides, similar to what was observed in the other pairs. Regarding the texts in the Methodology part of the slides, both single strategies and combined strategies were identified. As seen in Table 6.39, four single strategies and two combined strategies were found. The most frequent strategy this writer used was SS1. A closer examination of the instances of SS1 found that the texts directly quoted from the original thesis were the subheadings that indicated the data analysis procedures, which reveals that the writer prefers concise texts to full sentences when demonstrating the procedures of data analysis.

Table 6.39 Strategies Identified in the Methodology Part of PSMRD11

Single strategies	Occurrence
SS1 Directly quoting texts	5
SS4 Grafting texts	1
SS6 Extracting keywords or phrases to be listed items	1
SS7 Paraphrasing texts	1
CS13 Directly quoting and adding texts	1
CS21 Grafting and paraphrasing texts	1

In terms of the content in the integrated Results and Discussion part in the PSMRD11, both texts and graphics from the original MTRD11 were transferred to the slides. Nevertheless, only single strategies were identified during this genre transfer process. To be specific, SS9 *Directly copying graphic items* had nine occurrences and SS1 *Directly quoting texts* was observed in three instances. In other words, the graphics were selected from the original thesis to be presented in the slides without change. Moreover, the selected examples were directly demonstrated in the slides as well. These results echo the findings found in other pairs of the MTRDs and the PSRDs as reported in the preceding sections.

In short, this special case of PSMRD11 employed similar transfer strategies as others in terms of the moves/steps and the textual features. The only difference was the organization of the Methodology section and the integrated Results and Discussion section. Others tended to compose these two sections in a sequence, while this writer preferred to make them parallel.

6.6 The Conclusion Pair

6.6.1 Changes and Transfer Strategies of the Overall Structure

Comparing the subcorpora of the MTCs and the PSCs, it was found that 17 out of the MTCs (85%) were transferred to the corresponding slides, while three of them were not identified. It indicates that Conclusion is another significant part to be maintained during the genre transfer process. Accordingly, one genre transfer strategy was observed at the overall structure level, that is the omission of PSC. Nonetheless, this strategy was employed by only 15 % of the writers in the current corpus, thus, the omission of the PSC might not be a trend in the present discourse community.

Furthermore, most of the chapter titles "Conclusion" in the original MTCs were maintained in the slides to indicate the beginning of the corresponding Conclusion section. Nonetheless, two changes were identified in terms of the section heading in the slides. On the one hand, the chapter title "Conclusion" in MTC18 became "Conclusions" in the corresponding PSC18, which may be caused by the writer's carelessness. On the other hand, six PSCs omitted the chapter title and directly started to report the relevant content from the original Conclusion chapter. This result suggests that the chapter title could be omitted in the slides through the genre transfer.

6.6.2 Changes and Transfer Strategies of the Moves

As shown in Table 6.40, all the four moves were identified in the 17 pairs of the MTCs and PSCs. Move 1 was conventional in the MTCs with a frequency of 76.5%, while it was reduced to 23.5% in the corresponding PSCs. This result indicates that the structure of the Conclusion section in the slides, which might be addressed in the oral commentary, is not essential to be demonstrated, thus, it could be omitted from the transfer of the MTCs to the PSCs.

Table 6.40 Move Frequency in the 17 Pairs of MTCs and PSCs

Move	%(MTCs)	%(PSCs)
Move 1 Introducing the Conclusions chapter	76.5	23.5
Move 2 Summarizing the study	100	70.6
Move 3 Evaluating the study	100	58.3
Move 4 Deductions from the study	100	29.4

Furthermore, Move 2 *Summarizing the study*, being compulsory in the MTCs, turned to be conventional in the PSCs after the genre transfer. In spite of the fact that Move 2 was omitted by several PSCs, it was selected by the majority of the PSCs to be transferred, which reveals that Move 2 was essential to be maintained from the MTCs to the PSCs.

Moreover, both the obligatory Move 3 *Evaluating the study* and Move 4 *Deductions from the study* became optional when being transferred to the corresponding PSCs, which suggests that the evaluation of the study and the deductions from the writers' study were not necessary to be provided in the slides. However, the interviews with the supervisors reveal that these two moves are necessary to be provided in the slides to show the whole research completely. This result implies that the students are not clear about the expectations of this PSC since these two moves were found optional in their practices. Hence, to bridge this information gap between the supervisors and the students, the evaluation of the study and the deductions from the study need to be explicitly suggested to present in the PSCs in future instruction.

In terms of the move patterns, nine out of the 17 MTCs were configured by M1-M2-M3-M4. Nevertheless, most of the corresponding PSCs were composed of only one move after the genre transfer, which is caused by the omission of certain moves as mentioned in the preceding paragraphs. This result demonstrates that the majority of the writers in the present discourse community tended to maintain only one communicative purpose from the MTCs to the PSCs.

From the above changes, one transfer strategy, i.e., the omission of the move, was identified at the move level. The most frequently omitted move was Move 4 *Deduction from the study*. In addition, Move 1 *Introducing the Conclusions chapter* and Move 3 *Evaluating the study* were frequently omitted as well.

6.6.3 Changes and Transfer Strategies of the Steps

As for the steps, merely Move 3 *Evaluating the study* and Move 4 *Deductions from the study* contain step options for their realization. Hence, this section mainly demonstrates the comparison of the steps of Move 3 and Move 4. Table 6.41 lists the step frequency of Move 3 in both the MTCs and the PSCs.

Table 6.41 Step Frequency of Move 3 in the 17 Pairs of MTCs and PSCs

Step	%(MTCs)	%(PSCs)
S1 Indicating significance/advantage	52.9	11.8
S2 Indicating limitations	100	58.3
S3 Evaluating methodology	0	0

As shown in the table above, S1 remained optional when being transferred to the PSCs. Nevertheless, S2 which was obligatory in the original MTCs became optional in the PSCs after the genre transfer. It seems that the writers had less tendency to state the limitations of their study in the slides during the thesis defense. Nevertheless, a closer examination of the instances of this step found that the reduction of this step was caused by the frequent omission of Move 3 in the slides by which Move 3 became optional in the slides. Thus, this step was optional as well.

Table 6.42 Step Frequency of Move 4 in the 17 Pairs of MTCs and PSCs

Step	%(MTCs)	%(PSCs)
S1 Recommending further research	100	29.4
S2 Drawing pedagogical implications	11.8	0
S3 Making suggestions	5.9	0

Moreover, comparing the steps of Move 4 *Deductions from the study* in these two genres found that the frequency of S1 was largely reduced, as indicated in Table 6.42. The status of S1 changed from obligatory to optional after the genre transfer. This result manifests that the writers considered the recommendations for future studies not necessary and significant to be selected to the corresponding slides. The low frequency of S1 could be explained by the omission of Move 4 through the genre transfer process. This is because Move 4 only obtained a frequency of 29.4% in the PSCs, as mentioned in the preceding section. Additionally, S2 and S3 were not identified in the corresponding PSCs, maintaining the optional status as in the original MTCs.

To sum up, one transfer strategy was found at the step level, that is the omission of step. The most frequently omitted step was S1 *Recommending further research* of Move 4 *Deductions from the study*, followed by S2 *Indicating limitations* of Move 3 *Evaluating the study*.

6.6.4 Changes and Transfer Strategies of the Textual Features

Through the constant comparison of the texts between these 17 pairs of MTCs and PSCs, two changes in terms of the text forms were identified. Firstly, most of the texts were presented as listed items in the slides. The most frequently used form to list the items was the bullets which were observed in 11 PSCs, followed by the numbers employed in seven PSCs and the text boxes in two PSCs. Moreover, the content in the original MTC demonstrated by sentences was transferred to the slides in a diagram format. As shown in Figure 6.14 below, by the diagram, the lengthy description was clearly displayed. These results reveal that there was less restriction in terms of the text forms in the slides.

The comprehension of poetic metaphor, especially image metaphor, is enabled by **the hierarchy of conceptual system**. The hierarchy of concepts exists in and among mental domains with the connection and interaction of superior concept and **subordinate concept. Poetic metaphor** is at a more subordinate level while **conceptual metaphor** at superior level. (MTC06_p. 3)	(PSC06_S6)

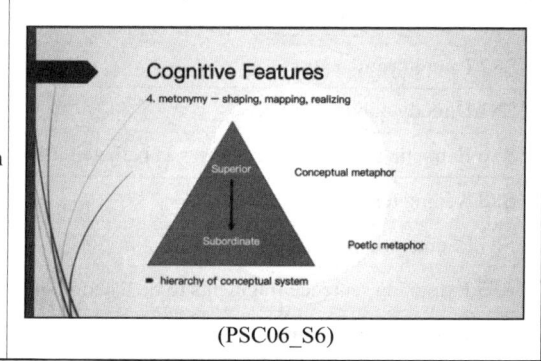

Figure 6.14 Example of Using Diagram to Present Texts

Accordingly, two transfer strategies related to the text forms were found during the genre transfer between the MTCs and the PSCs. One is to present the texts in listed items with bullets, numbers, and text boxes. The other one is to demonstrate the lengthy texts in a diagram that is concise and easy to comprehend instead.

Apart from the text forms, both single strategies and combined strategies were found to compose the items in the slides by the constant comparison of the MTCs and the PSCs. In total, 48 instances of the strategies were identified in these 17 pairs, ranging from one to seven strategies, averaging around three strategies per pair.

As for the single strategies, Table 6.43 below provides their occurrences and frequencies. It can be seen that the most frequently utilized single strategy was SS7

Paraphrasing texts, through which the writers paraphrased the selected sentence or sentences as a shorter sentence or sentence fragment to be a listed item in the slides. This result indicates that for this Conclusion section, the writers tended to provide more informative items rather than keywords or phrases as found in other sections, i.e., the Introduction, the Methodology, and the integrated Results and Discussion. It may be explained that in this ending section, the writers consider the elements to be presented in the slide significant for the audience to fully understand. Thus, for the significant information that needs the attention and comprehension from the audience, it is better to list it in full length and to paraphrase it into a concise item in the slides.

Table 6.43 Single Strategies Identified in the 17 Pairs of MTCs and PSCs

Single strategies	Occurrence	No. of pairs	%
SS7 Paraphrasing texts	20	10	58.8
SS1 Directly quoting texts	28	8	47.1
SS6 Extracting keywords or phrases to be listed items	24	4	23.5
SS8 Adding texts	4	3	17.6
SS12 Summarizing texts	3	3	17.6
SS5 Extracting sentence fragments to be listed items	8	2	11.8
SS9 Directly copying graphic items	2	1	5.9

The second frequently employed single strategy was SS1 *Directly quoting texts*, which was observed in eight PSCs (47.1%). It should be mentioned that in two out of these eight PSCs, merely the section headings from the original MTCs were directly cut and pasted to the slides to indicate what has been provided in the original MTCs, which may not be effective and informative for the audience, especially who has not read it in advance, to comprehend the writer's research.

Furthermore, the remaining five single strategies were used at a very low frequency, which shows that they were not preferred by the majority of the writers in the present discourse community.

Table 6.44 Combined Strategies Identified in the 17 Pairs of MTCs and PSCs

Combined strategies	Occurrence	No. of pairs	%
CS8 Extracting and adding texts	9	6	31.6
CS17 Extracting and paraphrasing texts	9	4	23.5
CS7 Extracting and rewording texts	2	2	11.8
CS1 Directly quoting and omitting texts	1	1	5.9
CS5 Paraphrasing and relocating texts	1	1	5.9
CS10 Extracting, rewording, and adding texts	1	1	5.9
CS21 Grafting and paraphrasing texts	1	1	5.9
CS22 Directly quoting and grafting texts	1	1	5.9

In terms of the combined strategies, as seen in Table 6.44, all of them had a far low frequency. The relatively frequently employed one was CS8 which was found in 6 out of the 17 pairs of the MTCs and the PSCs. In the instances of CS8, the writers usually extracted a part from a sentence and then added extra texts to this extracted part to be a listed item in the slide. The reason for this may be that the context in the presentation slides was not as comprehensive as that in the original thesis, hence, the writers tended to add more texts to the extracted texts to make the audience understand them during the thesis presentation.

In addition, CS17 and CS7 were observed in four PSCs and two PSCs, respectively. Moreover, the last five combined strategies, i.e., CS1, CS5, CS10, CS21, and CS22, were found in merely one PSC. These results demonstrate that these combined strategies were not a tendency for the writers in the present discourse community and their employment needs further practice.

In a nutshell, seven single strategies and eight combined strategies were identified in the Conclusion pair. Nevertheless, most of these strategies were used by less than half of the writers. The only one that was found in more than half of the PSCs was SS7 *Paraphrasing texts*, which suggests that the writer's paraphrasing skill is significant when composing a PSC.

With regard to the genre transfer from the MT to the PS, changes and strategies at the move-step level as well as the textual feature level were found. Table 6.45 below summarizes the changes and strategies at the rhetorical structure level. As for the strategies at the textual feature level, totally, 13 single strategies and 22 combined strategies were identified in the present corpora. SS6 *Extracting keywords or phrases to be listed items* was the most frequently used single strategy, which is in line with that from the interviews of the students that when transferring the MT to the PS, they usually select the key information to re-present in the slides and in order to make the slides concise, keywords and phrases were preferred, as mentioned by the student informant SS1 below.

> SS1: *I spent a lot of time thinking about what are the significant information that needs to be presented in the slides. I observed several slide sets produced by the seniors and then decided on what I wanted to select from the thesis. When demonstrating these selected contents, I prefer to extract only the keywords or phrases to make my slides concise and succinct.*

Table 6.45 Transfer Strategies of the Moves and Steps from the MT to the PS

Pair	Overall structure	Move	Step
Introduction (n=20)		Omission of move	Omission of step Addition of step Change of step
Literature Review (n=8)	Omission of LR Omission of Conclusion part Omission of Introduction part Addition of Introduction part Omission of Body part Reduction of thematic units	Omission of move Addition of move	Omission of step Addition of step
Theoretical Framework (n=7)	Omission of TF Addition of TF	Omission of move	Omission of step
Methodology (n=16)	Omission of Methodology	Omission of move	Omission of step Addition of step
Results and Discussion (n=20)		Omission of move	Omission of step
Conclusion (n=17)	Omission of Conclusion	Omission of move	Omission of step

From the findings reported in the above sections, it was identified that the changes and modifications through the genre transfer from the theses to the corresponding thesis defense presentation slides were mainly related to the textual features and the rhetorical structure, which is in agreement with what found in Dubios' (1986, as cited in Swales, 1990) study of the genre transfer between the research articles in journals and the corresponding news items in local papers that the differences were observed at both the language level and the structure level. Moreover, it is also in line with that of Pramoolsook (2007) who found the changes and modifications during the genre transfer from the thesis to the research articles were related to the content and language and the move/step structure. Besides, this result is partly in accordance with those found in other genre pairs. For example, Fahnestock (1986, as cited in Swales, 1990) and Piorno (2012) observed the differences at the language level, and Myers (1990), Mohamed (2000, as cited in Pramoolsook, 2007), as well as Zhang (2018) identified the changes at the structure level. These results demonstrate that the genre transfer between two closely related genres was conducted at two levels, i.e., the text and the structure, echoing the concepts of intertextuality and interdiscursivity, respectively, which will be provided in the following section.

6.7 Discussion on the Intertextuality and Interdiscursivity of the Current Genre Transfer

Intertextuality, as mentioned in Section 2.4, refers to the phenomenon in which one text is interrelated explicitly or implicitly with other texts at the textual level (Bazerman, 2004; Bhatia, 2010; Candlin & Maley, 2014; Deng et al., 2021 Devitt, 1991; Fairclough, 1992; Wu, 2011). The majority of the texts on the slides were identifiable in the original theses. Those texts were selected and transferred from the original text, i.e., the thesis. This is in line with the definition in that at the textual level, these two texts were interrelated with each other. Furthermore, those selected texts were mainly explicitly presented in the new text, i.e., the PS. This indicates what Fairclough (1992) called "manifest intertextuality" which happens when other texts are explicitly demonstrated in a new text.

To realize the intertextuality, 13 single strategies and 22 combined strategies employed by the writers were identified in the present study. Among the single strategies, SS1 *Directly quoting texts*, SS9 *Directly copying graphic items*, and SS7 *Paraphrasing texts* are consistent with the intertextual techniques, i.e., direct quotation and paraphrase, proposed by Bazerman (2004), Devitt (1991), and Tardy (2011). In addition, SS5 *Extracting sentence fragments to be listed items* and SS6 *Extracting keywords or phrases to be listed items* could be regarded as quotations as well. Moreover, SS12 *Summarizing texts* found in the current corpora is in line with what was claimed by Tardy (2011) that *Summary* is one of the intertextual strategies. The remaining seven single strategies were specifically identified in the genre transfer between the MT and the PS.

Furthermore, the combined strategies were only identified in the present corpora, which reveals that the transfer between these two genres is not an easy task because more than one strategy or action was required and employed to create the listed items in the slides. These strategies suggest that the intertextuality during the genre transfer along a genre chain needs much effort to accomplish, and the need to support the students to do this transfer is expected, which deserves more attention from the research field. The transfer strategies at the textual feature level found in the present research could facilitate the writers' comprehension of the intertextual links between these two genres, which in turn could support them in conducting the genre transfer more effectively.

Apart from the intertextuality, the current genre transfer indicates another concept as well, that is interdiscursivity. Simply put, interdiscursivity means the utilization of the characteristics of other genres, discourses, or styles to produce a new genre (Bhatia, 2010; Fairclough, 1992; Koller, 2010; Mäntynen & Shore, 2014; Wu, 2011). The two genres in the present study, i.e., the MT and the PS, are different genres as reviewed in Chapter 2. When producing the new genre PS, its structure or section organization closely followed the macrostructure of the original MT, i.e., the ILrTfMRDC structure. In other words, all the single chapters of the MT were found in the corresponding PS, although some students omitted the Literature Review section, the Theoretical Framework section, or the Conclusion section in the slides. Thus, it can be drawn that the organization of the MT was appropriated by the PS, which reveals the interdiscursive relation between these two genres.

Moreover, the move-step structure which is a convention of the original genre MT was appropriated as well. The moves and steps of the MT were identified in the PS. This demonstrates the interdiscursivity between these two genres. When borrowing the moves and steps, the writers employed several strategies, such as the omission of one move or step and the relocation or change of a step. This implies that in the process of interdiscursivity, modifications of the moves and the steps of the original genre can be found in order to better serve the new communicative purposes of the new genre. In addition, some of the citations in the original MT, which was a typical feature of the academic discourse, were observed to be maintained in the corresponding PS, revealing that the academic discourse was also appropriated in the composition of the PS. It can be seen that the characteristics of the original genre MT in terms of the macrostructure, moves/steps, and citations were appropriated in the new genre PS, which echoes the definition of the interdiscursivity in the previous studies (e.g., Bhatia, 2010; Fairclough, 1992; Mäntynen & Shore, 2014) and proves that the interdiscursivity can be observed in the process of the genre transfer from the MT to the PS as in the case of the present study.

In conclusion, with those links mapped and explained between Chapter 2 and the main findings, the present study is in line with and supports the theories of the intertextuality and the interdiscursivity. The transfer between two genres in a genre chain involves these two concepts, which in turn indicates that to investigate the genre transfer process, intertextuality, and interdiscursivity should be explored to shed more light on the understanding of the production of a new genre and the interrelationship between these two related genres.

6.8 Summary

This chapter demonstrated the detailed genre transfer process from the thesis to the corresponding thesis defense presentation slides, by which the changes and the transfer strategies of each chapter of the thesis in terms of the moves, the steps, and the textual features were provided and discussed. Then, the intertextuality and the interdiscursivity underpinning the current genre transfer were discussed according to the transfer strategies identified in the present corpora. The next chapter will delineate the conclusion of the whole research.

CHAPTER 7 Conclusion

This final chapter offers a summary of the major findings related to the three research questions of this current study. Specifically, the move-step structure of the master's thesis, the move-step structure of the corresponding thesis defense presentation slides, the changes and transfer strategies between these two closely related genres, and the intertextuality as well as the interdiscursivity underpinning the present genre transfer are provided concisely. Then, the pedagogical implications generated from the current research are demonstrated as well. Furthermore, this chapter ends with some suggestions for future studies based on the limitations of the present research.

7.1 Summary of the Findings

The present study examined two closely related genres, i.e., the master's thesis (MT) and the corresponding thesis defense presentation slides (PS), in terms of the move-step structure of the MT and the PS, respectively, as well as the genre transfer between them. The following sections provide a summary of these three aspects separately.

7.1.1 Summary of the Move-step Structure of the Master's Thesis

Based on the framework of Chen and Kuo (2012), the current research identified the moves and steps in each chapter of the 20 MTs in the present corpus. It should be mentioned that 12 out of the 20 MTs had a new chapter titled "Theoretical Framework". This current study attempted to analyze this chapter using the same move-step framework of the Literature Review chapter proposed by Chen and Kuo (2012) and found that this framework could explain the rhetorical structure of this extra chapter sufficiently. Table 7.1 provides the summary of the moves and steps found in each chapter, by which the frequency and the status of each move and step are displayed as well.

Table 7.1 The Proposed Move-step Structure of the MT in the Present Study

Chapter	Move and Step	%	Status
Introduction	**Move 1 Establishing a territory**	100	Obl.
	S1 Providing topic generalization/background	100	Obl.
	S2 Indicating centrality/importance of topic	90	Con.
	S3 Defining terms	35	Opt.
	S4 Reviewing previous research	80	Con.
	Move 2 Establishing a niche	100	Obl.
	S1 Indicating gaps in previous research	85	Con.
	S2 Continuing/extending a tradition	10	Opt.
	S3 Indicating a problem/need	65	Con.
	Move 3 Occupying the niche	100	Obl.
	S1 Indicating purposes/aims/objectives	100	Obl.
	S2 Indicating scope of research	35	Opt.
	S3 Indicating chapter/section structure	30	Opt.
	S4 Indicating theoretical position	10	Opt.
	S5 Announcing research/work carried out	85	Con.
	S6 Stating research questions/hypotheses	25	Opt.
	S7 Defining terms	75	Con.
	S8 Indicating research method	25	Opt.
	S9 Indicating value or significance	100	Obl.
	S10 Providing justification	30	Opt.
	S11 Indicating thesis structure	100	Obl.
Literature Review	**Move 1 Establishing one part of the territory of one's own research**	97.3	Con.
	S1 Surveying the non-research-related phenomena or knowledge claims	65.6	Con.
	S2 Claiming centrality	23.8	Opt.
	S3 Surveying the research-related phenomena	59	Opt.
	Move 2 Creating a research niche	68	Con.
	S1 Counter-claiming (weaknesses and problems)	24.7	Opt.
	S2 Gap-indicating (paucity or scarcity)	59.7	Opt.
	S3 Asserting confirmative claims about knowledge or research practices surveyed	29.9	Opt.
	S4 Asserting the relevancy of the surveyed claims to one's own research	3.9	Opt.
	S5 Abstracting or synthesizing knowledge claims to establish a theoretical position or a theoretical framework	10.4	Opt.
	S6 Concluding a part of literature review and/or indicating transition to review of a different area	33.8	Opt.

Cont.

Chapter	Move and Step	%	Status
Literature Review	**Move 3 Occupying the research niche**	36	Opt.
	S1 Indicating research aims, focuses, research questions or hypotheses	13.2	Opt.
	S2 Indicating theoretical positions/theoretical frameworks	20.8	Opt.
	S3 Indicating research design/processes	28.3	Opt.
	S4 Interpreting terminology used in the thesis	37.3	Opt.
Theoretical Framework (n=12)	**Move 1 Establishing one part of the territory of one's own research**	100	Obl.
	S1 Surveying the non-research-related phenomena or knowledge claims	100	Obl.
	S2 Claiming centrality	33.3	Opt.
	Move 2 Creating a research niche	83.3	Con.
	S1 Counter-claiming (weaknesses and problems)	16.7	Opt.
	S2 Asserting confirmative claims about knowledge or research practices surveyed	33.3	Opt.
	S3 Abstracting or synthesizing knowledge claims to establish a theoretical position or a theoretical framework	50	Opt.
	Move 3 Occupying the research niche	100	Obl.
	S1 Indicating research aims, focuses, research questions or hypotheses	16.7	Opt.
	S2 Indicating theoretical positions/theoretical frameworks	100	Obl.
	S3 Indicating research design/processes	25	Opt.
	S4 Interpreting terminology used in the thesis	25	Opt.
Methodology	**Move 1 Introducing the Method chapter**	95	Con.
	S1 Indicating chapter/section structure	80	Con.
	S2 Providing an overview of the study	80	Con.
	S3 Indicating theory/approach	10	Opt.
	Move 2 Describing data collection method and procedure(s)	100	Obl.
	S1 Describing the sample	100	Obl.
	S2 Describing methods and steps in data collection	100	Obl.
	S3 Justifying data collection procedure(s)	75	Con.
	Move 3 Delineating methods of data analysis	65	Con.
	S1 Presenting an overview of the design	55	Opt.
	S2 Explaining specific methods of data analysis	20	Opt.
	S3 Explaining variables and variable measurement	5	Opt.
	Move 4 Elucidating data analysis procedure(s)	100	Obl.
	S1 Relating (or recounting) data analysis procedure(s)	100	Obl.
	S2 Justifying the data analysis procedure(s)	5	Opt.
	S3 Previewing results	10	Opt.
	+ **Move 5 Providing chapter summary**	25	Opt.

Cont.

Chapter	Move and Step	%	Status
Results and Discussion	**Move 1 Introducing the Results-Discussion chapter**	100	Obl.
	S1 Providing background information	100	Obl.
	S2 Indicating chapter purposes and/or structure	100	Obl.
	S3 Indicating methods used or statistical procedure applied	100	Obl.
	Move 2 Reporting results	100	Obl.
	S1 Indicating section purposes/structure	90	Con.
	S2 Locating graphics	90	Con.
	S3 Reporting major findings	100	Obl.
	Move 3 Commenting on results	100	Obl.
	S1 Interpreting results	80	Con.
	S2 Comparing results with literature	35	Opt.
	S3 Accounting for results (giving reasons)	80	Con.
	Move 4 Summarizing results	95	Con.
	Move 5 Deductions from the (research) study	30	Opt.
	S1 Recommending further research	10	Opt.
	S2 Drawing pedagogical implications	10	Opt.
	S3 Making suggestions	20	Opt.
	+ Move 6 Providing chapter summary and/or next chapter introduction	45	Opt.
Conclusion	**Move 1 Introducing the Conclusions chapter**	80	Con.
	Move 2 Summarizing the study	100	Obl.
	Move 3 Evaluating the study	100	Obl.
	S1 Indicating significance/advantage	55	Opt.
	S2 Indicating limitations	100	Obl.
	Move 4 Deductions from the study	100	Obl.
	S1 Recommending further research	100	Obl.
	S2 Drawing pedagogical implications	15	Opt.
	S3 Making suggestions	10	Opt.

(Note: Obl. = Obligatory, Con. = Conventional, Opt. = Optional; The revised move or step is in italics; the + indicates the new move or step found in the present study)

It should be noticed that the majority of the Literature Review (LR) chapter had a structure of Introduction-Body-Conclusion, in which the Body part consisted of several thematic units. Thus, the frequency of the move in this LR chapter was calculated in terms of its percentage in all the thematic units rather than in the whole 20 LRs. Moreover, the frequency of the step was its percentage in all the instances of that move. Moreover, it should be noted that in the Introduction and Conclusion before and after the Body part, Move 2 and Move 3 could be found as well, thus, following Kwan's (2006) study, the current research excluded these two elements in the framework.

In total, 24 moves and 69 steps were identified in the 20 MTs, among which 3 moves and 18 steps were found in the Introduction, 3 moves and 13 steps in the Literature Review, 3 moves and 9 steps in the Theoretical Framework, 5 moves 12 steps in the Methodology, 6 moves and 12 steps in the integrated Results and Discussion, and 4 moves and 5 steps in the Conclusion.

Furthermore, these moves and steps show variations in terms of their statuses. Among the 24 moves, 13 of them are obligatory, 7 are conventional, and 4 are optional. In addition, 15 obligatory steps, 14 conventional steps, and 40 optional steps constitute the 69 steps found in the whole MTs in the present corpus. As for the obligatory moves and steps, they are recommended for the students to include when composing their own MTs. For the conventional ones, it is better for the students to present them as much as possible to make their MT more acceptable and effective to be used in this discourse community. Regarding the optional steps, they provide various possible options for the students to consider during their production of the MT, so the students can select the suitable ones to fulfill their particular intentions based on their research.

7.1.2 Summary of the Move-step Structure of the Thesis Defense Presentation Slides

The same framework proposed by Chen and Kuo (2012) for the thesis was adopted for the investigation of moves and steps of the corresponding thesis defense presentation slides and it was found to be able to explain the rhetorical structure of a different genre quite well. Table 7.2 displays the conclusion of the findings of the moves and steps. It should be pointed out that there were 20 PSs in total, however, the number of the separate sections varied widely. In addition, PS11 had a parallel structure of Methodology (PSM) and combined Results and Discussion (PSRD), which resulted in three recurrent structures of PSM-PSRD. Thus, these two sections in PS11 were reported separately rather than being integrated into the remaining PSMs and PSRDs.

Table 7.2 The Proposed Move-step Structure of the PS in the Present Study

Section	Move and Step	%	Status
Introduction (*n*=20)	**Move 1 Establishing a territory**	**80**	**Con.**
	S1 Providing topic generalization/background	70	Con.
	S2 Indicating centrality/importance of topic	25	Opt.
	S3 Reviewing previous research	20	Opt.
	Move 2 Establishing a niche	**55**	**Opt.**
	via Indicating gaps in previous research	55	Opt.
	Move 3 Occupying the niche	**100**	**Obl.**
	S1 Indicating purposes/aims/objectives	90	Con.
	S2 Indicating scope of research	5	Opt.
	S3 Indicating chapter/section structure	15	Opt.
	S4 Indicating theoretical position	10	Opt.
	S5 Announcing research/work carried out	10	Opt.
	S6 Stating research questions/hypotheses	75	Con.
	S7 Defining terms	10	Opt.
	S8 Indicating research method	5	Opt.
	S9 Indicating value or significance	40	Opt.
	S10 Indicating thesis structure	15	Opt.
Literature Review (*n*=8)	**Move 1 Establishing one part of the territory of one's own research**	**62.5**	**Con.**
	S1 Surveying the non-research-related phenomena or knowledge claim	62.5	Con.
	S2 Surveying the research-related phenomena	37.5	Opt.
	Move 2 Creating a research niche	**37.5**	**Opt.**
	S1 Gap-indicating	37.5	Opt.
	S2 Abstracting or synthesizing knowledge claims	12.5	Opt.
	Move 3 Occupying the research niche	**50**	**Opt.**
	S1 Indicating theoretical positions/theoretical framework	25	Opt.
	S2 Indicating research design/processes	12.5	Opt.
	S3 Interpreting terminology used in the thesis	12.5	Opt.
Theoretical Framework (*n*=8)	**Move 1 Establishing one part of the territory of one's own research**	**37.5**	**Opt.**
	via Surveying the non-research-related phenomena or knowledge claim	37.5	Opt.
	Move 2 Creating a research niche	**12.5**	**Opt.**
	via Counter-claiming	12.5	Opt.
	Move 3 Occupying the research niche	**100**	**Obl.**
	via Indicating theoretical positions/theoretical framework	100	Obl.

Cont.

Section	Move and Step	%	Status
Methodology (*n*=15)	**Move 1 Introducing the Method chapter**	**33.3**	**Opt.**
	S1 Indicating chapter/section structure	6.7	Opt.
	S2 Providing an overview of the study	26.7	Opt.
	S3 Indicating theory/approach	6.7	Opt.
	Move 2 Describing data collecting method and procedure(s)	**93.3**	**Con.**
	S1 Describing the sample	73.3	Con.
	S2 Describing methods and steps in data collection	60	Con.
	Move 3 Delineating methods of data analysis	**33.3**	**Opt.**
	S1 Presenting an overview of the design	13.3	Opt.
	S2 Explaining specific method(s) of data analysis	13.3	Opt.
	S3 Explaining variables and variable measurement	6.7	Opt.
	Move 4 Elucidating data analysis	**60**	**Con.**
	via Relating (or recounting) data analysis procedure(s)	60	Con.
Results and Discussion (*n*=19)	**Move 1 Introducing the Results-Discussion chapter**	**63.2**	**Con.**
	S1 Providing background information	31.6	Opt.
	S2 Indicating chapter purposes and/or structure	10.5	Opt.
	S3 Indicating methods used or statistical procedure applied	36.8	Opt.
	Move 2 Reporting results	**89.5**	**Con.**
	via Reporting major findings	89.5	Con.
	Move 3 Commenting on results	**10.5**	**Opt.**
	via Interpreting results	10.5	Opt.
	Move 4 Summarizing results	**21.1**	**Opt.**
Conclusion (*n*=17)	**Move 1 Introducing the Conclusions chapter**	**23.5**	**Opt.**
	Move 2 Summarizing the study	**70.6**	**Con.**
	Move 3 Evaluating the study	**58.3**	**Opt.**
	S1 Indicating significance/advantage	11.8	Opt.
	S2 Indicating limitations	58.3	Opt.
	Move 4 Deductions from the study	**29.4**	**Opt.**
	via Recommending further research	29.4	Opt.

(*Note: Obl. = Obligatory, Con. = Conventional, Opt. = Optional.*)

To sum up, the majority of the PSs followed the macrostructure of the original MTs which is organized by ILrTfMRDC. In addition, 21 moves and 41 steps were found in the corresponding PSs, most of which were optional ones. The special case of PS11 which had a recurrent structure of PSM and PSRD only consisted of the moves and steps identified in the remaining PSMs and PSRDs.

7.1.3 Summary of the Changes and Transfer Strategies from the MT to the PS

The MT and the corresponding PS are two closely related genres. Certain changes and the corresponding transfer strategies through the genre transfer between these two genres were identified in terms of the moves, the steps, and the textual features.

Regarding the strategies at the move-step level, as displayed in Table 6.45 in Chapter 6, omission and addition of move were identified during this genre transfer process. Moreover, omission, and addition of step and the change of one step to another step were found. The most frequently utilized transfer strategies at the move and step level were the omission of the move or the step, which could be ascribed to the limited time for the thesis presentation during the defense session so that merely the key information is presented. Moreover, the form of the new genre, i.e., the PS, which is organized by a sequence of slides, could be the possible reason for the omission of the moves or steps since the space in one single slide is limited as well. Apart from the moves and the steps, transfer strategies at the textual feature level were identified as well. Those strategies were divided into single strategies, which require single action involved, and combined strategies that require more than one action to fulfill. Table 7.3 below shows these strategies with their definitions.

Table 7.3   Transfer Strategies at the Textual Feature Level from the MT to the PS

Strategy	Definition
Single Strategy (SS)	
SS1 Directly quoting texts	To cut a full sentence or sentences from the original thesis and to paste it/them as a listed item in the slide
SS2 Rewording texts	To change certain word(s) of the sentence selected from the original thesis to form a listed item in the slide
SS3 Reordering texts	To reorganize the sequence of several sentences selected from the original thesis to form a listed item in the slide
SS4 Grafting texts	To extract a part from two different sentences in the original thesis and then combine them together to form a listed item in the slide
SS5 Extracting sentence fragments to be listed items	To extract a fragment from a full sentence in the original thesis to form a listed item in the slide
SS6 Extracting keywords or phrases to be listed items	To extract several keywords or phrases from the sentence(s) in the original thesis to form listed items in the slide
SS7 Paraphrasing texts	To paraphrase the sentence selected from the thesis to form a new sentence fragment or a sentence and present it as a listed item in the slide

Cont.

Strategy	Definition
SS8 Adding texts	To add new texts in the slide as a listed item, which are not found in the original thesis
SS9 Directly copying graphic items	To cut a graphic (e.g., table, figure) from the original thesis and paste it in the slide
SS10 Grafting graphic items	To extract several graphic items from different locations in the original thesis and then combines them as a new graphic item in the slide
SS11 Adding graphic items	To add a graphic item in the slide, which is not found in the original thesis
SS12 Summarizing texts	To summarize the sentences from the original thesis to form a listed item in the slide
SS13 Simplifying graphic items	To simplify a graphic item from the original thesis to be a graphic item in the slide
Combined Strategy (CS)	
CS1 Directly quoting and omitting texts	To cut a sentence or sentences from the original thesis, to omit the clause of the sentence or some sentence(s) in the middle, and to paste it/them as a listed item in the slide
CS2 Directly quoting and relocating texts	To cut a sentence or sentences, to move it/them from a location in the original thesis into a different location in the corresponding slides, and to paste it/them as a listed item in the slide
CS3 Rewording and relocating texts	To change certain word(s) of the selected sentence(s) to form a listed item, and to move it/them from a location in the original thesis into a different location in the corresponding slides
CS4 Grafting and adding texts	To extract a part from different sentences and combine them together, and then to add extra texts to it to form a listed item in the slide
CS5 Paraphrasing and relocating texts	To paraphrase a sentence or sentences to form a listed item, and to move it/them from a location in the original thesis into a different location in the corresponding slides
CS6 Extracting and relocating texts	To extract keywords, phrases, or fragments from the sentence(s) to form a listed item, and to move it/them from a location in the original thesis into a different location in the corresponding slides
CS7 Extracting and rewording texts	To extract a part from a full sentence or sentences in the original thesis and to change certain word(s) to form a listed item in the slide
CS8 Extracting and adding texts	To extract a part from a full sentence in the original thesis and to add extra texts to form a listed item in the slide
CS9 Extracting and restructuring texts	To extract a part or parts from a full sentence in the original thesis, and to reorganize it/them to form a listed item in the slide
CS10 Extracting, rewording, and adding texts	To extract a part from the selected sentence in the original thesis, then to change certain words and add extra texts to form a listed item in the slide
CS11 Extracting, restructuring, and rewording texts	To extract a part or parts from the selected sentence in the original thesis, to reorganize it/them and to change certain words to form a listed item in the slide

Cont.

Strategy	Definition
CS12 Extracting, adding, and relocating texts	To extract a part from the selected sentence in the original thesis, to add certain words into it to form a listed item, and to move it from a location in the original thesis into a different location in the corresponding slides
CS13 Directly quoting and adding texts	To cut a full sentence or sentences from the original thesis and add extra texts to form a listed item in the slide
CS14 Directly quoting and omitting the texts but keeping the citation(s)	To cut one sentence from one paragraph(s) and omit the remaining sentences but keep the citations as non-integral citations to be added to the end of that sentence or the relevant place to form a listed item in the slide
CS15 Directly quoting, omitting, and adding texts but keeping citation(s)	To cut one sentence(s) from one paragraph(s), omit the remaining sentences but keep the citation(s) as non-integral citations to be added to the end of that sentence or to the relevant place, and add extra texts to form a listed item in the slide
CS16 Rewording and omitting texts	To change certain word(s) and omit certain word(s) of the selected sentence(s) to form a listed item in the slide
CS17 Extracting and paraphrasing texts	To extract a part from one sentence in the original thesis and paraphrase it as a listed item in the slide
CS18 Directly copying and relocating graphic items	To copy a graphic from other chapters in the original thesis and then relocated it as a graphic item in the slide of the PSM
CS19 Grafting and rewording texts	To extract a part from different sentences and combine them together, then change certain word(s) to form a listed item in the slide
CS20 Extracting and simplifying texts	To extract a part from a sentence of the original sentence and simplify it to form a listed item in the slide
CS21 Grafting and paraphrasing texts	To extract a part from different sentences and combine them together and then paraphrase it to form a listed item in the slide
CS22 Directly quoting and grafting texts	To cut a sentence or sentences and then to extract a part (parts) from other sentence(s) to combine with the directly quoted sentence(s) to form a listed item in the slide

The main textual differences between these two closely related genres lie in the fact that the MTs were composed of the sentences and paragraphs in each chapter, whereas the PSs were presented by listed items in a sequence of slides. In short, at the textual feature level, 13 single strategies and 22 combined strategies were found through the constant comparison of the texts in the original MTs and the corresponding PSs in the present research. The most frequently used single strategy and combined strategy in the Introduction pair were SS6 *Extracting keywords or phrases to be listed items* and CS2 *Directly quoting and relocating texts*. In the Literature Review pair, the most frequently used strategies were SS1 *Directly quoting texts* and CS7 *Extracting and rewording texts*. In the Theoretical Framework pair, SS9 *Directly copying graphic items* and CS6 *Extracting and relocating texts* were found the most. Furthermore, in the Methodology pair and the integrated Results and Discussion pair, SS6 and CS7 were the most frequently used ones. In addition, in the Conclusion pair, SS7 *Paraphrasing texts* and CS8 *Extracting and adding texts* were identified the most. On the whole, SS6 *Extracting keywords or phrases to be listed items* and CS7 *Extracting and rewording texts* were the most frequently used strategies in the genre transfer process, which suggests that in order to better perform the genre transfer from the MT to the PS, students need to be equipped with the skills of extracting key information.

Furthermore, the changes and the transfer strategies between these two closely related genres indicate two concepts that play a key role in the genre transfer process as well, i.e., intertextuality and interdiscursivity. The majority of the texts in the PSs were identical to the original MTs, showing the intertextual relations between these two genres. In addition, the rhetorical structure of the MT was appropriated, to some extent, by the new PS genre, which indicates the interdiscursive practice conducted by the students during the genre transfer process. The findings reveal that the genre transfer process involves both intertextuality and interdiscursivity, which in turn demonstrates that the investigation of these two concepts would enhance our understanding of the relationship between two genres and the genre transfer practices.

7.2 Pedagogical Implications

The findings of the present research in terms of the move-step structure of the whole MT, the move-step structure of the corresponding PS, and the transfer strategies from the MT to the PS could benefit the thesis writers, the supervisors, the instructors, and the course designers.

Firstly, the changes and the transfer strategies from the MT to the PS, which, to the present researcher's knowledge, is the first attempt to investigate the transfer of this genre pair, add more insight to our knowledge of the genre transfer process. This could enhance the students' comprehension of the differences between these two closely related genres in terms of their communicative purposes and the targeted audience, and accordingly, the students can take effective actions to select the content from the MT to the PS. The identified transfer strategies in the present research demonstrate various options for the students to conduct this genre transfer more effectively. Moreover, the framework of the transfer strategies can support the supervisors as a reference to guide the students on their production of the PS. Besides, for the instructors, this finding manifests the specific skills that the students need to acquire in order to better transfer the contents of the MT to the PS. As a result, they could provide more specific instruction to the students. For example, the most frequently employed transfer strategy was the extraction of keywords, phrases, or sentence fragments. Accordingly, the instructors need to pay more attention to the development of the students' skills for extracting the most suitable and effective information appropriate for the new genre and provide more opportunities for the students to practice this skill.

Moreover, the discussion of the intertextuality and interdiscursivity underpinning the genre transfer from the MT to the PS demonstrates the appropriation of both the textual-internal resources and the textual-external resources from the original genre to the new genre during the transfer process, which indicates that the comprehension of these two concepts could equip the students to conduct the genre transfer more efficiently. Hence, these two concepts are suggested to be addressed through the instruction of genre transfer to raise the students' awareness of the appropriation of the textual-internal and textual-external resources.

Secondly, the complete picture of the moves and steps in each chapter of the MT explicitly provides the students with the specific communicative functions and the ways to accomplish these functions in that chapter. Thus, with a heightened awareness of the rhetorical structure of each chapter, the prospective students who may be inexperienced in writing such a lengthy text could compose the thesis effectively. Moreover, the supervisors will obtain a better comprehension of the real practice of the students' writing based on the move-step framework of the MT proposed in the present study, and accordingly, they could provide specific and effective suggestions to their supervisees through the supervision. In addition, the investigation of the moves and the steps of the MTs found that the writers had insufficient knowledge of how to comment on the results, which was confirmed by the interviews with the supervisors. The future instruction on thesis writing, therefore, needs to emphasize and pay more attention to the development of this skill of the students. The four steps to fulfill the communicative function of commenting on the results, i.e., *Interpreting results*, *Comparing results with literature*, *Evaluating results*, and *Accounting for results*, are suggested to be included and explicitly instructed in the classroom teaching to equip the students with various ways to comment the results found in their studies, as mentioned by Putri and Kurniawan (2021) as well as Ren and Li (2011) that making the writing knowledge explicit to the inexperienced writers could be an effective way to deal with their challenges.

Thirdly, the findings of the moves and steps of the PSs could raise students' genre awareness of this underexplored genre and contribute to their rhetorical knowledge of the communicative purposes, target audience, and the significant structural elements of the PS. Through the proposed framework, the students obtain a better understanding of the obligatory, conventional, and optional elements that could be included in the PS in order to produce a more acceptable and effective PS in the discourse community than simply following what the others did, as reported in the interviews. Furthermore, the supervisors might not pay due attention to the composition of the PS since the interviews with students reveal that they received no instruction on it. This current study, to a certain degree, therefore can increase the attention of the supervisors. They could use the findings of the rhetorical structure of the PS to guide the students on what needs to be selected from MT and re-presented in PS and where can be improved in the PS. In addition, given the pervasive employment of the PS in the thesis defense session, the integration of this genre into the writing syllabus by the course designers could largely benefit the students, as suggested by Hertz et el. (2016) that the instruction on how to design the slides and effective presentation with PowerPoint slides should be provided to the students. The instructors can make use of the findings of the present research as practical materials to teach the students in the classroom.

7.3 Limitations and Suggestions for Further Studies

After the investigation in the present research, certain limitations are identified, and thus, further studies are suggested for a better comprehension of the real practice in terms of the MT writing, the PS composition, and the transfer between two closely related genres.

With regard to the MT writing, the current research only examined its rhetorical structure, i.e., the moves and the steps, leaving the linguistic features of each move and step that could facilitate students' MT writing further out of the scope. Future studies, thus, can carry out the examination of the linguistic features that are frequently employed to realize each move and step in order to better equip the students for the challenging composition of this genre. Secondly, this study limits itself to the investigation of the MT produced by Chinese students. Through the comparison of the results of the present research with those in the previous studies (e.g., Chen & Kuo, 2012; Nguyen, 2014), cultural factors play a significant role in the employment of certain moves or steps. Therefore, it is suggested that a comparative analysis of the rhetorical structure of the MT written by writers from different cultural contexts should be conducted to add more insights to the comprehension of the MT practices. Thirdly, the majority of the MTs collected for the current study are qualitative studies and thus, some steps (e.g., S6 *Describing parameters of research* of Move 3 in Introduction) that are more likely identified in quantitative studies were scarcely found in the present corpus. Hence, more perspectives could be provided by the comparison of the move or step options between the qualitative-oriented and quantitative-oriented research to depict a clear picture of the choices by the writers holding different research paradigms.

Regarding the PS, this study only analyzed the moves and steps that fulfill the main communicative purposes of this particular genre, thus, other modes in the slides, such as the images and icons, which also facilitate the understanding of this genre are not included in the analysis. Further endeavors that touch upon the multimodal analysis of this genre would provide more valuable information for its production. Second, the data of the PS merely covered one discipline in the soft field, i.e., Foreign

Linguistics and Applied Linguistics, thus, to enhance the understanding of this practice, the rhetorical structure of the PS in other disciplines could be explored. Moreover, the comparison of the PS across different disciplines would expand our knowledge of the characteristics of the rhetorical structure of the PS in various disciplines, which would better support the teaching and learning of this genre. Third, the examination of the PS in the present study only focused on those composed by Chinese writers. As indicated in *Chapter 5*, cultural variation was observed when compared with those written by Iranian students. Therefore, further studies could benefit from the comparative analysis of the PS produced by writers from different cultural backgrounds to strengthen the comprehension of the production of the PS and to examine how the cultural factor exerts an influence on the employment of the moves and the steps. Finally, this study only explored the rhetorical structure of PS, whereas the various layouts and types, such as concise texts and heavy texts in the slides, employed by the writers are under-investigated. Hence, future research that demonstrates the perceptions of the target audience of the PS is suggested, which would bring into light what is the most expected form for the audience so as to make the PS more acceptable and effective among the discourse community members.

Furthermore, in terms of genre transfer, the current study only touched upon the transfer between the first two genres of the genre chain of the thesis defense, i.e., the transfer between the MT and the PS, while the transfer from the PS to the oral commentary is ignored. As mentioned in *Chapter 4*, the writers who presented heavy texts in the slides merely selected certain information to deliver orally given the limited presentation time, thus, further studies can be conducted to investigate the genre transfer between the PS, a written genre, and the oral commentary which is a spoken genre to reveal the complex interrelation of these two closely related genres, which could further unveil the process of the genre transfer and in turn could support the composition of the PS and the preparation of the oral commentary for the thesis defense. Secondly, the exploration of the genre transfer between the MT and the PS which was supplemented by the interviews with supervisors reveals that there is an information gap between the supervisors, who are the target audience of the PS, and the students. To illustrate, the Literature Review chapter of the original MT was necessary to be presented in the slides from the perspective of the supervisors, whereas it was optional to be included in the PS through the investigation of the genre transfer conducted by the students. To bridge this information gap, more studies need to be conducted to explore the expectations of the target audience, especially the supervisors and the committee members, and their perceptions towards the real practice of genre transfer produced by the students, which will facilitate the students' comprehension of the expectations of the audience and thus, to better equip them with explicit instruction on the significant elements to be selected to the PS. Thirdly, the present research merely focused on the genre transfer from the MT to the PS composed by the master's students. Nevertheless, this kind of genre transfer is also essential for the doctoral students who are required to transfer their lengthy dissertation to oral presentation with slides during the final defense. Further studies that examine this similar genre transfer conducted by the doctoral students, who are more experienced than the master's students, could be a worthy inquiry line and the comparison of it with that produced by master's students would provide more perspectives for the improvement of the genre transfer conducted by the master's students. Finally, the framework of the transfer strategies at the textual feature level was absent in the previous studies, thus, there are some limitations on the description and labelling of each strategy since it is primarily based on the researcher's own understanding and vocabulary. Accordingly, more endeavors that adopt this framework to the investigation of the genre transfer in similar contexts could make it more refined and applicable.

Furthermore, as shown in *Chapter 1*, the whole research was a case study that was situated in a single institution in China. Moreover, only 20 pairs of the MT and PS were investigated. The research acknowledges that the findings of the current study might not be generalized to the wider EFL contexts. As a result, future research that include more data sources and a larger sample size to make the sample more representative of the population would be of great importance.

7.4 Summary

The current chapter concluded the major findings related to the proposed three research questions at the beginning, i.e., the move-step structure of the thesis, the move-step structure of the thesis defense presentation slides, and the changes and transfer strategies between them. Based on these major findings, pedagogical implications for the students, the supervisors, and the instructors were demonstrated. Finally, the limitations of the present study were put forward and accordingly, the future studies were recommended.

REFERENCES

[1] ABDEL-MALEK M. Empowering Arabic learners to make meaning: A genre-based approach[J]. System, 2020, 94: 1-11.

[2] AGUILAR M. The peer seminar, a spoken research process genre[J]. Journal of English for Academic Purposes, 2004, 3(1): 55-72.

[3] ANDERSON T, OKUDA T. Temporal change in dissertation macrostructures[J]. English for Specific Purposes, 2021, 64: 1-12.

[4] APPERSON J M, LAWS E L, SCEPANSKY J A. An assessment of student preferences for PowerPoint presentation structure in undergraduate courses[J]. Computers & Education, 2008, 50(1): 148-153.

[5] ATAI M R, TALEBZADEH H. Exploring visual and textual discourse of applied linguistics PowerPoint conference presentations[J]. ESP across Cultures, 2012, 9: 7-26.

[6] AZIZIFAR A, KMALVAND A, GHORBANZADE N. An investigation into visual language in PowerPoint presentations in Applied Linguistics[J]. Asian Journal of Social Sciences & Humanities, 2014, 3(3): 84-96.

[7] BAKER J P, GOODBOY A K, BOWMAN N D, et al. Does teaching with PowerPoint increase students' learning? A meta-analysis[J]. Computers & Education, 2018, 126: 376-387.

[8] BASTURKMEN H. Commenting on results in published research articles and Master's dissertations in Language Teaching[J]. Journal of English for Academic Purposes, 2009, 8(4): 241-251.

[9] BAWARSHI A S, REIFF M J. Genre: An introduction to history, theory, research, and pedagogy[M]. Anderson: Parlor Press, 2010.

[10] BAZERMAN C. Systems of genres and the enactment of social intentions[M]//

FREEDMAN A, MEDWAY P. Genre and the new rhetoric. United Kingdom: Taylor & Francis, 1994: 79-101.

[11] BAZERMAN C. Intertextuality: How texts rely on other texts[M]// BAZERMAN C, PRIOR P. What writing does and how it does it: An introduction to analyzing texts and textual practices. Mahwah: Lawrence Erlbaum Associates, 2004: 83-96.

[12] BERK R A. Research on PowerPoint: From basic features to multimedia[J]. International Journal of Technology in Teaching and Learning, 2011, 7(1): 24-35.

[13] BHATIA V K. Analysing genre: Language use in professional settings[M]. London: Longman, 1993.

[14] BHATIA V K. Worlds of written discourse: A genre-based view[M]. New York: Continuum, 2004.

[15] BHATIA V K. Interdiscursivity in professional communication[J]. Discourse & Communication, 2010, 4(1): 32-50.

[16] BHATIA V K. Profession written genres[M]// GEE J P, HANDEFORD M. The Routledge handbook of discourse analysis. London: Routledge, 2012: 47-65.

[17] BIBER D, CONNOR U, UPTON T. Discourse on the move: Using corpus analysis to describe discourse structure[M]. Amsterdam: John Benjamins Publishing Company, 2007.

[18] BITCHENER J, BASTURKMEN H. Perceptions of the difficulties of postgraduate L2 thesis students writing the discussion section[J]. Journal of English for Academic Purposes, 2006, 5(1): 4-18.

[19] BITCHENER J, BASTURKMEN H, EAST M. The focus of supervisor written feedback to thesis/dissertation students[J]. International Journal of English Studies, 2010, 10(2): 79-97.

[20] BOLTON K, GRADDOL D. English in China today[J]. English Today, 2012, 28(3): 3-9.

[21] BREMNER S, COSTLEY T. Bringing reality to the classroom: Exercises in

intertextuality[J]. English for Specific Purposes, 2018, 52: 1-12.

[22] BUCHER H J, NIEMANN P. Visualizing science: the reception of PowerPoint presentations[J]. Visual Communication, 2012, 11(3): 283-306.

[23] BULLO S. Investigating intertextuality and interdiscursivity in evaluation: The case of conceptual blending[J]. Language and Cognition, 2017, 9(4): 709-727.

[24] BUNTON D. Generic moves in Ph.D. thesis introductions[M]// FLOWERDEW J. Academic discourse. London: Pearson Education Limited, 2002: 57-75.

[25] BUNTON D. The structure of Ph.D. conclusion chapters[J]. Journal of English for Academic Purposes, 2005, 4(3): 207-224.

[26] CALLAGHAN M, ROTHERY J. Teaching factual writing: A genre-based approach[J]. Metropolitan East Disadvantaged Schools Program, 1988.

[27] CANDLIN C N, MALEY Y. Intertextuality and interdiscursivity in the discourse of alternative dispute resolution[M]// GUNNARSSON B L, LINELL P, NORDBERG B. The construction of professional discourse. London: Routledge, 2014: 201-222.

[28] CARBONELL-OLIVARES M, GIL-SALOM L, SOLER-MONREAL C. The schematic structure of Spanish Ph.D. thesis introductions[J]. Spanish in Context, 2009, 6(2): 151-175.

[29] CASANAVE C P. Performing expertise in doctoral dissertations: Thoughts on a fundamental dilemma facing doctoral students and their supervisors[J]. Journal of Second Language Writing, 2019, 43: 57-62.

[30] CASTELLÓ A, CHAVEZ D, CLADELLAS R. Association between slides-format and Major's contents: Effects on perceived attention and significant learning[J]. Multimedia Tools and Applications, 2020, 79(33): 24969-24992.

[31] CHANG J. Globalization and English in Chinese higher education[J]. World Englishes, 2006, 25(3-4): 513-525.

[32] CHEN C W Y. PowerPoint as a multimodal retelling tool: Students' slide design, collaboration, and goal-setting[J]. Innovation in Language Learning

and Teaching, 2023, 17(1):1-14.

[33] CHEN T Y, KUO C H. A genre-based analysis of the information structure of master's theses in applied linguistics[J]. The Asian ESP Journal, 2012, 8(1): 24-52.

[34] CHENG A. EAP at the tertiary level in China: Challenges and possibilities[M]// HYLAND K, SHAW P. The Routledge handbook of English for academic purposes. London: Routledge, 2016: 97-108.

[35] CHENG A. Genre and graduate-level research writing[M]. Michigan: University of Michigan Press, 2018.

[36] COE R M. The new rhetoric of genre: Writing political briefs[M]// JOHNS A M. Genre in the classroom. Mahwah: Lawrence Erlbaum, 2002: 195-205.

[37] COE R M, FREEDMAN A. Genre theory: Australian and North American approaches[M]// KENNEDY M. Theorizing composition. Westport: Greenwood Publishing Company, 1998: 136-147.

[38] COHEN L, MANION L, MORRISON K. Research methods in education [M]. Sixth edition. London: Routledge, 2007.

[39] COTOS E, HUFFMAN S, LINK S. Furthering and applying move/step constructs: Technology-driven marshalling of Swalesian genre theory for EAP pedagogy[J]. Journal of English for Academic Purposes, 2015, 19: 52-72.

[40] CRESWELL J W. Qualitative inquiry and research design: Choosing among five approaches[M]. Second edition. Thousand Oaks, California: Sage Publications, 2007.

[41] CRESWELL J W, CRESWELL J D. Research Design: Qualitative, quantitative, and mixed methods approaches[M]. Fifth edition. Thousand Oaks, California: Sage Publications, 2018.

[42] CRYER P. The research student's guide to success[M]. New York: McGraw-Hill Education, 2006.

[43] CRYSTAL D. The Cambridge encyclopedia of the English language[M]. Second edition: Cambridge: Cambridge University Press, 2003.

[44] DASTJERDI Z S, TAN H, ABDULLAH A N. Rhetorical structure of

integrated results and discussion chapter in master's dissertations across disciplines[J]. Discourse and Interaction, 2017, 10(2): 61-83.

[45] DENG L, LAGHARI T, GAO X. A genre-based exploration of intertextuality and interdiscursivity in advertorial discourse[J]. English for Specific Purposes, 2021, 62: 30-42.

[46] DEVITT A. Intertextuality in tax accounting: Generic, referential, and functional[M]// BAZERMAN C, PARADIS J. Textual dynamics of the professions: Historical and contemporary studies of writing in professional communities. Madison: University of Wisconsin Press, 1991: 336-357.

[47] DEVITT A, REIFF M J, BAWARSHI A. Scenes of writing: Strategies for composing genres[M]. Pearson Education, 2004.

[48] DIANI G. Visual communication in Applied Linguistics conference presentations[M]// CAMICIOTTOLI B C, FORTANET-GÓMEZ I. Multimodal analysis in academic settings: From research to teaching. London: Routledge, 2015: 83-107.

[49] DONG J, LU X. Promoting discipline-specific genre competence with corpus-based genre analysis activities[J]. English for Specific Purposes, 2020, 58: 138-154.

[50] DONG Y R. Non-native graduate students' thesis/dissertation writing in science: Self-reports by students and their advisors from two US institutions[J]. English for Specific Purposes, 1998, 17(4): 369-390.

[51] DUBOIS B L. The use of slides in biomedical speeches[J]. The ESP Journal, 1980, 1(1): 45-50.

[52] DUDLEY-EVANS T. Genre analysis: An investigation of the introduction and discussion sections of M.Sc. dissertations[M]// COULTHARD M. Talking about text. Birmingham: English Language Research, University of Birmingham, 1986: 128-145.

[53] DUDLEY-EVANS T. The dissertation: A case of neglect?[M]// THOMPSON P. Issues in EAP writing research and instruction. Reading: Centre for Applied Language Studies, University of Reading, 1999: 28-36.

[54] DUDLEY-EVANS T. Genre analysis: An approach to text analysis for ESP[M]// COULTHARD M. Advances in written text analysis. London: Routledge, 1994: 219-228.

[55] DUFF P. Case study research in applied linguistics[M]. New York: Routledge, 2018.

[56] FAIRCLOUGH N. Discourse and social change[M]. Cambridge: Polity Press, 1992.

[57] FAIRCLOUGH N. Analyzing discourse: Textual analysis for social research[M]. London: Routledge, 2003.

[58] FAIRCLOUGH N. Genres of political discourse[M]// BROWN K. Encyclopedia of language and linguistics. Oxford: Elsevier, 2006: 32-38.

[59] FAKHRUDDIN W F W W, HASSAN H. A review of genre approaches within linguistic traditions[J]. LSP International Journal, 2015, 2(2): 53-68.

[60] FEEZ S. Text-based syllabus design[M]. Sydney: McQuarie University/ AMES, 1998.

[61] FLOWERDEW L. An integration of corpus-based and genre-based approaches to text analysis in EAP/ESP: Countering criticisms against corpus-based methodologies[J]. English for Specific Purposes, 2005, 24(3): 321-332.

[62] FLOWERDEW L. Using corpus-based research and online academic corpora to inform writing of the discussion section of a thesis[J]. Journal of English for Academic Purposes, 2015, 20: 58-68.

[63] FLOWERDEW L. A genre-inspired and lexico-grammatical approach for helping postgraduate students craft research grant proposals[J]. English for Specific Purposes, 2016, 42: 1-12.

[64] FLOWERDEW J, FOREST R W. Schematic structure and lexico-grammatical realization in corpus-based genre analysis: The case of research in the Ph.D. Literature Review [M]// CHARLES M, PECORARI D, HUNSTON S. Academic writing: At the interface of corpus and discourse. London: Continuum, 2009: 15-36.

[65] FOREY G, FENG D. Interpersonal meaning and audience engagement in academic presentations[A]. In HYLAND K, SHAW P (Eds.). The Routledge handbook of English for Academic Purposes[C]. Routledge, 2016: 416-430.

[66] FROW J. Genre[M]. London: Routledge, 2013.

[67] GAO Y, BARTLETT B. Opportunities and challenges for negotiating appropriate EAP practices in China [M]// LIYANAGE I, WALKER T. English for academic purposes (EAP) in Asia. Rotterdam: Sense Publishers, 2014: 13-31.

[68] GARDNER S. Genres and registers of student report writing: An SFL perspective on texts and practices[J]. Journal of English for Academic Purposes, 2012, 11(1): 52-63.

[69] GREEN E P. Healthy presentations: How to craft exceptional lectures in Medicine, the Health Professions, and the Biomedical Sciences[M]. Berlin: Springer, 2021.

[70] GÜNTHER K, RAITAKARI S, JUHILA K. From plan meetings to care plans: Genre chains and the intertextual relations of text and talk[J]. Discourse & Communication, 2015, 9(1): 65-79.

[71] HALLEWELL M J, CROOK C. Performing PowerPoint lectures: Examining the extent of slide-text integration into lecturers' spoken expositions[J]. Journal of Further and Higher Education, 2020, 44(4): 467-482.

[72] HERMANSSON C, JONSSON B, LEVLIN M, et al. The (non) effect of Joint Construction in a genre-based approach to teaching writing[J]. The Journal of Educational Research, 2019, 112(4): 483-494.

[73] HERTZ B, KERKOF P, VAN WOERKUM C. PowerPoint slides as speaking notes: The influence of speaking anxiety on the use of text on slides[J]. Business and Professional Communication Quarterly, 2016, 79(3): 348-359.

[74] HEWINGS M. The end! How to conclude a dissertation [M]// BLUE G. Language, learning and success: Studying through English. London: Macmillan, 1993: 105-112.

[75] HO V. What functions do intertextuality and interdiscursivity serve in request

e-mail discourse?[J]. Journal of Pragmatics, 2011, 43(10): 2534-2547.

[76] HOLMES R. Genre analysis, and the social sciences: An investigation of the structure of research article discussion sections in three disciplines[J]. English for Specific Purposes, 1997, 16(4): 321-337.

[77] HOPKINS A, DUDLEY-EVANS T. A genre-based investigation of the discussion sections in articles and dissertations[J]. English for Specific Purposes, 1988, 7(2): 113-121.

[78] HU G. English language education in China: Policies, progress, and problems[J]. Language Policy, 2005, 4(1): 5-24.

[79] HU G, LIU Y. Three-minute thesis presentations as an academic genre: A cross-disciplinary study of genre moves[J]. Journal of English for Academic Purposes, 2018, 35: 16-30.

[80] HUMPHREY S L, ECONOMOU D. Peeling the onion–A textual model of critical analysis[J]. Journal of English for Academic Purposes, 2015, 17: 37-50.

[81] HUMPHREY S, MACNAUGHT L. Revisiting joint construction in the tertiary context[J]. Australian Journal of Language and Literacy, 2011, 34(1): 98-115.

[82] HYLAND K. A genre description of the argumentative essay[J]. RELC Journal, 1990, 21(1): 66-78.

[83] HYLAND K. Disciplinary discourses: Social interaction in academic writing[M]. London: Longman Pearson Education, 2000.

[84] HYLAND K. Genre: Language, context, and literacy[J]. Annual Review of Applied Linguistics, 2002, 22(1): 113-135.

[85] HYLAND K. Graduates' gratitude: The generic structure of dissertation acknowledgements[J]. English for Specific Purposes, 2004, 23(3): 303-324.

[86] HYLAND K. English for academic purposes: An advanced resource book[M]. London: Routledge, 2006.

[87] HYLAND K. Genre pedagogy: Language, literacy and L2 writing instruction[J]. Journal of Second Language Writing, 2007, 16(3): 148-164.

[88] HYLAND K. Academic publishing and the myth of linguistic injustice[J]. Journal of Second Language Writing, 2016, 31: 58-69.

[89] HYON S. Introducing genre and English for specific purposes[M]. London: Routledge, 2018.

[90] JALILIFAR A R, FIRUZMAND S, ROSHANI S. Genre analysis of problem statement sections of M.A. proposals and theses in Applied Linguistics[J]. Language, Society and Culture, 2011, 33: 85-93.

[91] JOHNS A M. Rhetorical Genre Studies (RGS) and the teaching of EFL reading and writing–or genre is much more than text structure [C]. In Proceedings of the CELC Symposium Bridging Research and Pedagogy. Singapore: National University of Singapore, 2013: 1-7.

[92] JOHNS A M, BAWARSHI A, COE R M, et al. Crossing the boundaries of genre studies: Commentaries by experts[J]. Journal of Second Language Writing, 2006, 15(3): 234-249.

[93] JORDAN R R. English for academic purposes: A guide and resource book for teachers[M]. Cambridge: Cambridge University Press, 1997.

[94] JOYNER R L, ROUSE W A, GLATTHORN A A. Writing the winning thesis or dissertation: A step-by-step guide[M]. Thousand Oaks, CA: Corwin Press, 2018.

[95] KANOKSILAPATHAM B. Rhetorical structure of biochemistry research articles[J]. English for Specific Purposes, 2005, 24(3): 269-292.

[96] KATHPALIA S S, KHOO C S. Generic structure and citation functions in introductions of biological science articles in English-medium international journals[J]. Iberica, 2020, 40: 123-147.

[97] KAWASE T. Metadiscourse in the introductions of Ph.D. theses and research articles[J]. Journal of English for Academic Purposes, 2018, 20: 114-124.

[98] KOLLER V. Lesbian nation: A case of multiple interdiscursivity [M]// DE CILLIA R, GRUBER H, MENZ F, KRZYZANOWSKI M. Discourse, politics, identity. Tübingen: Stauffenburg, 2010: 369-381.

[99] KOSKELA M. Same, same, but different: Intertextual and interdiscursive

features of communication strategy texts[J]. Discourse & Communication, 2013, 7(4): 389-407.

[100] KRISTEVA J. Semiotics[M]. Paris: Editions du Seuil, 1969.

[101] KRISTEVA J. Word, dialogue and novel [M]// ROUDIEZ L S. Desire in language: A semiotic approach to literature and art. New York: Columbia University Press, 1980: 64-91.

[102] KWAN B S C. The schematic structure of literature reviews in doctoral theses of applied linguistics[J]. English for Specific Purposes, 2006, 25(1): 30-55.

[103] LEVASSEUR D G, KANAN SAWYER J. Pedagogy meets PowerPoint: A research review of the effects of computer-generated slides in the classroom[J]. The Review of Communication, 2006, 6(1-2): 101-123.

[104] LI L, FRANKEN M, WU S. Bundle-driven metadiscourse analysis: Sentence initial bundles in Chinese and New Zealand postgraduates' thesis writing [M]// HATIPOGLU C, AKBAS E, BAYYURT Y. Metadiscourse in written genres: Uncovering textual and interactional aspects of texts. Berlin: Peter Lang, 2017: 251-283.

[105] LI L, FRANKEN M, WU S. Bundle-driven move analysis: Sentence initial lexical bundles in Ph.D. abstracts[J]. English for Specific Purposes, 2020, 60: 85-97.

[106] LI Q, ZHANG X. An analysis of citations in Chinese English-major master's theses and doctoral dissertations[J]. Journal of English for Academic Purposes, 2021, 51: 100982.

[107] LIM J M H. Method sections of management research articles: A pedagogically motivated qualitative study[J]. English for Specific Purposes, 2006, 25(3): 282-309.

[108] LINELL P. Discourse across boundaries: On recontextualizations and the blending of voices in professional discourse[J]. Text & Talk, 1998, 18(2): 143-158.

[109] LIU Y, BUCKINGHAM L. The schematic structure of discussion sections in

applied linguistics and the distribution of metadiscourse markers[J]. Journal of English for Academic Purposes, 2018, 34: 97-109.

[110] LIU Z, LIU H. How is meaning constructed multimodally? — A case study of PowerPoint presentations in an M.A. thesis defense[J]. Journal of Language Teaching and Research, 2021, 12(6): 969-978.

[111] MACKIEWICZ J. Comparing PowerPoint experts' and university students' opinions about PowerPoint presentations[J]. Journal of Technical Writing and Communication, 2008, 38(2): 149-165.

[112] MAHER P, MILLIGAN S. Teaching master thesis writing to engineers: Insights from corpus and genre analysis of introductions[J]. English for Specific Purposes, 2019, 55: 40-55.

[113] MÄNTYTHEN A, SHORE S. What is meant by hybridity? An investigation of hybridity and related terms in genre studies[J]. Text & Talk, 2014, 34(6): 737-758.

[114] MARTIN J R, CHRISTIE F, ROTHERY J. Social processes in education: A reply to Sawyer and Watson (and others) [M]// REID I. The place of genre in learning: Current debates. Geelong: Deakin University Press, 1987: 46-57.

[115] MATZLER P P. Grant proposal abstracts in science and engineering: A prototypical move-structure pattern and its variations[J]. Journal of English for Academic Purposes, 2021, 49: 100938.

[116] MILLER C R. Genre as social action [M]// FREEDMAN A, MEDWAY P. Genre and the new rhetoric. London: Taylor & Francis, 1994: 23-42.

[117] MITCHELL T D, PESSOA S, GÓMEZ-LAICH M P. Know your roles: Alleviating the academic-professional tension in the case analysis genre[J]. English for Specific Purposes, 2021, 61: 117-131.

[118] MONREAL C S. A move-step analysis of the concluding chapters in computer science Ph.D. theses[J]. Ibérica, 2016, 32: 105-132.

[119] MORELL T. International conference paper presentation: A multimodal analysis to determine effectiveness[J]. English for Specific Purposes, 2015, 37: 137-150.

[120] MOSQUERA H J, TULUD D. Methodology section of graduate school thesis manuscripts: A genre analysis probe of rhetorical structure[J]. Journal of English Language Teaching and Applied Linguistics, 2021, 3(9): 36-52.

[121] NEGRETTI R, KUTEVA M. Fostering metacognitive genre awareness in L2 academic reading and writing: A case study of pre-service English teachers[J]. Journal of Second Language Writing, 2011, 20(2): 95-110.

[122] NGAI C S B, SINGH R G, KWAN B S C. A comparative study of the linguistic manifestations of intertextuality in corporate leaders' messages of global corporations in the US and China[J]. English for Specific Purposes, 2020, 60: 65-84.

[123] NGUYEN T T L. Move-step structures and citation practice in English TESOL master's theses by Vietnamese students [D]. Nakhon Ratchasima: Suranaree University of Technology, 2014.

[124] NGUYEN T T L, PRAMOOLSOOK I. A move-based structure of the master's thesis literature review chapters by Vietnamese TESOL postgraduates[J]. LangLit: An International Peer-Reviewed Open Access Journal, 2014a, 1(2): 282-301.

[125] NGUYEN T T L, PRAMOOLSOOK I. Rhetorical structure of introduction chapters written by novice Vietnamese TESOL postgraduates[J]. 3L: The Southeast Asian Journal of English Language Studies, 2014b, 20(1): 61-74.

[126] NGUYEN T T L, PRAMOOLSOOK I. A move analysis of method chapters by Vietnamese TESOL master's students[J]. Research Scholar: An International Refereed e-Journal of Literary Explorations, 2015a, 3(1): 14-28.

[127] NGUYEN T T L, PRAMOOLSOOK I. Move analysis of results-discussion chapters in TESOL master's theses written by Vietnamese students[J]. 3L: The Southeast Asian Journal of English Language Studies, 2015b, 21(2): 1-15.

[128] NISBET J, WATT J. Case study [M]// BELL J, BUSH T, FOX A, GOODEY J, GOULDING S. Conducting Small-Scale Investigations in Educational

Management. London: Harper & Row, 1984: 79-92.

[129] NODOUSHAN M A S, KHAKBAZ N. Theses 'Discussion' sections: A structural move analysis[J]. International Journal of English Studies, 2011, 5(3): 111-132.

[130] NOURI H, SHAHID A. The effect of PowerPoint presentations on student learning and attitudes[J]. Global Perspectives on Accounting Education, 2005, 2(1): 53-73.

[131] NTALALA S G, ORWENJO D O, ERASTUS F K. Rhetorical moves of Kenyan Parliamentary Committee Reports[J]. Applied Linguistics Research Journal, 2020, 4(3): 65-85.

[132] NWOGU K N. The medical research paper: Structure and functions[J]. English for Specific Purposes, 1997, 16(2): 119-138.

[133] PALTRIDGE B. Genre and the language learning classroom[M]. Ann Arbor, MI: University of Michigan Press, 2001.

[134] PALTRIDGE B. Thesis and dissertation writing: An examination of published advice and actual practice[J]. English for Specific Purposes, 2002, 21(2): 125-143.

[135] PALTRIDGE B. Genre and English for Specific Purposes [M]// PALTRIDGE B, STARFIELD S. The handbook of English for specific purposes. Oxford: John Wiley & Sons, 2014: 347-366.

[136] PALTRIDGE B, STARFIELD S. Thesis and dissertation writing in a second language: A handbook for supervisors[M]. London: Routledge, 2007.

[137] PHILLIPS E M, PUGH D S. How to get a Ph.D.: A handbook for students and their supervisors[M]. Maidenhead: Open University Press, 2010.

[138] PI Z, HONG J. Learning process and learning outcomes of video podcasts including the instructor and PPT slides: A Chinese case[J]. Innovations in Education and Teaching International, 2016, 53(2): 135-144.

[139] PIKETALEYEE A, BAZARGANI D T. Exploring the moves and steps in TEFL M.A. theses introduction and review of literature PowerPoint presentations: A genre analysis approach[J]. Theory and Practice in

Language Studies, 2018, 8(9): 1186-1194.

[140] PIORNO P E. An example of genre shift in the medicinal product information genre system[J]. Linguistica Antverpiensia, New Series-Themes in Translation Studies, 2012, 11: 167-187.

[141] PRAMOOLSOOK I. Genre transfer from dissertation to research article: Biotechnology and environmental engineering in a Thai university context [D]. Coventry: University of Warwick, 2007.

[142] PUTRI T D, KURNIAWAN E. Rhetorical move and genre knowledge development in local and international graduates' thesis and dissertation Abstracts[J]. LLT Journal: A Journal on Language and Language Teaching, 2021, 24(2): 324-336.

[143] RAO P S. The importance of English in the modern era[J]. Asian Journal of Multidimensional Research (AJMR), 2019, 8(1): 7-19.

[144] RAO X. University English for academic purposes in China: A phenomenological interview study[M]. Berlin: Springer, 2018.

[145] RAU G, SHIH Y S. Evaluation of Cohen's kappa and other measures of inter-rater agreement for genre analysis and other nominal data[J]. Journal of English for Academic Purposes, 2021, 53: 101026.

[146] RAWDHAN A, EBADI S, LOAN N T T. Rhetorical structure variations in Literature Review chapters of Applied Linguistics master's theses by Iraqi and international students[J]. International Journal of Instruction, 2020, 13(4): 849-866.

[147] REN H, LI Y. A comparison study on the rhetorical moves of Abstracts in published research articles and master's foreign-language theses[J]. English Language Teaching, 2011, 4(1): 162-166.

[148] ROBERTS C, HYATT L. The dissertation journey: A practical and comprehensive guide to planning, writing, and defending your dissertation[M]. Third edition. Thousand Oaks, CA: Corwin Press, 2019.

[149] ROBSON C. Real world research[M]. Second Edition. Oxford: Blackwell, 2002.

[150] ROTHERY J. Making changes: Developing an educational linguistics [M]// HASAN R, WILLIAMS G. Literacy in society. London: Longman, 1996: 86-123.

[151] ROTHERY J, STENGlin M. Exploring literacy in school English (Write it right resources for literacy and learning)[M]. Sydney: Metropolitan East Disadvantaged Schools Program, 1995.

[152] ROWLEY-JOLIVET E. Visual discourse in scientific conference papers: A genre-based study[J]. English for Specific Purposes, 2002, 21(1): 19-40.

[153] ROWLEY-JOLIVET E, CARTER-THOMAS S. The rhetoric of conference presentation introductions: Context, argument and interaction[J]. International Journal of Applied Linguistics, 2005, 15(1): 45-70.

[154] RUSSELL-PINSON L, HARRIS M L. Anguish and anxiety, stress and strain: Attending to writers' stress in the dissertation process[J]. Journal of Second Language Writing, 2019, 43: 63-71.

[155] SADEGHI K, SHIRZAD K A. Thesis writing challenges for non-native M.A. students[J]. Research in Post-Compulsory Education, 2015, 20(3): 357-373.

[156] SAMRAJ B. A discourse analysis of master's theses across disciplines with a focus on introductions[J]. Journal of English for Academic Purposes, 2008, 7(1): 55-67.

[157] SCHMIED J. Graduate academic writing in Europe in comparison: A research-based approach to metalanguage and genre[J]. Research in English Language and Linguistics, 2015, 8: 1-24.

[158] SCHOENEborn D. The pervasive power of PowerPoint: How a genre of professional communication permeates organizational communication[J]. Organization Studies, 2013, 34(12): 1777-1801.

[159] SELONI L. "I'm an artist and a scholar who is trying to find a middle point": A textographic analysis of a Colombian art historian's thesis writing[J]. Journal of Second Language Writing, 2014, 25: 79-99.

[160] SHIN D S, CIMASKO T, YI Y. Development of metalanguage for multimodal composing: A case study of an L2 writer's design of multimedia

texts[J]. Journal of Second Language Writing, 2020, 47: 100714.

[161] SOLER-MONREAL C. Announcing one's work in Ph.D. theses in computer science: A comparison of Move 3 in literature reviews written in English L1, English L2 and Spanish L1[J]. English for Specific Purposes, 2015, 40: 27-41.

[162] SOLER-MONREAL C. A move-step analysis of the concluding chapters in computer science Ph.D. theses[J]. Ibérica, 2016, 32: 105-132.

[163] SOLER-MONREAL C, CARBONELL-OLIVARES M, GIL-SALOM L. A contrastive study of the rhetorical organization of English and Spanish Ph.D. thesis introductions[J]. English for Specific Purposes, 2011, 30(1): 4-17.

[164] SWALES J M. Genre analysis: English in academic and research settings[M]. Cambridge: Cambridge University Press, 1990.

[165] SWALES J M. Research genres: Explorations and applications[M]. Cambridge: Cambridge University Press, 2004.

[166] SWALES J M. A text and its commentaries: Toward a reception history of 'genre in three traditions' (Hyon, 1996)[J]. Ibérica, 2012, 24: 103-116.

[167] TARDY C M. Expressions of disciplinarity and individuality in a multimodal genre[J]. Computers and Composition, 2005, 22(3): 319-336.

[168] TARDY C M. Building genre knowledge[M]. West Lafayette, IN: Parlor Press, 2009.

[169] TARDY C M. Genre analysis [M]// HYLAND K, PALTRIDGE B. Continuum companion to discourse analysis. London: Continuum, 2011: 54-68.

[170] TARDY C M. Beyond convention: Genre innovation in academic writing[M]. Ann Arbor, MI: University of Michigan Press, 2016.

[171] TEACHING ADVISORY COMMITTEE FOR TERTIARY ENGLISH MAJORS. English Teaching Syllabus for English Majors (ETSEM)[M]. Beijing: Foreign Language Teaching and Research Press, 2000.

[172] THE SIXTH DISCIPLINE EVALUATION GROUP OF THE STATE COUNCIL ACADEMIC DEGREES COMMITTEE. Basic Requirements for

Doctor's Degree and Master's Degree in First-level Discipline[M]. Beijing: Higher Education Press, 2014.

[173] THOMPSON P. Achieving a voice of authority in Ph.D. theses [M]// HYLAND K, GUINDA C S. Stance and voice in written academic genres. Basingstoke: Palgrave MacMillan, 2012: 119-133.

[174] THOMPSON P. Thesis and dissertation writing [M]// PALTRIDGE B, STARFIELD S. The handbook of English for Specific Purposes. Oxford: John Wiley & Sons, 2013: 283-299.

[175] THOMPSON S. Frameworks and contexts: A genre-based approach to analysing lecture introductions[J]. English for Specific Purposes, 1994, 13(2): 171-186.

[176] THONGCHALERMS S, JARUNTHAWATCHAI W. The impact of genre-based instruction on EFL learners' writing development[J]. International Journal of Instruction, 2020, 13(1): 1-16.

[177] WANG Q. The national curriculum changes and their effects on English language teaching in the People's Republic of China [M]// CUMMINS J, DAVISON C. International handbook of English language teaching. New York: Springer, 2007: 87-105.

[178] WECKER C. Slide presentation and speech suppressors: When and why learners miss oral information[J]. Computers and Education, 2012, 59(2): 260-273.

[179] WEISSBERG B. The graduate seminar: Another research-process genre[J]. English for Specific Purposes, 1993, 12(1): 23-35.

[180] WU J. Understanding interdiscursivity: A pragmatic model?[J]. Journal of Cambridge Studies, 2011, 6(2-3): 95-115.

[181] XIE J. Evaluation in moves: An integrated analysis of Chinese M.A. thesis Literature Reviews[J]. English Language Teaching, 2017, 10(3): 1-20.

[182] XU X, LOCKWOOD J. What's going on in the chat flow? A move analysis of e-commerce customer service webchat exchange[J]. English for Specific Purposes, 2021, 61: 84-96.

[183] YANG R, ALLISON D. Research articles in applied linguistics: Moving from results to conclusions[J]. English for Specific Purposes, 2003, 22(4): 365-385.

[184] YASUDA S. Toward a framework for linking linguistic knowledge and writing expertise: Interplay between SFL-based genre pedagogy and task-based language teaching[J]. TESOL Quarterly, 2017, 51(3): 576-606.

[185] YATES J, ORLIKOWSKI W. The PowerPoint presentation and its corollaries: How genres shape communicative action in organizations [M]// ZACHRY M, THRALLS C. The Cultural turn: Communicative practices in workplaces and the professions. Amityville, NY: Baywood Publishing, 2007: 67-92.

[186] YEUNG L. In search of commonalities: Some linguistic and rhetorical features of business reports as a genre[J]. English for Specific Purposes, 2007, 26(2): 156-179.

[187] YIN R. Applications of case study research[M]. Second edition. Thousand Oaks: Sage Publications, 2003a.

[188] YIN R. Case study research: Design and methods[M]. Third edition. Thousand Oaks: Sage Publications, 2003b.

[189] YOON J, CASAL J E. Rhetorical structure, sequence, and variation: A step-driven move analysis of applied linguistics conference abstracts[J]. International Journal of Applied Linguistics, 2020, 30(3): 462-478.

[190] YUNICK S. Genres, registers and sociolinguistics[J]. World Englishes, 1997, 16(3): 321-336.

[191] ZAINUDDIN S Z, SHAARI A H. A genre-inspired investigation of Establishing the Territory in thesis Introductions by Malaysian ESL writers[J]. 3L: Southeast Asian Journal of English Language Studies, 2021, 27(2): 144-160.

[192] ZAREVA A. Self-mention and the projection of multiple identity roles in TESOL graduate student presentations: The influence of the written academic genres[J]. English for Specific Purposes, 2013, 32(2): 72-83.

[193] ZAREVA A. Multi-word verbs in student academic presentations[J]. Journal of English for Academic Purposes, 2016, 23: 83-98.

[194] ZDANIAUK A, GRUMAN J A, CASSIDY S A. PowerPoint slide provision and student performance: The moderating roles of self-efficacy and gender[J]. Journal of Further and Higher Education, 2019, 43(4): 467-481.

[195] ZHANG J. A cross-cultural study of generic structure and linguistic patterns in M.A. thesis acknowledgements[J]. The Asian ESP Journal, 2012, 8(1): 141-165.

[196] ZHANG L J. Reflections on the pedagogical imports of western practices for professionalizing ESL/EFL writing and writing-teacher education[J]. Australian Review of Applied Linguistics, 2016, 39(3): 203-232.

[197] ZHANG Y. Retailing science: Genre hybridization in online science news stories[J]. Text & Talk, 2018, 38(2): 243-265.